DESIGNING DEMOCRATIC INSTITUTIONS

NOMOS

XLII

NOMOS

Harvard University Press

The Liberal Arts Press

Atherton Press

Aldine-Atherton Press

Lieber-Atherton Press

New York University Press

NOMOS XLII
Yearbook of the American Society for Political and Legal Philosophy

DESIGNING DEMOCRATIC INSTITUTIONS

Edited by

Ian Shapiro, *Yale University*
and
Stephen Macedo, *Princeton University*

NEW YORK UNIVERSITY PRESS　　•　　*New York and London*

NEW YORK UNIVERSITY PRESS
New York and London

Library of Congress Cataloging-in-Publication Data
Designing democratic institutions / edited by Ian Shapiro and
Stephen Macedo.
p.   cm. — (Nomos ; 42)
Includes bibliographical references and index.
ISBN 0-8147-9773-3 (cloth : alk. paper)
1. Democracy. 2. Democratization.   I. Shapiro, Ian. II. Macedo,
Stephen, 1957– III. Series.
JC423 .D4887 2000
321.8—dc21   00-009268

New York University Press books are printed on acid-free paper,
and their binding materials are chosen for strength and durability.

Manufactured in the United States of America
10 9 8 7 6 5 4 3 2 1

CONTENTS

PREFACE

This volume grew out of the annual meeting of the American Society for Political and Legal Philosophy held in conjunction with the annual meeting of the Association of American Law Schools, held in San Francisco, California, in January 1998. The society's membership selected the topic "Designing Democratic Institutions" by ballot. Stephen Macedo, the incoming editor of NOMOS, worked with me to put together an excellent program. I note with appreciation the help I received from Kellianne Farnham and Stuart Chinn in putting together this, my final, volume of the annual. The NYU Press production team, consisting of Niko Pfund and Despina Papazoglou Gimbel, deserve our thanks for their usual, yet uncommon, efficiency in guiding the manuscript into print.

Ian Shapiro

CONTRIBUTORS

BROOKE A. ACKERLY
Department of Political Science, University of California, Los Angeles

IAN AYRES
Yale Law School

GEOFFREY BRENNAN
Research School of Social Sciences, Australian National University

JOHN FEREJOHN
Department of Political Science, Stanford University

ALAN HAMLIN
Department of Economics, University of Southampton

RUSSELL HARDIN
Department of Politics, New York University

DONALD L. HOROWITZ
Department of Political Science and Law School, Duke University

STEPHEN MACEDO
Department of Politics, Princeton University

PHILIP PETTIT
Research School of Social Sciences, Australian National University

ROBERT POST
  University of California, Berkeley, School of Law

PHILIPPE C. SCHMITTER
  Department of Political Science, European University Institute

IAN SHAPIRO
  Department of Political Science, Yale University

PHILIPPE VAN PARIJS
  Department of Philosophy, Universite Catholique de Louvain

IRIS MARION YOUNG
  Department of Political Science, University of Chicago

INTRODUCTION

IAN SHAPIRO AND STEPHEN MACEDO

The principles and practices of democracy continue to spread ever more widely, and it is hard to imagine that there is a corner of the globe into which they will not eventually penetrate. But the euphoria of democratic revolutions is typically short-lived, and its attainment seems typically to be followed by disgruntlement and even cynicism about the actual operation of democratic institutions. It might be widely accepted that democracy is a good thing, yet it is equally apparent that democrats have much work to do in improving the performance of democratic institutions. Of course, it is far easier to perceive the need for reform than to prescribe specific proposals.

The essays in this volume focus on this difficult but vital challenge: how to improve the design of democratic institutions. There are important insights to be gleaned here about democratic principles as well, but the focus is on how democratic principles work or fail to work in practice. How can public deliberation in democracies be enhanced? How can elections be reformed so as to dampen the excessive influence of special interests, and especially those with money? How can democratic institutions be reformed so as to be able to deal with political issues that transcend the boundaries of nation states? And how can democratic practices better take account of the internal plurality of societies that are ethnically or otherwise divided?

I. Deliberation, Decision, and Enforcement

Deliberation is the lifeblood of democratic politics, and the lack of adequate deliberation therefore a perpetual threat to it. What counts as adequate deliberation is much debated and difficult to specify, but few would disavow the proposition that the quality of deliberation in most modern democracies is less than fully adequate. As two commentators on the American democracy recently put it: "In the practice of our democratic politics, communicating by sound bite, competing by character assassination, and resolving political conflicts through self-seeking bargaining too often substitute for deliberation on the merits of controversial issues."[1]

Lamentations of this sort abound, yet constructive responses are less easily located. Grotesque multimillion-dollar election campaigns are invariably followed by posturing and hand-wringing on the part of politicians and commentators about the need for campaign finance reform, reversal of the Supreme Court's 1976 decision to outlaw limits on campaign expenditures, and the importance of regulations mandating increased disclosure of campaign contributions.[2] It is difficult to imagine, however, that the reforms that are standardly proposed could have much of an impact on the problem. Indeed, the ritualistic, not to say hackneyed, character of calls for reform followed by inaction suggests that attempts at significant change are not taken seriously among America's political elites. It is therefore as refreshing as it is arresting to encounter the novel argument put forward by Ian Ayres in chapter 1. It turns on the intuition that the secret ballot is a better model for thinking about campaign contributions than is the First Amendment. Introduction of the secret ballot was justified, in part, by the aspiration to prevent corruption of the political process. "Voting booth privacy disrupted the economics of vote buying," Ayres notes, "making it much more difficult for candidates to buy votes because, at the end of the day, they could never be sure who voted for them."

Were we to conceive of campaign contributions along the same lines as the secret ballot, Ayres argues, it would enable us to derive comparable anonymity benefits by means of a "donation booth." Donors would be forced to channel campaign contributions through blind trusts, keeping candidates ignorant of the identities of their supporters. There would be no need to try to limit the amounts of campaign contributions on this scheme because donors would never be sure who had in fact made contributions of different amounts, or indeed whether those who claimed to have contributed had in fact made any contribution at all. "Just as the secret ballot makes it more difficult for candidates to *buy* votes, mandating anonymous donations through a system of blind trusts might make it harder for candidates to *sell* access or influence because they would never know which donors had paid the price." Ayres explores the constitutionality of this proposal in the United States, as well as its institutional practicality, making a strong case for its superiority over the going alternatives.

Geoffrey Brennan and Alan Hamlin take issue with Ayres's argument in chapter 2. Conceding Ayres's case that anonymity in campaign contributions might deter the corruption that currently accompanies them, they wonder, nonetheless, whether the cure might not be worse than the disease. Pursuing Ayres's analogy, they note that the secret ballot comes at a price: "Secret voting breaks the most obvious connection between argument and vote, and undermines the reliability of the vote as a serious and responsible political input. If individuals are not held responsible for their vote, at least to the extent of being called upon to defend their stated opinion," we should not be surprised if voting tends to be less responsible as a result. This is surely a cost of secret voting. Brennan and Hamlin contend that in the campaign contributions area the costs, in terms of lost openness and information, may be unacceptably high.

Brennan and Hamlin are skeptical, moreover, of the alleged benefits of Ayres's proposal. They worry that rather than lead to a culture of privacy, as the secret ballot does, anonymous campaign contributions will create a culture of deception in which people lie about whom they support because they no longer have incentives to be truthful. Brennan and Hamlin also make the case that in responding to the most venal form of corruption, Ayres's proposal would wipe out other incentives in the open-contribution regime, such as that for politicians to provide incidental constituency services. Most seriously, however, they ask whether

Ayres's proposed reform would eliminate the corrupting effects of campaign contributions at the price of creating incentives for an even worse form of corruption: straightforward bribery. No doubt many politicians are beyond bribery, but Brennan and Hamlin contend that an Ayres regime might, perversely, "select for" venal candidates, who can be bribed, and against virtuous ones, who cannot. They also identify other possible defects in Ayres's proposal, such as a net reduction in campaign contributions that might, in turn, strengthen the hands of incumbents. There might be answers to these difficulties, such as public funding for challengers, but Brennan and Hamlin make a strong prima facie case that Ayres's proposal needs to be evaluated in a larger context of cost-benefit considerations before its desirability can be established.

Most discussions of political deliberation focus on increasing either its quantity or its quality. In chapter 3 John Ferejohn questions the desirability of trying to institutionalize increased, or improved, deliberation (as distinct from promoting ethical norms favoring deliberation in the population or among elites). Sidestepping the debate over whether the deliberative democratic ideal is attainable, he poses the question Assuming it is attainable, is it desirable? In Ferejohn's view, proponents of deliberative democracy embrace the sociological hypothesis that increased deliberation will lead to convergence, if not on a single view of the common good, at least on a small class of reasonable views that everyone will "own" and thus be willing to help implement. He adduces several reasons for harboring skepticism of the sociological hypothesis. In a world in which there is enduring value pluralism, deep differences must be predicted to survive the deliberative process. Moreover, in representative democracies, even if deliberation leads representatives to converge on reasonable compromises, it is by no means clear that the populations they represent will alter *their* beliefs and preferences accordingly, so that coercive enforcement by government will still be required.

Some have suggested decentralized decision making as a response to this difficulty, but Ferejohn notes that it is not a panacea. For one thing, the possibility of collective-action problems means that even decentralized decisions must be enforced.

For another, "minorities within smaller political units and associations lack the protections of publicity and formality that are available to those in larger associations," so that decentralized decision making "can be an invitation to local tyranny."

The greatest difficulty with institutionalizing enhanced deliberation under conditions of value pluralism, on Ferejohn's account, is that it makes decisive action by government difficult and it tends to favor the status quo. Reforms of the Progressive period that were intended to enhance deliberation "seem, in retrospect, to have had the effect of emasculating government capabilities and permitting unjustifiable social and economic conditions to persist and develop." Accordingly, he concludes that, when thinking about reforms that enhance deliberation in the political institutions of an actual world beset by enduring disagreements of interest and value, "it is vital that democratic reform preserve the capacity of government to act decisively on important occasions."

Whereas Ferejohn explores the difference between democracy's representative and deliberative institutions, in chapter 4 Philip Pettit explores the related contrast between its electoral and "contestatory" dimensions. Like Ferejohn, Pettit takes the presence of pervasive value pluralism seriously, but he thinks that it should not lead us to abandon the notion that all law in a democracy should be geared to "empowering the common, recognizable interests of ordinary people, and nothing else besides." It is possible that a group of people has no common interests; in that case they could not live together under a common government. Generally in democracies people do share common interests, at least in solving collective action problems of coordination, free riding, compromise, and commitment. Moreover, Pettit contends (perhaps more controversially), they share common interests in a certain amount of redistribution to facilitate risk spreading in social insurance, protection of minority rights, and positive-sum welfare improvements.

Democratic institutions should be designed to track common interests thus conceived, Pettit argues, and this requires two complementary types of political institutions: electoral institutions, whose function is to attract and express putative expressions of common interest, and contestatory institutions, geared to ensuring that decisions that are implemented really do really reflect common interests. Democratic institutions must have both a "positive search-and-identify dimension" as well as a "negative scrutinize-and-disallow dimension." The first of these "will guard against false negatives, by allowing every possible common-interest policy into consideration." The other dimension, by contrast, "will guard against false positives by subjecting the policies adopted and their mode of implementation to a rigorous testing and filtering procedure."

Pettit details a number of institutional innovations to help foster this dual result: procedural and consultative constraints on lawmaking, and appellate constraints on implementation. Thus, on the electoral side, he argues against referenda because they invite expressive (as opposed to reflective) voting, and they are easily manipulated by particular interests. He favors depoliticizing matters such as interest-rate policy and criminal sentencing guidelines for similar reasons. He favors compulsory voting because it gives politicians incentives to propose policies that appeal to all population groups, and he favors bicameral legislatures with mixed electoral systems to capture multiple possible bases of representation. On the contestatory side, he favors devices of deliberative consultation in both the policy-making and policy-implementation stages, as well as various measures to empower community movements, given how difficult it is "for an individual to garner the information or marshal the expertise required to make a significant input" into consultative or appellate processes. There is no ideal outcome of democratic politics, but Pettit makes a strong case that reforms of this kind will move us closer to a world in which "what touches all" will be "considered and approved by all."

II. DEMOCRACY BEYOND THE NATION-STATE

The discussions by Ayres, Brennan and Hamlin, Ferejohn, and Pettit are principally directed at national political institutions. It is increasingly clear, however, that the nation-state is diminishing in efficacy as an instrument of democratic politics. Its capacity for effective action is challenged by transnational political and economic forces, at the same time that mushrooming movements for greater local autonomy—sometimes even secession—

threaten its integrity from within.[3] In chapter 5 Iris Marion Young makes the case that this reality demands fundamental rethinking of both the goals and means of democratic political association.

To motivate this claim, Young exposes inadequacies in the views of both camps in the debate between cosmopolitan individualists and liberal nationalists. She agrees with the liberal nationalists that cosmopolitan individualists take too little account of the importance of group membership in shaping people's lives and identities. But she resists the liberal nationalist alternative on the grounds that it is morally arbitrary to cede national states exclusive sovereignty over particular territories. On the one hand, she argues, liberal nationalists such as David Miller, Yael Tamir, and Will Kymlicka advance circular arguments when distinguishing national groups (which reasonably aspire to statehood) from ethnic groups (which do not). In fact, the claims made for national groups could just as reasonably be made for ethnic groups. Yet there are many thousands of such groups in the world, far more than could reasonably exist with their own nation-states. On the other hand, pragmatic defenses of nation-states on the grounds that they promote redistribution strike her as both philosophically and politically dubious. Philosophically, they make the obligation to redistribute dependent on sentiment rather than on what justice requires. Politically, not only do they promote ignoring obligations to outsiders, they supply ballast for the tendency to dismiss the claims of disadvantaged insiders who belong to stigmatized minority groups.

As a "third way," Young proposes recognition of the rights of "peoples" rather than nations, as entities that are prima facie deserving of self-government. Peoples, she argues, should be comprehended in relational rather than substantive terms. A relational conception "does not posit a social group as having an essential nature composed of a set of attributes defining only that group." A group is instead conceived as specific "only in interactive relations with others." Thus while the Scots might distinguish themselves from the English by reference to history, religious affiliation, language to some extent, and territory, when comparing themselves to Russians or Chinese they might think of themselves "as more like English than not." And as the reference to Scottish language indicates, "peopleness" is a matter of degree rather than kind, and it changes over time.

The presumption that peoples should have the right to local self-government does not imply any right to territorial sovereignty, however, and Young believes it should be regulated by a series of global regimes to attenuate the possibilities of domination. These regulatory regimes should have distinct "functional jurisdictions" over such issues as the environment, trade and finance, peace and security, investment and capital utilization, communications and transportation, citizenship and migration, and human rights—understood to include labor standards and welfare rights. Each regulatory regime should provide "a thin set of general rules that specify ways that individuals, organizations, and governments are obliged to take account of the interests and circumstances of one another." They should "deterritorialize" sovereignty by affirming the rights of peoples to govern themselves at the local level, provided they do so democratically within a set of federalist global arrangements. The regulatory regimes themselves should be more democratic and transparent than many—such as the International Monetary Fund, the World Bank, and the Security Council of the United Nations—are today, and open to influence by peoples through their local collective institutions. In this way, the model of international regulation as the product of treaties among sovereign states should be eroded.

In chapter 6 Russell Hardin makes the case that Young's defense of local autonomy in defense of group values is as vulnerable to objection as the liberal nationalist views that she rejects. Both views, Hardin submits, are vitiated by fallacies of composition: they mistakenly impute "group interests" to the individuals who constitute the groups in question. Hardin agrees that in certain cases it might sometimes be defensible to argue for group autonomy of "externally defined" groups, if second-class citizenship has been foisted on them in virtue of an arbitrary characteristic such as race. The difficulty is that, once empowered as political entities, the governments of such groups will have the power to oppress subsets of their memberships. With "internally defined" aspirational groups, the difficulty is no less serious, and there is not even the saving grace of remedying the injustice of discrimination. In all but the most rudimentary forms of association, members have diverse interests that may or may not be accommodated by those who have political power to act in the name of the group in question. Indeed, Hardin argues, such diversity is generally necessary for group health. Allowing local authorities a monopoly over the definition of group values all too easily reduces to the purchase of group autonomy at the price of individual oppression. It binds dissenters, and children (who might not appreciate the costs of disassociation from the larger political entity), not to mention future generations.

Hardin usefully reminds us that the idea of the self-determination of peoples was introduced into modern politics by Woodrow Wilson "in a racist, elitist era, and arguably in keeping with the racist views of his time." Those who defend group autonomy in the abstract forget this history too easily. The idea of group autonomy "sounds okay, perhaps even lovely, when it is kept unspecific and glib. But it sours quickly when we try to imagine it on the ground." The view of cosmopolitan individualism that Young and the liberal nationalists both dismiss looks a good deal more inviting from this practical perspective. Liberal nationalism, Hardin concludes. "is too good to be true." But ordinary nationalism "is too true to be good."

Robert Post questions Young's assault on the idea of sovereignty in chapter 7. Rather than think of sovereign power as power that trumps all other commitments, Post argues that we should think of it as originary authority. In a democracy such as the United States, for example, it is not the state that is sovereign but rather the people. Some of their power is delegated to the federal government and some to the states, but the people remain the sources of all sovereign authority. Thinking of sovereignty within nations, on this conception, in no way precludes the possibility that nations can be bound by transnational regimes. These might be regimes to which they have committed themselves as nations (as in treaty arrangements), or rules that emanate from an overlapping sovereign source, as in legislation that emerges from the European Parliament.

Young is misguided, Post thinks, to believe that sovereignty can ever be done away with; it can only be relocated. And when we maintain that it should be relocated, it behooves us, he argues, to attend to the institutions through which this can be given efficacy. Writing from the perspective of a lawyer whose characteristic focus is on implementation, Post is skeptical that global regulatory institutions can themselves be democratic without the prior emergence of a global democratic culture. He also worries that Young's contention that "distinct peoples" should become what are effectively sovereign entities is not accompanied by a description of institutions that could make this viable in practice.

Like Young, Philippe Schmitter is concerned with democracy beyond the nation state, and like Post he is concerned with its institutional embodiments. In chapter 8 he takes up the increasingly debated and pressing issue of the "democratic deficit" that attends the institutions of the European Union. The EU presents an ambiguous and novel set of challenges for democratic theorists on his telling. They are ambiguous because although the EU is notoriously undemocratic, it has provided a powerful stimulus for the transformation of authoritarian regimes in eastern and southern Europe into democracies, and many believe that it remains "one of the best insurance policies that a nascent democracy can take out to prevent its eventual regression to autocracy." The challenges are novel because the EU consists of a set of institutions that are sui generis in their history, purpose, and relations to existing democratic states.

Democrats often criticize the EU as drifting toward a centralized "superstate," run by faceless Eurocrats who act in secret and are in any case only minimally accountable to the populations affected by their decisions. Schmitter paints a more nuanced picture: "What seems to be asserting, and even consolidating, itself is a plurality of polities at different levels of aggregation—national, subnational, and supranational." Apart from the atypical case of the European Court of Justice, EU authorities have few exclusive competencies, and they have not managed to assert hierarchical authority over the domestic political systems of member states. Instead, the multiple authority levels "negotiate with one another in a continuous way in order to perform common tasks and resolve common problems across an expanding range of issues."

Lacking sovereignty, the EU really is more of a process than an entity. This partly explains why there is "no definite person or body that can be held accountable for its actions in the public realm." Yet Schmitter argues that it is important, nonetheless, to think creatively about democratizing the EU process, given the declining democratic legitimacy of national governments and the growing perception of uncontrolled regulatory power in Brussels. In addition, we should add the consideration that it may be easier to insist on democratizing institutions as they are emerging than to try to change them once they have been entrenched. To these ends, Schmitter suggests a series of democratic reforms. In the area of enhancing democratic citizenship, he suggests referenda with Euro-wide elections, improved status for denizens, dual voting for deputies, and electronic or "mail-in" voting. In the area of representation, he proposes universal membership in the European Parliament, reform of its committee system, European Parliamentary control over EU election funds, and a secondary citizenship voucher scheme. And in the realm of decision rules, he advocates "proportional proportionality" (whereby votes in both the Council of Ministers and the European Parliament would be proportional to the populations of the citizenries in member states), three Colegii (groupings) determined by size of country, concurrent majorities, and a tripartite commission. These reforms, he contends, are likely to be the best means for holding rulers accountable.

III. Limits to Institutional Design?

Desirable as Schmitter's proposed reforms might be, he concedes that they lack an effective agent: a force that has both the incentive and the authority to enact them. Enter Horowitz, much of whose previous work has also been on electoral engineering and institutional design in varying political settings where the persistent differences Ferejohn refers to take the form of strong ethnic attachments.[4] In chapter 9 Horowitz develops his earlier critique of consociational democracy as an ineffective solution to the political challenges of deeply divided societies. Consociationalism has been described by its best-known proponent as a system of government based on "a cartel of elites."[5] This reflects the fact that the groups whose rights it is designed to protect are defined by leaders, who are then forced by such devices as concurrent majorities or minority veto powers to rule by agreement with one another. (This thought seems also to inform several of Schmitter's prescriptions.)[6] The motivating idea is that in deeply divided societies majority-rule elections amount to little more than an "ethnic census," so that, without these devices, minorities will always lose in democratic politics. Accordingly, they will have no incentive to participate in hopes of working their will through the process in the future. Instead they will defect if they can, and democracy will break down.

Horowitz contends that consociational solutions are more often "the product of resolved struggles or of relatively moderate cleavages" than means to "to resolve struggles and to moderate cleavages." In fact, there is not a single case on record of a deeply divided society in which consociational solutions have been successful at ameliorating conflict. This is not surprising, in Horowitz's view, because they depend on cooperation among elites from different groups in circumstances where mutual trust is almost by definition unlikely to be forthcoming. More likely to be effective, Horowitz claims, are systems that shape the behavior of elites from one group toward the grassroots members of other groups. This can be achieved in a variety of ways, all of which require politicians to compete for votes among politicized groups other than their own. The most obvious is a combination of coalition politics and heterogeneous constituencies. Elsewhere, Horowitz has described a successful example of this kind from Malaysia, in which Malay and Chinese politicians were forced to rely in part on votes delivered by politicians belonging to the other ethnic group. The votes would not have been forthcoming "unless leaders could portray the candidates as moderate on issues of concern to the group that was delivering its votes across ethnic lines." In this type of situation, which Horowitz identifies as having operated for considerable periods (and then failed) in countries as different as Lebanon, Sri Lanka, and Nigeria, compromises at the top of a coalition are reinforced by electoral incentives at the bottom.[7]

Another possible device is geographical distribution requirements, such as the Nigerian formula for presidential elections employed in 1979 and 1983, in which the winning candidate had to get both the largest number of votes and at least 25 percent of the vote in two-thirds of the then-nineteen states of the Nigerian Federation. When territorial dispersion of politicized groups undermines the effectiveness of geographical distribution requirements, other forms of electoral engineering must be sought. The two most promising candidates are proportional representation utilizing the single transferable vote system, and an alternative vote rule that also lists more than one ordered preference but declares elected only candidates who receive a majority, rather than a plurality, of votes. Both systems require politicians to cater to voters' choices other than their first preferences, assuming heterogeneous constituencies, so that the politicians' incentives work in the appropriate moderating directions.[8]

Horowitz is convincing that such vote-pooling systems are more likely to achieve interethnic political cooperation than consociational arrangements. But this does not mean they are likely to be adopted. As he argues here, decision makers may lack the relevant knowledge of how different systems are likely to operate and overestimate the sui-generis character of their particular circumstances. The "expert" consultants are often not much better informed, and they tend to reach for the familiar—which frequently makes things worse.

Perhaps the severest obstacle to adopting coherent institutional reform packages is that the rules of the game are generally agreed on in negotiations among players who have at least one eye fixed firmly on short-term electoral consequences for themselves and their adversaries. What these players can agree on in the high-stakes context of transition negotiations may buy peace in the short term, but there is no reason to believe that they will converge on a solution that best manages the divisions in the society. Enlightened statesmen are seldom at the helm. Accordingly, Horowitz is not optimistic. The existing practice, in which elements of different schemes are forced into incoherent packages that are not well suited to ameliorating ethnic conflict, is likely to persist.

In chapter 10 Brooke Ackerly makes the case that Horowitz overestimates the importance of ethnic cleavage, and hence of the need for institutions to ameliorate it. This, she contends, is partly due to his tendency to select on the dependent variable rather than consider a broader class of cases of democratic breakdown that might reveal factors other than ethnic division to be at work. Drawing on the scholarship of Diamond and others, she argues against Horowitz that in countries like Nigeria, socioeconomic inequality and centralized political competition for economic benefits seem to have had more to do with the political breakdown than the imperfectly realized constitutional arrangements Horowitz identifies. Tackling these causes of democratic breakdown may be no easier than responding to the defects in electoral institutions, but her argument might be thought to suggest that the considerable attention that is devoted to different electoral devices as mechanisms for alleviating ethnic conflict may be misplaced. On Ackerly's telling, intensification of ethnic conflict may be more the result of intense elite political competition (principally for economic advantage) than a cause of it.

Philippe Van Parijs criticizes Horowitz from a different perspective in chapter 11. Drawing on the examples of Holland and Belgium, he makes the case that Horowitz's preoccupation with failures in attempts at democratic constitutional engineering in the face of profound ethnic division blinds him to possibilities of success. Accordingly, Van Parijs, argues, Horowitz's pessimism is unwarranted. He takes exception, moreover, to the all-or-nothing approach implicit in Horowitz's distinction between coherent and incoherent packages of reforms, arguing that, at least as far as the history of Belgium is concerned, pragmatic mixes of different schemes of ethnic accommodation have in fact been remarkably effective at attenuating ethnic conflict and achieving ethnic accommodation.

In reply in chapter 12, Horowitz disputes Van Parijs's evidence about Belgium, pointing out that when proportional representation was adopted, the ethnic conflicts there were not severe. This supports his general contention that where consociational arrangements appear to work, they have not been introduced as an antidote to deep ethnic divisions. Once conflicts become polarized, it is too late. Hence Horowitz's skepticism about consociationalism in deeply divided societies, and his "provisional pessimism" about all forms of constitutional engineering in polarized ethnic conflicts. The pessimism is provisional because he notes some possibilities that a degree of learning is in fact taking place, so that the advice given to constitutional engineers in different settings may actually be improving. And while enlightened statesmen are seldom at the helm, it is not true that they are never at the helm.

It should also be emphasized that Horowitz does not reject Ackerly's view that institutional arrangements may be only a small piece of the puzzle as far as limiting ethnic conflict is concerned. During periods of transition, however, it is institutional arrangements that are up for grabs. Even if their influence is marginal, "their impact remains important because marginal change is valuable and because formal institutions are amenable to deliberate intervention." Socioeconomic variables might ultimately be more consequential, but "those who wish to intervene deliberately in severe conflicts have to use the tools at hand." Admittedly this leaves open the question whether electoral arrangements are the most important institutions to focus on, but surely they are not irrelevant. And once they have been put into place and legitimated, they become exceedingly difficult to change. From this perspective, even if they are of modest significance, this does not detract from the importance of trying to get them right.

The controversies that divide Horowitz from his critics underscore the fact that abstract debates about democratic ideals are of limited value when conducted apart from serious efforts at institutional design, and from serious attention to the varying contexts in which democracy must be realized if it is to be realized at all. Few things are easier than celebrating rule by the deliberate sense of the people, and few things are harder than designing institutions to bring this about in practice. The essays that follow are written in a spirit of constructive, if cautious, hope about the possibility of democratic improvement. They help us understand the difficulty of implementing democratic ideals better, without falling prey to a complacent cynicism about the shortcomings of democratic life.

NOTES

1. Amy Gutmann and Dennis Thompson, *Democracy and Disagreement* (Cambridge: Harvard University Press, 1996), 12.

2. In *Buckley v. Valeo* 424 U.S. 1 (1976), the Supreme Court held, inter alia, that although Congress may regulate financial contributions to political parties or candidates, it cannot otherwise regulate private expenditures on political speech, which latter are protected by the First Amendment. Although the Court has since allowed some minor constraints on corporate expenditures, in *Austin v. Michigan State Chamber of Commerce*, 110 S.Ct. 1391 (1990), for all practical purposes the *Buckley* rule makes it impossible to limit privately funded political advertising

3. See Ian Shapiro and Lea Brilmayer, eds., *NOMOS XLI: Global Justice* (New York: New York University Press, 1999).

4. See Donald L. Horowitz, *Ethnic Groups in Conflict* (Berkeley: University of California Press, 1985), and *A Democratic South Africa? Constitutional Engineering in a Divided Society* (Berkeley: University of California Press, 1991).

5. Arendt Lijphardt, "Consociational Democracy," *World Politics* 4:2 (January 1969): 213–15, 222.

6. The cartel of elites idea may be contrasted with the model of "circulating elites" of classic pluralist theory, according to which different coalitions of elites control different parts of the political process at different times. See Robert Dahl, *Who Governs?* (New Haven: Yale University Press, 1961).

7. Horowitz, *Democratic South Africa?* 154–55.

8. Horowitz thinks this will be accentuated further by the alternative vote system, assuming that parties proliferate. Ibid., 184, 166, 187–96.

PART I

DELIBERATION, DECISION, AND ENFORCEMENT

1

DISCLOSURE VERSUS ANONYMITY IN CAMPAIGN FINANCE

IAN AYRES

INTRODUCTION

About the only campaign finance issue on which there is a strong consensus is the belief that the law should force candidates to disclose the identity of their contributors. The Supreme Court in *Buckley v. Valeo* has signed off on such regulation as a means of deterring candidates from selling access and influence in return for contributions. Today there are calls for "instantaneous" disclosure via the Internet. Indeed, a growing group of scholars and advocates are coming to believe that mandated disclosure should be the *only* campaign finance regulation. For example, Representative John Doolittle has proposed "The Citizen Legislature and Political Freedom Act," which essentially would repeal all limits on political campaign contributions and merely require immediate disclosure by candidates when they do receive contributions.[1] This type of "pure disclosure" reform has garnered support from a wide spectrum of both liberals and conservatives—including the CATO Institute, Senator Mitch McConnell, and Kathleen Sullivan.[2] People who want to repeal all campaign finance regulation save mandatory disclosure have come to believe that other restrictions are counterproductive because they tend to shift money to less accountable forms of political speech—such as "independent expenditures" and "issue advocacy."

A set of enduring poetic images for the advocates of mandated disclosure was provided by Justice Brandeis:

> Publicity is justly commended as a remedy for social and industrial diseases. Sunlight is said to be the best of disinfectants; electric light the most efficient policeman.

But there exists in our polity a counterimage—the voting booth—that stands against this cult of disclosure. Ballot secrecy was adopted toward the end of the nineteenth century to deter political corruption. "Before this reform, people could buy your vote and hold you to your bargain by watching you at the polling place."[3] Voting booth privacy disrupted the economics of vote buying, making it much more difficult for candidates to buy votes because, at the end of the day, they could never be sure who voted for them.

A similar proanonymity argument can be applied to campaign finance. We might be able to harness similar anonymity benefits by creating a "donation booth": a screen that forces donors to funnel campaign contributions through blind trusts. Like the voting booth, the donation booth would keep candidates from learning the identity of their supporters. Just as the secret ballot makes it more difficult for candidates to *buy* votes, mandating anonymous donations through a system of blind trusts might make it harder for candidates to *sell* access or influence because they would never know which donors had paid the price. Knowledge about whether the other side actually performs his or her promise is an important prerequisite of trade. People—including political candidates—are less likely to deal if they are uncertain whether the other side performs. The secret ballot disrupts vote buying because candidates are uncertain how a citizen actually voted; anonymous donations disrupt influence peddling because candidates are uncertain whether contributors actually contributed.

So which is better: mandated disclosure or mandated anonymity? Each holds the potential for disrupting political corruption. This Article tries to imagine the effects of pure disclosure and anonymity regimes.[4] If we were to repeal all contribution or expenditures limitations and were going to regulate only information, which should we prefer? I tentatively argue that mandated anonymity is preferable. It is a less restrictive alternative that is more likely to deter political corruption.

Critics are quick to point out that mandated anonymity is likely to convert some direct contributions into independent, "issue-advocacy" expenditures (where anonymity cannot be required), but they fail to see that mandated disclosure, if it were effective in deterring political corruption, would also be likely to shift some direct contributions toward issue ads (where disclosure cannot be required). The simple reason that mandated disclosure is unlikely to hydraulically push money toward issue advocacy is that disclosing the identity of donors deters very little corruption. Disclosure regimes may make us feel good about ourselves but they probably do not produce very different results than a true laissez-faire regime, where contributors have complete freedom to remain anonymous or to disclose their identity to the candidate and/or the public. Thus, while the Article nominally confronts the choice between mandated anonymity and mandated disclosure, in most cases this is essentially the same as a choice between mandated anonymity and informational laissez-faire. At the end of the day, reasonable people could disfavor mandated anonymity—for example, because of the predictable shift of resources toward less accountable independent issue advocacy—but they should not particularly favor mandated disclosure because it generates substantial benefits beyond a regime that declined to mandate either disclosure or anonymity.

Several states have already experimented with prohibiting judicial candidates from learning who donates to their (re)election campaigns.[5] The rationale, of course, is that judges do not need to know the identity of their donors: Judicial decisions should be based on cases' merits, not contributors' money. But there is no good reason that legislators or the executive need to know the identity of their donors. An individual's power to influence government should not turn on personal wealth. Small donors are already effectively anonymous because $100 is not going to buy very much face time with the President. Mandating anonymity is likely to level the influence playing field by making small contributions count for relatively more. Anonymous donors can still signal the intensity of their preferences by marching on Washington—barefoot, if need be.

In what has become a postelection ritual, politicians wring their hands about the problem of campaign donors buying unwarranted "access." Candidates assert that contributions do not affect their political positions. Nonetheless, the suspicion that "access" leads to corruption persists. If candidates really want to stop themselves from selling influence or access, they should forgo finding out the identity of their contributors.

The idea of mandating anonymity at first strikes many readers as a radical and dangerous departure from the current norm of disclosure. The metaphors of "sunshine" and "open air" are currently very powerful. But to assess the anonymity idea fairly, it is necessary to free ourselves from what might be little more than the happenstance of history. The public ballot was similarly accepted as a natural and necessary part of democracy for roughly half of our nation's history. This system produced "the common spectacle of lines of persons being marched to the polls holding their colored ballots above their heads to show that they were observing orders or fulfilling promises."[6] These spectacles put such pressure on the disclosure norm that, ultimately, the secret "Australian ballot" caught on and spread like wildfire at the end of the nineteenth century.[7] Readers need to consider whether the current spectacle of campaign corruption might be sufficient to overturn our deeply ingrained disclosure norm.

This Article is divided into three parts. Part I compares how mandated anonymity and disclosure regimes might disrupt the market for political influence. Part II then describes in more detail how a system of mandated anonymity might operate. To avoid the "nirvana fallacy" of comparing an idealized reform to a real-world market failure, this part assesses whether the private efforts to evade anonymity—by means of "independent expenditures" or "issue advocacy"—undermine the usefulness of the proposal. Part III argues that mandated anonymity is clearly constitutional. Indeed, appreciating the possibility of anonymity may even undermine *Buckley v. Valeo*'s conclusion that mandated disclosure is constitutional.

I. MITIGATING THE PROBLEMS OF POLITICAL CORRUPTION

The corrupting influence of campaign contributions has been a central concern of finance reform.[8] The notion that wealthy

TABLE 1. THREE INFORMATIONAL REGIMES

Disclosure Regime	Donor, candidate, and public know
Laissez-Faire Regime	Donor and candidate know
Anonymity Regime	Only donor knows

donors are able to purchase political access or influence is antithetical to our ideal of equal citizenship.[9] As Cass Sunstein has observed, "[T]here is no good reason to allow disparities in wealth to be translated into disparities in political power. A well-functioning democracy distinguishes between market processes of purchase and sale on the one hand and political processes of voting and reason-giving on the other."[10] Bruce Ackerman also advocates separating market and political processes: "A democratic market society must confront a basic tension between its ideal of equal citizenship and the reality of market inequality. It does so by drawing a line, marking a political sphere within which the power relationships of the market are kept under democratic control."[11] The most popular reforms for decoupling these spheres operate by regulating money: They either limit the amount that donors can give or they limit the amount that candidates can spend.

But there is another way to decouple private wealth from public power. Instead of limiting money, we might limit information. Since Watergate, the only informational reforms have been those that have increased the amount of mandated disclosure. Discussions of disclosure often assume that we must choose between a world in which everyone knows of a gift (the disclosure regime) and a world in which only a donor and her candidate know the source of a gift (the laissez-faire regime). But as shown in Table I, this analysis overlooks the possibility of moving toward a world in which only the donor knows about a gift. In fact, there are several different continua of possible informational regulations. For example, we could require the blind trusts that received a candidate's contributions to publicly disclose the identity of all donors but not the amounts that the individuals gave.[12] For specificity, I will image a "mandated anonymity" regime where the donor has the option of remaining completely anonymous or having the blind trust verify publicly that she gave up to $200. The trust would never disclose whether a donor had given more than $200. It is my thesis that the failure of scholars and courts to consider these alternative informational regimes is largely responsible for the strong consensus in favor of public disclosure.

The impetus for disclosure is that a public armed with knowledge about political contributions will be able to punish candidates who sell their office or who are otherwise inappropriately influenced. It has, however, proved exceedingly difficult to infer inappropriate influence from the mere fact of contributions. Politicians claim they would have acted the same way regardless of whether a questionable contribution had been made. Moreover, we have been unwilling to prohibit selling access (re: face time) in return for contributions. The attorney general has flatly concluded that such quid pro quo agreements are legal.[13] And today's jaded citizenry imposes hardly any electoral punishment on candidates known to have sold political access. In sum, public disclosure produces very little deterrent benefit: types of corruption that can be proved (contributions for access) are legal, and types of corruption that are illegal (contributions for influence) can't be proved. At most, disclosure deters only the most egregious and express types of influence peddling.

In contrast, a regime of mandated anonymity interferes with an informational prerequisite of corruption. Put simply, it will be more difficult for candidates to sell access or influence if they are unsure whether a donor has paid the price. Of course, much turns on whether government can actually keep candidates uninformed about who donates to their campaigns. But to begin, this section considers what an idealized regime of mandated anonymity—without evasions or substitute speech—can and cannot accomplish.

An idealized donation booth would severely impede quid pro quo corruption, the trading of contributions for political access or influence. This effect would encompass not only explicit trades (donations for nights in the Lincoln bedroom, presidential coffees, legislative activity), but also a large range of implicit deals, including sequential action whereby either the politician or donor "performs" in expectation of subsequent performance by the other side. The Supreme Court's concern with the corrupting effects of "political debts"[14] would also be neutralized by the donation booth for the simple reason that politicians would be unable to determine to whom they were indebted. This rationale was explicitly used to justify a proposed system of anonymous donations to presidential legal defense funds. In 1993, the Office of Government Ethics ("OGE") reasoned, "Anonymous private paymasters do not have an economic hold on an employee because the employee does not know who the paymasters are. Moreover, the employee has no way to favor the outside anonymous donors."[15]

Mandated anonymity could also deter politicians from extorting donations. The popular discussion of quid pro quo corruption focuses solely on campaign contributions in return for legislative favors. In the terminology of public choice theory, donors would be engaged in a kind of "rent seeking." But there is a radically different kind of quid pro quo corruption. Politicians engage in "rent extraction" when they threaten potential donors with unfavorable treatment unless a sufficiently large contribution is made.[16] Rent extraction almost surely explains some of the anomalous patterns of giving—particularly, the "everybody loves a winner" phenomenon. The high level of contributions made to incumbents with safe seats is consistent with rent extraction because incumbents have the greatest ability to extort donations.[17] Understanding rent extraction also explains why several corporations have privately agreed not to make soft money contributions.[18] Fear of rent extraction may even keep private interest groups from organizing because politicians will have a harder time shaking down an unorganized mass.[19] Mandated donor anonymity would allow private interests to organize without fear of being targeted for extortion.

Just as the secret ballot substantially deterred vote buying, mandating secret donations might substantially deter both forms of quid pro quo corruption: rent seeking and rent extraction. There is a lively academic debate about how much current campaign donations are intended to garner access or influence or to avoid unfavorable treatment.[20] Since mandated anonymity is better suited than mandated disclosure to deter quid pro quo corruption, an important part of its justification must turn on the extent to which this form of corruption is truly a problem.

However, the problems of "monetary influence corruption" or "inequality" also plague our current system of campaign finance.[21] Although mandated anonymity would not eliminate these problems, a regime of mandated anonymity is likely to mitigate these problems much more than a regime of mandated disclosure. Even when politicians don't condition their behavior on contributions, they may nonetheless expect that taking certain positions will cause donors to give more money. This is the problem of "monetary influence." And even when wealthy donors don't expect their giving to change a candidate's behavior, they may reasonably believe that giving to a candidate with whom they agree will increase that candidate's chance of (re)election. This at times is referred to as the inequality problem. In the first instance, there is the possibility that a contribution has a corruptive influence on the candidate's behavior. In the second, even though the candidate's positions are uncorrupted (read "unchanged") by the contribution, the contributions of those with disproportionate wealth corrupt the process by increasing the likelihood that positions favored by the wealthy will be disproportionately favored in our political sphere.

Some might argue, however, that monetary influence is not a problem because donors' willingness to pay usefully informs candidates about the intensity of voter preferences. Yet there is strong consensus from a broad range of scholars that politicians should not choose their policies with an eye toward campaign contributions.[22] Not all interest groups can readily organize to compete for candidates' monetary interests. A concentrated interest group advocating a law that decreases social welfare may be able to donate more money than can more diffuse interests opposing the measure. Under such conditions, donations may give candidates a false signal of citizens' intensity of preference. Insulating candidates from the influence of donations may lead toward legislation that more truly reflects the preference intensity of voters.[23] Monetary-influence corruption, like vote buying, is rejected because the legitimate preferences of citizens with unequal abilities to pay or unequal opportunities to pay are given undue influence.[24]

Scholars have also rejected the notion that contributions should influence politicians in part because contributions tend to reduce independent deliberation and reason giving.[25] David Strauss, in particular, has argued:

> [O]n any plausible conception of representative government, elected representatives sometimes should exercise independent judgment. . . . Campaign contributions do not create the possibility that representatives will follow instead of lead; that is an unavoidable (and to some extent desirable) part of any democracy. But because contribution-votes can be so much better targeted than votes at the ballot box, a system in which contributions are explicitly exchanged for official action will accentuate this tendency of representative government.[26]

Under this view, the monetary influence of contributions impedes the deliberative processes of democracy. At times, representatives should take positions that are not merely aggregations of their constituents' preferences.

Mandated anonymity would reduce the corrupting influence of contributions on candidates' behavior by reducing both the candidates' feedback about how particular positions affect giving and the willingness of donors to make large donations to influence candidate behavior. Candidates would still learn the total amount of money that had been contributed to their campaigns, but they wouldn't learn how particular positions translate into particular contributions. Mandated anonymity would create a kind of Tiebout model[27] for candidates' policies. In the original Tiebout model, different towns committed to particular taxes and amenities, and then potential citizens voted with their feet by moving to the towns with the tax and expenditure package they most preferred. Mandated anonymity would push the contribution market in the same direction. Politicians would announce policies and then wait to see whether those policies garnered financial support. This is not true independent leadership, but it is likely to be more independent than the current regime—one in which private interests can bestow gifts on a politician in full expectation that she will see and appreciate on which side her bread is buttered.

Past giving would be a poor guide for predicting future donations under a mandated anonymity regime because donor anonymity would exacerbate the "donor's paradox." Just as it is irrational to vote when there is an infinitesimal chance that one's vote will affect the election, it is irrational to give if one's gift imperceptibly increases the chance of a candidate's victory. Under the current regime, politicians overcome the donor's paradox by developing a reputation for giving donors special consideration; large donors expect their contributions to yield concrete benefits concerning a candidate's policy, legislative activity, or at the very least, the candidate's willingness to meet with the donor. But mandated anonymity greatly diminishes the expected return on an individual donation and thus, in all likelihood, will substantially reduce the number of large donations. It would be difficult for candidates to provide favors or special access for individual contributors without knowing the contributors' identities.

Mandating donor anonymity would reduce the disproportionate influence of wealth in our political system not only by reducing the number of large donations, but also possibly by increasing the number of small donations. While mandating anonymity exacerbates the donor's paradox for large donors, the same anonymity might mildly mitigate the paradox for small donors. Under the current system, small donors have virtually no impact on the electoral process. "For example in the 1996 election cycle less than one-fourth of 1 percent of the American people gave contributions of $200 or more to a federal candidate," but this tiny group of donors generated an astonishing eighty percent of total donations.[28] By reducing the importance of large donations, mandated anonymity would make small donors relatively more important and thus might induce less affluent donors to give more.

Mandated anonymity—even if perfectly implemented—is not a panacea. Candidates would still have a muted incentive to take certain positions in order to generate contributions, and the wealthy would continue to have a disproportionate voice in electioneering. But by (1) making it harder for politicians to reward their contributors, (2) substantially reducing the number of large donors, and (3) possibly increasing the number of small donors, a regime of mandated anonymity could mitigate the problems of monetary influence and inequality.

In contrast, mandated disclosure is much less likely to affect these problems. Monetary influence and inequality could be deterred only if voters punished candidates who pandered to contributors or received disproportionate contributions because of their position favoring wealthy contributors. Our experience with mandated disclosure is that the benefits to a candidate of having extra contributions for the campaign almost always outweigh any the possibility that some voters will be put off by the fact of the contribution itself. At the end of the day, a workable regime of mandated anonymity is likely to have a much larger effect than mandated disclosure on monetary influence and inequality for the simple reason that it is likely to reduce the number of five- and six-figure contributions.

II. Confronting Practical Problems
of Implementation

The preceding part considered the effects of an idealized system of mandated anonymity. But to avoid the nirvana fallacy, one must consider whether and how anonymity could be implemented. If candidates could easily decode the identity of their contributors, then the superficial requirement of anonymity would be counterproductive; we would lose the limited benefits of public disclosure and gain nothing, thus permitting quid pro quo corruption to proceed unabated. This part considers the details of implementation, assesses the extent to which anonymity can be maintained, and ultimately concludes that, even given predictable evasions, mandating donor anonymity is sufficiently workable to remain a plausible candidate for reform.

While it has been difficult to force candidates to disclose meaningful and timely information about the identity of their contributors, implementing a regime that keeps candidates in the dark is potentially even more daunting. To mitigate problems of implementation, the implementation rules in this section are organized around a "mimicry" principle. Contributions are kept effectively anonymous not by restricting the signals that true donors can send to candidates but, instead, by allowing faux donors to send identical signals. As long as faux donors can mimic the signals of true donors, candidates will have difficulty discerning whether a contribution was actually made.

A. Details of Implementation

Mandated donor anonymity might be applied to any election. As mentioned above, some judicial election reforms have already successfully prevented candidates from learning the identity of their donors. For concreteness, this section considers how to implement a regime of mandated donor anonymity in federal elections.

1. Private versus public administration. One could imagine a system of literal donation booths controlled by the government: Once the curtain closed, people could drop their cash donations into a slot for the candidate of their choice, and the government would periodically pass these contributions on to the appropriate candidates. Just as there is a "ceremonial aspect[ ] of voting . . . [that] is to some degree a self-conscious act of citizenship,"[29] visiting a government donation booth might in time also come to be viewed as a constitutive act of citizenship.

Donation booths—whether publicly or privately administered—run greater risks of fraud than do voting booths. For either "booth" to be effective, we must trust the administrator (1) not to reveal for whom citizens vote or to whom they donate, and (2) not to misapply the donation or vote to an unintended candidate. But with donations—unlike votes—there is the added risk that the administrator will convert the gift to her own private benefit.

Because of this embezzlement risk, we tentatively prefer a privatized system of blind trusts, operated by seasoned trust companies (say, those in existence for at least ten years) with substantial, pre-existing assets (of more than, say, $100,000,000).[30] More than one thousand financial institutions satisfy these requirements. Requiring the trust companies to be seasoned and large would make donors, candidates, and the public more likely to trust the participating institutions. The diversity of qualifying institutions would help ensure that all candidates are treated fairly. But because the threat of defalcation is so high, the trusts' records should be publicly audited ten years after each election. This ex-post auditing would inform donors whether their donations had been properly routed and would allow the public to assess whether donations were—notwithstanding the trust—purchasing access or influence. Computer encryption software might make it possible for donors to verify anonymously that their contributions were credited to the appropriate campaign funds.

2. Mechanics of blind trust operation. Each candidate, political party, and PAC would choose a qualified institution to establish a separate blind trust account. Representatives of the blind trust could not be employed in positions influencing access or policy and, as a prophylactic, should be prohibited from privately communicating with candidates or campaign workers. The core regulation would require all donations to individual candidates, political parties, or PACs to be made to the blind trusts by mail. Campaigns would no longer be allowed to accept money in cash or by check. Campaigns would still need check books, but not deposit slips. The blind trusts would conceal the source of all contributions larger than $200. Large donors would have the option of having the trust disclose that they had given up to $200, but under no circumstance would the trust identify a donor as having contributed more than $200. Allowing donors to prove that they have contributed to a particular campaign mitigates the free-speech burden of the regulation. The exact dollar amount for the anonymity threshold is unimportant, but the notion is that small donations pose a much smaller threat of corruption.

The blind trusts would then report to the candidates on a weekly or biweekly basis how much money had been donated, but would not detail the amounts given by large donors. The frequency of reporting would have to balance the candidate's need to know how much she could spend against the desire to impede candidates from decoding the identity of particular donors. Hourly disclosure of amounts available would allow a donor to say, "I bet your total went up $100,000 during the past hour." Large donations on Israel's independence day might analogously signal contributors' interest in pro-Israel policies. One way to shorten the time between disclosures would be to require that trusts intentionally obscure the presence of large donations. Trusts might even be allowed to report the daily amount available for spending, but this amount might be calculated using a randomizing procedure that breaks up unusually large contributions for future disclosure.

3. Donor speech. One might consider reinforcing the anonymity of the blind trust by prohibiting donors from discussing their

contributions with the candidate or others. Such a prohibition could be backed up by criminal penalties, civil penalties, or both. But such a regulation is fraught with problems of enforcement and constitutionality. The law can do little to stop private, one-on-one conversations between donors and candidates. Even if such conversations could be regulated, the resulting burden on donors' free speech rights may not be compatible with the First Amendment.

A "cheap talk" regime is preferable. Just as anyone can tell Clinton she had voted for him, allowing anyone to tell Clinton she had given him money would not give Clinton a very good idea of who his true contributors were. For the blind trusts to be effective, it is only necessary that donors cannot credibly communicate whether they have contributed. As long as the candidate cannot verify whether a donor's representation is true, the blind trust can impede influence peddling. Some will argue that it is simply wrong for the government to tacitly promote lying. However, it can be a civic virtue to dissemble in order to disrupt criminal activity. The possibly apocryphal World War II story of the Danish king wearing—and urging other Christians to wear—the Jewish yellow star is a prime example of the virtue of social "ambiguation."[31] More prosaically, the ubiquitous (and oftentimes false) cab sticker "Not more than $20 kept by driver" shows that lying to discourage crime is an acceptable exception to truth telling.

Donors wishing to prove they donated to a particular candidate may brandish a canceled check showing the amount of the donation. To mitigate this problem, trusts should be required to provide a check cashing service for nondonors. A faux donor could mail a check to a trust with a note asking the trust to deposit the check and (once it had cleared) to mail back to the faux donor a reimbursement check. The faux donor requesting reimbursement would receive both a canceled check from her bank and a reimbursement check from the trust. A candidate seeing a canceled check made out to a blind trust couldn't be sure whether the canceled check evidences a contribution or merely a cash conversion. And since the trust's reimbursement check could be cashed or posted to a different account, showing the candidate a bank statement or audited books would not prove that a contribution had been made. As with cheap talk, appropriate regulation could undermine the credibility of canceled checks.

Donors wanting to signal their gift credibly might instead mail the check to the blind trust while in the presence of a campaign representative (or simpler yet, give the check to the campaign worker to mail to the trust on the donor's behalf). We favor prohibiting such behavior. Yet even here, a system of mandated anonymity does not need to rely solely on the deterrent effect of ex-post penalties. It might be advisable to give donors a ten-day cooling-off period, during which they could cancel any donation. As long as a period exists in which donors can privately cancel their contributions, the credibility of previous public signals will be attenuated.

4. Soliciting contributions. The fundamental requirement would be that, in fund-raising, no one from the candidate's campaign could accept contributions; only representatives of the blind trust could accept checks (via the mail). Candidates could still ask individuals for support, but they could not close the deal. George Bush could still have fund-raisers and limit invitations to rich, registered Republicans. But under this regime of mandated anonymity, the invitations could not be conditioned on a campaign contribution, and the dinner could not be priced above cost. Instead, campaign workers could do no more than distribute postage-free envelopes addressed to the blind trust so that attendees could later mail in a contribution. Making it more difficult for candidates (and their political opponents) to solicit funds personally from wealthy contributors might alleviate the current fund-raising marathon.[32]

This scheme of mandated anonymity would go a long way toward eliminating the long-standing practice of rewarding successful fund-raisers with ambassadorships. The representatives of the trust could not take jobs or even consult with the administration. A candidate might observe a fund-raiser's inputs (how many New Hampshire coffees she hosted) but not her output (how many donations she generated).

5. Drawing the line. In deciding what types of contributions to subject to the anonymity requirement, we will be obliged to distinguish close cases. Line drawing is a necessary feature of any reform program trying to constrain the influence of money in

the political sphere. To begin, the in-kind contribution of services by political volunteers would not be made anonymously because it would be impossible for a candidate not to know their identities. Thus, people could still volunteer in order to receive undeserved access or influence. There is also no practicable way to stop candidates from knowing how much they contribute to their own campaign.[33]

Benefit concerts present a difficult issue. If Barbra Streisand performs a series of concerts to benefit the Clinton campaign, Clinton could easily estimate how much revenue is being generated. Allowing benefit concerts would provide an easy end run around the rule mandating that fund-raising dinners must be priced at cost. Many of today's $1,000-a-plate fund-raising dinners could become tomorrow's $1,000-a-seat benefit concerts with only nominal entertainment. Accordingly, performers should be prohibited from contractually dedicating the proceeds from an event to a political campaign. The performer or audience could independently contribute or claim that they gave or will give the proceeds; they just couldn't enter into an enforceable contract ensuring that attendance ensures contribution. We would still allow politically motivated concerts and rallies, but any profit would need to escheat to the state (or possibly to a nonpolitical charity).

B. Can Anonymity Be Maintained?

The metaprinciple of implementation is to allow nondonors to ape easily any signal that true donors might try to send. If nondonors can mimic the signals of donors, then donors will have difficulty credibly communicating their contributions. This principle explains the specific regulations regarding donor speech, check cashing, and cooling-off periods. Instead of prohibiting donors from speaking, the regime allows nondonors to use the same words. To undermine the credibility of a donor's canceled check, the regime gives nondonors the option of acquiring an identical canceled check by merely cashing a check with the blind trust. And to undermine the credibility of mailing a check in the presence of a campaign worker, the cooling-off period allows nondonors to publicly donate and then privately cancel.

There are, however, limitations to the mimicry principle. A poor person cannot credibly mimic the representations of a rich person—saying that she donated $100,000, for example. But it is unlikely that ability to pay is a close enough proxy for willingness to pay to cause politicians to kowtow to rich people generally. For example, if a law mandated that sellers of Cadillacs could not learn the identity of their customers, sellers would not respond by giving Cadillacs to the universe of rich people. Even if wealth (ability to pay) signals something about whether a donor actually gave, the important point is that the signal would be much weaker than it is now. Similarly, it would not be credible for liberals to represent that they contributed to conservatives (or vice versa). In the shadow of a donation booth, Ralph Nader could not credibly represent that he had donated to the Republican Party. At the end of the day, rich conservatives are the only people who would potentially make large soft money contributions to the Republicans. Therefore, it is reasonable to ask who among this group would be willing to go to the trouble of becoming a faux donor—to noise up the system, for example, by making the ratio of canceled checks to net donations fairly high. My answer is that the current class of Republican contributors who either feel they are being extorted or think they are paying for favors are prime candidates to fake donation. Victims of extortion are likely to have few qualms about lying to avoid the political shakedown, and even those contributors who are trying to corrupt the system by buying political favoritism may prefer to get the same favoritism for a reduced price.

Although this proposal tries to undermine a donor's ability to communicate her contribution credibly, I am under no illusion that this (or any other) system of anonymity would be completely successful in keeping candidates uninformed. Some inventive donors, with the aid of inquiring candidates, will undoubtedly devise methods to credibly signal. For example, donors or candidates may bribe a representative of the blind trust to violate her fiduciary duty and disclose donor identities.[34] Undoubtedly, incumbents will have an easier time than nonincumbents discovering the identity of their contributors because a previous history of giving provides a stronger basis for belief; nonincumbents often must start with no track record of fund-raising. But simply relying on reputation will not suffice. A history of giving when donations were public does not create a very strong reputation for continuing to give once contributions become anonymous. Candidates will rightfully be concerned that even faithful contributors, once behind the cloak of anonymity, will decide to chisel on their past tradition of giving.

The most predictable and serious evasions of mandated anonymity is likely to be a substitution toward "independent expenditures" or "issue advocacy." The test for what constitutes independence turns on who controls the content of the speech. Independent expenditures—in contradistinction to "coordinated expenditures"—fund political expression that is not controlled by a candidate's campaign. Independent expenditures are made without "prearrangement and coordination." The test for "issue advocacy" turns on the content of the speech itself. Issue advocacy—in contradistinction to "express advocacy"—does not expressly advocate the election of a particular candidate.

Because the Supreme Court has shown greater willingness to protect political speech that it deems either "issue advocacy" or an "independent expenditure," mandating donor anonymity for large gifts would undoubtedly cause more extensive use of these two end runs. And it is clear that independent expenditures and issue advocacy still pose some danger of corruption. "Candidates often know who spends money on their behalf, and for this reason, an [independent] expenditure may in some contexts give rise to the same reality and appearance of corruption."[35]

As shown in figure 1, these two dichotomous categories create four permutations of control and content. Coordinated express advocacy, like candidate express advocacy, is the most regulated type of political speech. One might initially predict a hydraulic response if donor anonymity were applied to this category: Every dollar of direct contribution that the donation booth deterred might simply reemerge in one of the three other boxes—as an independent expenditure, an issue advocacy campaign, or both. Recent history has already provided ample evidence of substitution toward these three categories.[36] What is more, because candidates are not accountable for "independent" ad campaigns,

FIGURE 1

		Content Test	
		Express Advocacy	Issue Advocacy
Control Test	Independent	///////	
	Coordinated	///////	///////

Mandated Contributor Anonymity Constitutionally Permissible	///////
Mandated Contributor Anonymity Not Constitutionally Permissible	

these campaigns are likely to be particularly negative and reckless. It is not surprising, therefore, that the infamous "Willie Horton" ads were independent expenditures.[37]

If mandated anonymity is likely to produce anything like a dollar-for-dollar hydraulic shift from direct contributions to independent expenditures or issue advocacy, the benefits of mandated anonymity reform would largely be lost. However, (1) mandated anonymity can be extended to reduce the possibility of an end run, and (2) where mandated anonymity is not constitutionally permissible, existing structural factors may ensure that independent or issue advocacy will not be a perfect substitute for corrupt, direct contributions. What would it mean to extend mandated anonymity? To begin, it is straightforward to cover coordinated issue advocacy. As a constitutional matter, coordinated speech can be regulated as much as direct candidate speech.[38] And although there is currently a lively debate about whether current law regulates coordinated issue advocacy,[39] there is little question that informational regulation (such as mandated disclosure or mandated anonymity) is constitutional.

Independent express advocacy poses a harder problem. This circumvention, however, could also be substantially reduced by requiring that such campaigns be funded solely by contributions from individuals (not corporations or unions) funneled through blind trusts.[40] Under such a regime, organizations could establish committees to orchestrate independent express advocacy ad campaigns, but the funding for such campaigns would need to come from individuals' donations to blind trusts. As with the earlier anonymity proposal, individuals would be able to communicate credibly that they had contributed (up to $200) and thus, for example, have their names appear in a newspaper advertisement saying, "We support candidate x." But such individuals would not be able to signal the amount of a large contribution.

Requiring that independent express advocacy be funded by individual anonymous donations would substantially reduce the viability of this circumvention. To be sure, some wealthy individuals would still be able to completely fund an independent express advocacy campaign.[41] But given the costs of effective advertising, we predict that it would be difficult to raise individual contributions in the shadow of a blind trust. Those donors who are deterred by mandated anonymity from contributing directly to a candidate's campaign are unlikely to give to a blind trust that needs numerous contributions for effective independent express advocacy. And few individuals have the wherewithal to individually fund effective independent ads.

The most unyielding problem concerns substitution toward the upper-right box in figure 1, that is, substitution toward independent issue advocacy. This combination of content and control has proven constitutionally unregulable. *Buckley v. Valeo* suggests that mandated disclosure of speaker identity in this quadrant is unconstitutional, and mandated anonymity would fare no better. Still, some progress might be made by expanding the definition of what counts as express advocacy. The Supreme Court might accept a broader definition than the "magic words" test suggested in *Buckley*. The McCain-Feingold bill attempts just this broadening by defining as express advocacy any advertisements picturing or naming a candidate within thirty days of a primary election or sixty days of a general election. But instead of capping such expenditures or requiring disclosure of the names of the people who fund such campaigns, mandating contributor anonymity would more effectively balance the government's interest in deterring corruption with the First Amendment interest in allowing unfettered discussion of political issues.

Even under the broadest imaginable constitutional definition of express advocacy, there will still be significant opportunity to use independent issue ads to affect the outcome of an election. But independent issue ads are not perfect substitutes for direct donations, especially donations made as part of quid pro quo corruption. As the Supreme Court has repeatedly emphasized:

> Unlike contributions, such independent expenditures may well provide little assistance to the candidate's campaign and indeed may prove counterproductive. The absence of prearrangement and coordination of an expenditure with the candidate or his agent not only undermines the value of the expenditure to the candidate, but also alleviates the danger that expenditures will be given as a quid pro quo for improper commitments from the candidate.[42]

This quotation nicely underscores the procedural and substantive differences between direct contributions and independent expenditures. Procedurally, the absence of prearrangement and coordination makes it more difficult for candidates and contributors to agree on the terms of quid pro quo corruption. The inability of candidates to solicit these expenditures, in particular, is likely to reduce a candidate's ability to extort (extract rent from) potential donors. Substantively, the absence of prearrangement and coordination makes it more likely that the independent expenditure will be spent differently than the candidate would have spent a direct contribution. The Supreme Court is overly sanguine in suggesting that "independent expenditures may well provide little assistance to the candidate's campaign and indeed may prove counterproductive." But because candidates would often use the money differently—for example, on express advocacy—candidates will tend to value $1,000,000 of independent issue ads less than $1,000,000 of direct contributions.[43]

Under a regime of mandated anonymity, candidates might still take positions in order to induce independent issue ads on their behalf (and vice versa), but the prohibition of both coordination and express advocacy acts as a tax on such indirect giving, tending to reduce its value to the candidate. Because mass communication exhibits dramatic economies of scale, it may be much more difficult for individuals who had been giving, say, $10,000 or $20,000 to the Democratic Party (and its candidates) to find an equally effective issue-ad substitute. To be sure, independent issue-ad organizations will start soliciting contributions, but these organizations are likely to find it more difficult to persuade the erstwhile political donor to contribute.

While I concede mandated anonymity would lead to an increase in independent issue ads, I simultaneously predict that a regime of mandated anonymity would nevertheless reduce quid pro quo and monetary-influence corruption by reducing the overall level of direct and indirect (such as issue advocacy) contributions. A donation booth is likely to dramatically reduce the number of five- and six-figure "soft money" contributions. Moreover, mandated anonymity would prohibit the current practice of PAC bundling, whereby PACs gain influence with candidates by bundling together contributions from individual donors.

The predictable, hydraulic shift of contributions toward less accountable issue advocacy—even if only partial—is a reasonable ground for ultimately opposing a mandated anonymity regime. But this hydraulic criticism perversely should also undermine the conviction that mandated disclosure by itself will be effective in deterring corruption. If mandated disclosure could deter corrupt direct giving, the hydraulic critics would have to fear that the same corrupt contributions would reappear as anonymous "issue advocacy" ads.[44] Mandated disclosure might not deter corruption but merely shift it to less accountable independent expenditures. Proponents of mandated disclosure must admit either that finance regulation can sometimes deter unwanted direct contributions without creating an unacceptable substitution or that mandated disclosure is simply window dressing that is not really expected to deter unwanted contributions. My intuition is that the hydraulic response is not a concern when it comes to mandated disclosure because we do not believe that disclosure deters very many direct contributions in the first place.

C. Is the Game Worth the Candle?

This section will consider three additional drawbacks of the scheme, beyond the shift of money to less accountable issue advocacy. While this article has previously argued that a candidate has a legitimate interest in learning the identity of her contributors, the donation booth also denies identity information to voters and other donors. This section considers whether preventing these people from learning donor identities undermines the usefulness of mandated anonymity. But first the section considers an even more fundamental problem: Whether anonymity would unduly limit a candidate's ability to speak.

1. Less candidate speech. The claim that mandated anonymity could cause a campaign-financing crisis must be taken seriously. Anonymity exacerbates the donor's paradox for large donors and might lead to a dramatic drop-off in giving. As a general matter, donors like to be recognized for their charity. The donation booth may have an overbreadth problem in that contributors who currently give, in part, to acquire status among their peers may be deterred from giving through blind trusts. Even donors who are not motivated by a desire to corruptly influence policy may thus be chilled by mandated anonymity.

Access to the media requires funding. A reduction in donations could mean a reduction in media access. In this regard, mandated anonymity could limit a candidate's ability to speak— and thereby the public's right to listen. Indeed, the very uncertainty of the effect of mandated anonymity on contributions could give policy makers pause.

A related concern is that, by reducing the ability of candidates to speak, mandated anonymity will unduly increase the influence of other speakers, such as the media, unions, and rich, self-funded candidates. Media speech, the quintessential independent expenditure, will go unregulated under any reform proposal. We might worry about who will be next in line to influence the candidate corruptly if anonymity undermines the influence of large donors. Candidates unable to sell influence in exchange for contributions might begin to kowtow to the image makers of the mass media. It might be better to countenance the undue influence of large donors under the current system than to transfer this influence to an even smaller media oligarchy. Under this theory, the contributions of James Riady and the millions of other millionaires among us may provide a Jeffersonian counterweight against the potentially disproportionate influence of Citizens Hearst or Murdoch—or the even less accountable corporations and unions that bankroll issue ads.

Nevertheless, facilitating quid pro quo and monetary influence corruption is too high a price to pay for political speech. The Constitution doesn't require Congress to facilitate corruption in order to subsidize political speech. Prohibiting quid pro quo deals might also substantially reduce the ability of candidates to speak, but the First Amendment doesn't mandate generating money to produce a meaningless debate in which donors have already purchased candidates' positions outside the realm of open deliberation. If noncorrupt private donations do not sufficiently fund campaigns or offset the undue influence of media moguls, we should supplement private contributions with public money. A belief that mandated anonymity would produce far fewer net political expenditures than a mandated disclosure should be a signal that disclosure by itself would not be effective in deterring corruption.

2. Less donor information for voters. Mandated anonymity keeps voters—as well as candidates—in the dark about donors' identities. Denying voters this information could be problematic. The Supreme Court in *Buckley* identified two adverse effects:

> [Disclosing the identity of a candidate's donors] allows voters to place each candidate in the political spectrum more precisely than is often possible solely on the basis of party labels and campaign speeches. The sources of a candidate's financial support also alert the voter to the interests to which a candidate is most likely to be responsive and thus facilitate predictions of future performance in office.[45]

The second advantage of donor identity is absent under a system of mandated anonymity: Candidates are not "more likely to be responsive" to donors if they don't know who their donors are. Moreover, it is unclear whether the first effect of donor identification—more precisely placing the candidate in the political spectrum—should be classified as an advantage. It might be more conducive to democratic deliberation for voters to learn about a candidate's positions on policy matters rather than to learn whether Jane Fonda or the NRA contributed to the candidate's campaign. Individual donors at times may have better information—possibly based on private conversations with the candidates—about a candidate's true intentions than could be gleaned from the public record. But because there are other avenues of gaining this information, the government's interest in contributor identity as a proxy for candidate beliefs is less compelling than its interest in deterring corruption.

The proposed regime of mandated anonymity also partially accommodates the voters' interest in donor identity. Under the proposal, a contributor would have the option of having the blind trust disclose the amount of her contribution up to $200. Given the pervasive interest of donors in identifying themselves, it is likely that the vast majority of donors would opt to be identified as having given something. Given that voter knowledge of donor identity is less important in a regime in which candidates as well as voters are kept in the dark, and given that some voter information about donor identity would be generated under the proposed system of optional partial disclosure, the public's interest in donation information does not ultimately militate against the proposed anonymity regime.

3. Less donor information for PAC contributors. Finally, mandated anonymity will make it more difficult for donors to monitor how PACs and other political intermediaries spend their money. Under the proposed system, PACs would have only the option of disclosing a donation of $200 or less to any one candidate. Prospective PAC donors would have more difficulty assessing whether the PAC had served their interests effectively.

For those who think PAC influence is a destructive force in our polity, disrupting donors' ability to monitor PACs is all to the good because potential PAC donors who are unable to monitor are less likely to contribute. One might argue that mandated anonymity goes too far in impeding the ability of insular groups to organize and influence government. But while mandated anonymity creates this potential harm, I believe this effect would be relatively minor. Restricting PAC donor information is unlikely to disrupt PAC formation because most PAC donors don't avail themselves of this information.[46] Most donors give to Newt Gingrich's leadership PAC, for instance, because they trust his ideological and political instincts, not because they have microanalyzed the effectiveness of the way in which his PAC allocates its contributions. Mandated anonymity might disrupt PACs because donors would not be as willing to donate to an organization that can no longer corrupt/influence politicians, but this effect is a benefit rather than a cost of the proposal.

III. CONSTITUTIONALITY

Mandated anonymity is clearly constitutional. It burdens speech less than mandated disclosure and is more likely to further the government's compelling interest in deterring corruption. And while the Supreme Court upheld the constitutionality of mandated disclosure, appreciating the possibility of mandated anonymity calls into question whether a disclosure regime constitutes the least restrictive alternative required by the First Amendment.

In locating the exact anonymity burden, we should begin by remembering what the proposal does not do. It does not affect how much a donor can contribute, and it does not limit the words a donor might say. The regime would even allow a donor to prove she had given up to $200. The only burden of the anonymity proposal is that donors could not credibly signal that they had given more than $200. The inability to prove a large contribution certainly burdens a donor's ability to communicate. Reducing the "expressive value" of a contribution might deter some large donors from giving.

However, the Supreme Court's jurisprudence suggests that the size of this burden is rather marginal, particularly because donors can prove they contributed $200. In discussing the burden of contribution limits, the Court in *Buckley* found that

> a limitation upon the amount that any one person or group may contribute to a candidate or political committee entails only a marginal restriction upon the contributor's ability to engage in free communication. A contribution serves as a general expression of support for the candidate and his views, but does not communicate the underlying basis for the support. The quantity of communication by the contributor does not increase perceptibly with the

size of his contribution, since the expression rests solely on the un-differentiated, symbolic act of contributing. . . . A limitation on the amount of money a person may give to a candidate or campaign organization thus involves little direct restraint on his political communication, for it permits the symbolic expression of support evidenced by a contribution but does not in any way infringe the contributor's freedom to discuss candidates and issues.[47]

This analysis suggests that a donor's burden of proving that she gave Clinton $1,000 instead of $200 should be considered only "a marginal restriction upon the contributor's ability to engage in free communication." The quantity of communication involved in proving that a donor gave a larger amount "does not increase perceptibly." And the effect of the restriction is mitigated by the donor's unrestricted ability to speak independently in favor of a particular candidate.

Ackerman's "brute property" argument[48] correctly identifies a deeply held impulse in our polity: "It's my property and I have a right to use it to support any candidate I want." The donation booth accommodates this impulse while simultaneously restraining property's influence. The donation booth does not affect how property can be used, nor does it limit the words (or other signals) a donor may employ to describe her use. A donor may even have a First Amendment right to truthfully claim she gave the Democratic Party a million dollars, but the constitution does not give her a right to stop a faux donor from making the same claim. Because the ability to prove credibly how one uses one's property is not a firmly established concomitant of ownership, the donation booth does not directly contradict the "brute property" impulse.

The constitutionality of mandated anonymity can most clearly be demonstrated by comparing the constitutional costs and benefits of the specific proposal to two other free speech restrictions that have passed constitutional scrutiny: mandated voter anonymity and compelled disclosure of donor identity (reporting requirements). By showing that mandated anonymity is less burdensome and more supportive of the government's interest in preventing corruption, these comparisons provide two *a fortiori* arguments for the constitutionality of anonymity regulation.

First, the constitutionality of the voting booth—that is mandated voting anonymity—suggests that mandated donor anonymity is also constitutional. The voting booth also burdens political expression. No matter how much a conservative wants, she can never prove she did not vote for McGovern, nor can a liberal prove he did not vote for Reagan. Since voting is the quintessential act of political expression, denying citizens the right to prove for whom they voted is surely more burdensome than denying citizens the right to prove they gave a candidate more than $200.[49]

Although the privacy of the voting booth is an innovation of fewer than one hundred years' standing, we cannot conceive that the Supreme Court would strike down this form of mandated anonymity as unduly burdening voters' free speech rights. Opponents of mandated donor anonymity will be hard pressed to explain why a donation booth is unconstitutional but a voting booth is not.

Second, the Supreme Court's willingness in *Buckley* to approve compelled disclosure of donor identity suggests that compelled nondisclosure is all the more constitutional. Mandated nonanonymity is more burdensome than mandated anonymity. The Supreme Court has traditionally protected the right to silence or anonymity much more than the right to speak credibly. Plenty of cases can be found where the Supreme Court has struck down regulations requiring speakers to identify themselves.[50] But it is hard to find cases where the First Amendment has been abridged because a statute would not allow a speaker to prove what he says is true. Indeed, the strong antilibel impulse enunciated by Justice Hugo Black and others makes it harder for speakers to signal the truth of their allegations credibly because false statements often do not expose the speaker to monetary damages. Mandated disclosure may deter potential donors from giving to unpopular causes for fear of retaliation or ostracism; in comparison, the chilling effect on those legitimate donors who want to prove they gave more than $200 should be considered only a secondary concern.

Mandated disclosure is also less likely to further the government's interest in preventing corruption. Even though the Supreme Court suggested that mandated disclosure could deter corruption, it has proved exceedingly difficult to prove either quid pro quo or monetary-influence corruption from the mere knowledge of identity. As adumbrated in part I, donor anonymity is more likely to deter corruption because uninformed candidates have less opportunity to peddle influence or change their positions in the hope of garnering greater contributions—and this effect is likely to be stronger than any voter discipline caused by a mandatory disclosure regime.

Indeed, the possibility of mandated anonymity calls into question the constitutionality of mandated disclosure. The First Amendment requires not only that the effect of furthering the government's compelling interest outweigh the speech burden, but that government choose the least restrictive alternative for achieving its compelling interest.[51] *Buckley* did not discuss this additional "least restrictive alternative" requirement in constitutionalizing mandated disclosure, probably for the simple reason that the Court thought that lawmakers' only relevant informational regulatory options were mandated disclosure or laissez-faire regimes. But once we appreciate that mandated anonymity can provide a smaller speech burden and more strongly deters corruption, it becomes difficult to characterize mandated disclosure as the least restrictive alternative.

Conclusion

This Article stands against the strong consensus in favor of disclosure, but then again, so does the secret ballot. The strategy of keeping the candidate as well as the public in the dark has a long pedigree. Maimonides long ago extolled the benefits of anonymous charity.[52] We should remind ourselves why we chose to make voting a solitary act. Indeed, anyone opposing mandated donor anonymity needs to explain why we should not also jettison mandated voting anonymity.

Mandated anonymity also provides a useful perspective from which to rethink whether mandated disclosure can be defended. In the end, reasonable people might reject the donation booth because of the likely increase in issue advocacy. If mandated anonymity induces even a partial shift of contributions toward this form of reckless and unaccountable speech, we might not want to extend the voting booth rationale to campaign finance. But mandated disclosure regimes—if effective—should give rise to similar hydraulic effects. The visceral sense that mandated disclosure has not created a similar shift probably stems from the sense that few corrupt donations would in fact be deterred by a disclosure requirement. For the CATO Institute, which favors the move to a pure disclosure regime largely on libertarian grounds, a pure anonymity regime fosters arguably even more donor freedom. It is difficult to advance a priori arguments against mandated anonymity while at the same time advancing a priori arguments in favor of mandated disclosure.[53] The donation booth is not a panacea, but it keeps faith with the simple and widely held belief that the size of your purse should not determine your access to government.

NOTES

Bruce Ackerman, Jennifer Brown, Tom Campbell, Joshua Cohen, Steve Gotlieb, Peter Harris, John Langbein, Larry Lessig, John Lott, Bob Munch, Richard Posner, Jay Pottenger, E. Joshua Rosenkranz, Steve Ross, Ian Shapiro, Victor Stone, David Strauss, Kathleen Sullivan, Cass Sunstein, Tom Ulen, Fred Wertheimer, and seminar participants at the American Bar Foundation and the University of Chicago provided helpful comments. Sarah Goddard and Andrea Rottinger provided excellent research assistance.

1. See Pete du Pont, "Campaign Finance Defies a Complicated Solution," *Tampa Tribune*, 7 September 1997, 6.

2. See, e.g., Kathleen M. Sullivan, "Political Money and Freedom of Speech," *U.C. Davis L. Rev.* 30 (1997): 663, 688–89; "Campaign Finance: Full Disclosure, More Options Might Help," *Dallas Morning News*, 12 October 1997, 2j, col. 1.

3. Bruce Ackerman, "Crediting the Voters: A New Beginning for Campaign Finance," *American Prospect* 13 (1993): 71; see also Ashley C. Wall, "The Money of Politics: Financing American and British Elections," *Tul. J. Int'l & Comp. L.* 5 (1997): 489, 503 (commenting that the Ballot Act of 1872 "brought into existence the secret ballot, which had long term effects on curbing bribery").

4. In an earlier article that forms the basis for much of the present analysis, Jeremy Bulow and I argued that mandated anonymity would be a useful complement to the current limitation on contributions. See Ian Ayres & Jeremy Bulow, "The Donation Booth: Mandating Donor Ano-

nymity to Disrupt the Market for Political Influence," *Stanf. L. Rev.* 50 (1998): 837. The idea that mandating donor anonymity might deter corruption has been discussed previously by a number of authors. See, e.g., Saul Levmore, "The Anonymity Tool," 144 *U. Pa. L. Rev.* (1996): 2191, 2222. "It should not be surprising to find a system that made political contributions anonymous by channeling them to candidates through intermediaries. . . .") and sources cited in Ayres & Bulow at note 4.

5. The commentary to the 1972 Code of Judicial Conduct ("CJC") stated, "[T]he [judicial] candidate should not be informed of the names of his contributors unless he is required by law to file a list of their names." E. Wayne Thode, Reporter's Notes to Code of Judicial Conduct 99 (1973). This provision was subsequently adopted—and, to varying degrees, applied—in ten states. Stuart Banner, "Note, Disqualifying Elected Judges from Cases Involving Campaign Contributors," *Stan. L. Rev.* 40 (1988): 449, 473 n.130 (identifying the ten adopting states as Arkansas, Nebraska, North Dakota, South Carolina, South Dakota, Tennessee, Utah, Washington, West Virginia, and Wyoming) 470 (1988); see also 1978 N.Y. St. Comm. on Jud. Conduct Ann. Rep. 63 (1979) ("The intent behind keeping a judge from knowing his contributors is obvious: to avoid the impression that, if elected, the judge will administer his office with a bias toward those who supported his candidacy."). See also Ayres & Bulow, supra note 4, at 870 for an assessment of the ultimate effectiveness of these judicial regulations.

6. Wayne Andrews, Voting, in *Concise Dictionary of American History*, ed. Wayne Andrews (New York: Scribner, 1962), 989. The thesis that the Australian ballot was adopted in order to deter vote buying specifically—and cleanse the political system generally—is hotly contested. An alternative interpretation is that these voting reforms were motivated, at least in part, to dampen mass political activism. The "spectacle" of lines of voters marching to the polls with colored ballots in hand might not have indicated that their votes were bought but, instead, that their votes were not for sale—a symbol of the solidarity between voters and labor or other mass political movements. See, e.g., Michael E. McGerr, *The Decline of Popular Politics: The American North, 1865–1928* (New York: Oxford University Press, 1986), 12; Walter Dean Burnham, "The Changing Shape of the American Political Universe," *Am. Pol. Sci. Rev.* 59 (1965): 7. Even if this alternative reading of the Australian ballot is correct as an historical matter, the donation booth (unlike the secret ballot) has the potential to dampen the political power of those with disproportionate wealth and thereby increase the incentives for wider popular politics.

7. John H. Wigmore, *The Australian Ballot System as Embodied in the Legislation of Various Countries*, 2d ed. (1889), 1–57.

8. See Cass R. Sunstein, "Political Equality and Unintended Consequences," *Colum. L. Rev.* 94 (1994): 1390, 1391 (identifying corruption as the "[f]irst and most obvious, perhaps," ground for campaign finance reforms).

9. See Daniel Hays Lowenstein, "On Campaign Finance Reform: The Root of All Evil Is Deeply Rooted," *Hofstra L. Rev.* 18 (1989): 301, 302 ("[P]ayment of money to bias the judgment or sway the loyalty of persons holding positions of public trust is a practice whose condemnation is deeply rooted in our most ancient heritage.").

10. Sunstein, supra note 8, at 1390.

11. Ackerman, supra note 3, at 71.

12. Richard Craswell has also suggested in comments that it might be possible to use a modified version of the donation booth to give candidates information about voters' aggregate preferences but not voters' identities. If the blind trusts solicited donors' policy preferences and revealed these preferences to the candidates—for example, if the trusts revealed that $300,000 of total donations support NAFTA—the mandated anonymity regime might reveal something more to the candidates about the intensity of the donors' aggregate preferences while still disrupting the market for quid pro quo corruption.

13. Letter from Janet Reno, United States Attorney General, to Rep. Henry J. Hyde, House Judiciary Chairman, reprinted in *New York Times*, 4 October 1997, A9.

14. *First National Bank of Boston v. Bellotti*, 435 U.S. 765, 788 n.26 (1978).

15. OGE Inf. Adv. Ltr. 93x21 (Aug. 30, 1993), available in 1993 WL 721241, at *4. See generally Kathleen Clark, "Paying the Price for Heightened Ethics Scrutiny: Legal Defense Funds and Other Ways That Government Officials Pay Their Lawyers," *Stan. L. Rev.* 50 (1997): 65.

16. See Fred S. McChesney, "Rent Extraction and Rent Creation in the Economic Theory of Regulation," *J. Legal Stud.* 16 (1987): 101, 102.

17. See Frank J. Sorauf, *Inside Campaign Finance: Myths and Realities* (New Haven: Yale University Press, 1992), 60–97.

18. See Richard J. Mahoney, "Letter to the Editor, A Corporate Mood," *New York Times*, 30 January 1997, A14.

19. See Fred S. McChesney, "Rent Extraction and Interest-Group Organization in a Coasean Model of Regulation," *J. Legal Stud.* 20 (1991): 73, 85–89.

20. See generally Stephen G. Bronars & John R. Lott, Jr., "Do Campaign Donations Alter How a Politician Votes? Or, Do Donors Support Candidates Who Value the Same Things That They Do?" *J.L. & Econ.* 40 (1997): 317.

21. See Thomas F. Burke, "The Concept of Corruption in Campaign Finance Law," *Contst. Commentary* 14 (1997): 127, 131 (arguing that Supreme Court decisions have identified "three distinct standards of corruption," which the author labels "quid pro quo," "monetary influence," and "distortion"). Thomas Burke shows how each of these effects has been characterized as a problem of corruption, although the last possibility—"distortion"—is more often described as the problem of inequality. See id.

22. For example, even market-oriented scholars such as James Buchanan and Gordon Tullock have argued that contributions might not accurately measure intensity of preferences because of "market imperfections." James M. Buchanan & Gordon Tulloch, *The Calculus of Consent: Logical Foundations of Constitutional Democracy* (Ann Arbor: University of Michigan Press, 1962), 272.

23. The possibility of rent extraction also militates against using donations to register the preference intensity of voters. Politicians trying to extort donations under threat of harmful laws are likely to pass a retaliatory law from time to time in order to make their threats credible. An uninsulated system of monetary influence might therefore lead to worse policies than one that insulates candidates from the preference intensity of voters.

24. See generally Daniel R. Ortiz, "The Democratic Paradox of Campaign Finance Reform," *Stan. L. Rev.* 50 (1998): 893. Moreover, citizens can credibly signal the intensity of their preferences by engaging in other activities, such as marching on Washington, that are more generally available to a large proportion of the populace. Even if citizens wish to signal the intensity of their preferences by spending money, it is not clear that donating money is superior, literally, to burning the money for a cause. It is one thing for a candidate to change positions because her constituents are willing to part with considerable money. Such behavior is consistent with the idea that politicians should faithfully represent the aggregate preferences of their constituents. But it is another thing to change positions in order to receive this money. Because there is no natural way to aggregate preferences, it is suspect for a candidate to choose an aggregation that self-interestedly increases her chance of election.

25. See Burke, "The Concept of Corruption," 148 ("[W]here contributor-influenced representatives predominate, legislative deliberation becomes a sham.").

26. David A. Strauss, "Corruption, Equality and Campaign Finance Reform," *Colum. L. Rev.* 94 (1994): 1369, 1375–76.

27. See generally Charles M. Tiebout, "A Pure Theory of Local Expenditures," *J. Pol. Econ.* 64 (1956): 416.

28. David Donnelly et al., "Going Public," *Boston Review* 22 (April–May, 1997).

29. Strauss, "Corruption, Equality and Campaign Finance Reform," 1376 n.18.

30. Similar requirements have been imposed on trusts serving as corporate fiduciaries. See Cal. Fin. Code 1500-1591 (West 1989) (imposing requirements such as security deposits on trust companies); John H. Langbein, "The Contractarian Basis of the Law of Trusts," *Yale L.J.* 105 (1995): 625, 638–39, & n.64 (describing modern-day, institutional trusteeships).

31. See Lawrence Lessig, "The Regulation of Social Meaning," *U. Chi. L. Rev.* 62 (1995): 943, 1010–11, & n.225 (1995) (citing Jorgen H. Barfod, Norman L. Kleebatt & Vivian B. Mann, eds., *Kings and Citizens: The History of the Jews in Denmark, 1622–1983* (New York: Jewish Museum, 1983).

32. Under a regime of mandated anonymity, candidates are likely to spend less time fund-raising because this activity would be less productive and because the candidate would need fewer funds to effectively compete with an opponent who faces similar constraints. There is the theoretical possibility—called an "income effect"—that if anonymity causes less giving generally, then candidates will respond by engaging in more fund-raising. As an empirical matter, however, economists typically find that substitution effects dominate income effects—that is, when fund-raising becomes more difficult, politicians are likely to spend less time on it (especially when their opponents' fund-raising also becomes more difficult).

33. But as the Supreme Court has noted, contributing to yourself does not present the same risks of quid pro quo or monetary-influence corruption. See *Buckley v. Valeo*, 424 U.S. 1, 53 n.59 (1976) (per curiam). Self-contribution, however, often exacerbates problems of inequality.

34. The FEC could be empowered to audit campaigns for compliance with the anonymity regulations. Much like Fair Housing tests, such audits could determine whether campaign officials are willing to conspire with purported donors or trust representatives to learn donor identities.

35. Sunstein, supra note 8, at 1395.

36. Both Clinton and Dole orchestrated the use of party soft money to fund coordinated issue campaigns. See Jill Abramson, "1996 Campaign Left Finance Laws in Shreds," *New York Times*, 2 November 1997 ("[T]he Democratic committee spent at least $32 million on early issue advertising. The advertisements, which began airing in mid-1995, were created by the Clinton-Gore team and prominently featured the Presi-

dent in patriotic settings."). Labor and business spent millions on independent issue campaigns in the 1996 election cycle. See Eliza Newlin Carney, "Campaign Reform Debate Will Linger," *Nat'l J.* 22 (1997): 2026.

37. See Richard L. Hasen, "Clipping Coupons for Democracy: An Egalitarian/Public Choice Defense of Campaign Finance Vouchers," *Calif. L. Rev.* 84 (1996): 1, 19 n.79.

38. See *Colorado Republican Fed. Campaign Comm. v. FEC*, 518 U.S. 604, 619 (1996) (plurality opinion) indicating that the Court has treated coordinated expenditures as contributions, which Congress may constitutionally regulate.

39. See, e.g., Jill Abramson, "Tape Shows Clinton Involvement in Party-Paid Ads: Legal Line Is Unclear," *New York Times*, 21 October 1997, A1 (discussing television issue ads that "advanced the Democratic Party's agenda as well as Mr. Clinton's").

40. See *Austin v. Michigan State Chamber of Commerce*, 494 U.S. 652, 654–55 (1990) (prohibiting independent political expenditures from a corporation's general treasury is constitutional); *Buckley*, 424 U.S. at 80–82 (mandating disclosure with regard to independent express advocacy is constitutional).

41. For example, Michael R. Goland, "apparently motivated by the pro-Israel policies of Senators Paul Simon and Alan Cranston, funded large independent expenditure campaigns against their opponents." Hasen, "Clipping Coupons for Democracy," 19 n.79 (1996).

42. *Buckley*, 424 U.S. at 47.

43. An exception to this tendency might occur when the independent expenditure is used for purposes the politician supports but doesn't want attributed to herself—for example, "going negative" by attacking her opponent. See text accompanying note 37 supra (discussing the Willie Horton ads). Yet the fact that independent expenditures are attributed to another speaker can often be a political liability. An independent ad campaign paid for by, say, Jane Fonda or tobacco interests might alienate as many voters as it persuades. Hence, independent expenditures by well-heeled but unpopular speakers would be much less valuable then direct contributions.

44. See Sullivan, "Political Money and Freedom of Speech," 690 ("[C]ompelled disclosure avoids a regime of absolute laissez-faire. Even this partial deregulation might have unintended consequences.").

45. *Buckley*, 424 U.S. at 67.

46. Joseph P. Kalt & Mark A. Zupan, "Capture and Ideology in the Economic Theory of Politics," *Am. Econ. Rev.* 74 (1984): 279, 283.

47. *Buckley*, 424 U.S. at 20–21.

48. See Ackerman, supra note 3, at 78.

49. The government's interest in preventing vote as compared to donation corruption cannot easily explain why the voting booth would stand on a firmer constitutional footing than the donation booth. The danger of donation corruption is greater than the danger of voting corruption because wealth is much more concentrated than votes. The transaction costs of vote corruption are much higher because candidates would need to cut deals with many more people for vote corruption to have an effect.

50. See, e.g., *McIntyre v. Ohio Elections Comm.*, 514 U.S. 334, 353 (1995) (striking down an Ohio statute that prohibited the distribution of anonymous campaign literature as a violation of the First Amendment); *Talley v. California*, 362 U.S. 60, 66 (1960) (striking down a city ordinance that forbade the distribution of anonymous handbills).

51. See *Central Hudson Gas & Elec. Corp. v. Public Serv. Comm'n of N.Y.*, 447 U.S. 557 (1980). See generally Eugene Volokh, "Freedom of Speech: Permissible Tailoring and Transcending Strict Scrutiny," *U. Pa. L. Rev.* 144 (1996): 2417.

52. See Moses Ben Maimon, *The Laws of Hebrews Relating to the Poor and the Stranger*, trans. James W. Peppercorne (1840), 67–68.

53. At a minimum, Congress should change the law to give individual candidates the option of using blind trusts to finance their campaigns. The first question candidates should be asked when they announce their candidacy is whether they will commit to donor anonymity. We hope that candidates would voluntarily comply in order to avoid explaining why they need to know the identity of their donors. But we fear the issue can be demagogued. Opponents of mandated anonymity are likely to respond, "What do the proponents have to hide? Why aren't they willing to reveal who their contributors are?" Of course, these same questions were asked of those early proponents of the secret ballot.

2

PAYING FOR POLITICS

GEOFFREY BRENNAN AND
ALAN HAMLIN

I. Introduction

In "Disclosure v. Anonymity in Campaign Finance," Ian Ayres broaches a very particular issue in the design of democratic institutions, discusses that issue in a very particular context, and advocates a very particular institutional remedy. The specific issue concerns the regulation of information concerning political donations. The specific context has two relevant dimensions. Ayres is clearly concerned with the case of the United States, and, implicitly and explicitly, the discussion takes many other aspects of the U.S. political environment as the relevant background. At the same time, Ayres is primarily concerned with the prevention of corruption, so that the relevant criterion by which alternative institutional regimes are judged is just the extent to which corruption is deterred. Within this context, Ayres argues that the norm of full anonymity with respect to political donations would operate more effectively to prevent corruption than would the norm of full disclosure; so that rather than "sunlight [being] the best of disinfectants; electric light the most efficient policeman," Ayres argues that total darkness is the real cure for corruption. Ayres's constructed "veil of ignorance" is nothing like Rawls's, but it does involve a putatively constructive use of ignorance in the same way that Rawls's construction does.

55

The essential argument is simple enough. Under full information, all campaign donations are matters of public record, so that there can be nothing covert about the funding process; nevertheless, the possibility of buying political favors is still present. Indeed, in the limit, one might imagine that competitive political donations constitute a straightforward market for political influence that operates alongside the electoral process to determine political outcomes. Whether or not we describe open financial transactions in such a market as "corrupt,"[1] or "unfair" (given an unequal distribution of income and wealth), there is certainly a presumption that such a "market" might be expected to influence political outcomes and so reduce the reliance of political outcomes on the electoral process and other more strictly "political" mechanisms. At the other extreme, under perfect anonymity, campaign donations are organized in such a way that no one (other than the donor—and specifically not the recipient) has any reliable information about the existence, or size, of any individual donation. In this case, so the argument goes, since there can be no proof that a donation has been made, there can be no political deals struck: it is impossible to buy influence if it is impossible to demonstrate payment.

Of course, this sketch does not do full justice to Ayres's argument, but we believe that it suffices to focus attention on the key issues: the idea that corruption takes the form of market-like deals that "pervert" the democratic process in the sense that political outcomes differ from those that would be realized under a purely political process; and the argument that such deals are effectively ruled out by complete anonymity. We also note that Ayres's discussion is informed by a recurring analogy with the process of voting itself—and with the idea, in particular, that the secret or "Australian" ballot provides an appropriate exemplar for secrecy in the political process. We will return to the significance of this analogical reasoning and to other aspects of Ayres's specific argument in due course, but first we wish to make some effort to widen the discussion a little.

The design of democratic institutions may be approached in either of two styles: a "piecemeal" style or a "synoptic" one. A piecemeal style characteristically focuses on this or that piece of institutional practice and subjects it to scrutiny. A synoptic style is one that attempts to work from general principles in developing an overview of the operation of democratic institutions and to develop thereby implications for the design of particular institutional devices.[2] Clearly, neither style holds a monopoly on usefulness, and it is likely that the iteration between these styles offers the most plausible route to reasonable conclusions. It is for this reason that, initially at least, we wish to respond to Ayres's piecemeal proposal in a rather more synoptic mode.

Even if we narrow our range of concern to the institutional framework for financing democratic politics, we must recognize that a number of interrelated issues are raised: the relative merits of private and state funding of political parties or candidates; the possibility of regulating either the set of agents who may make political contributions or the size of the political contributions they may make; the possibility of regulating the flow of information about the financial affairs of donors, parties, or candidates; the possibility of regulating expenditures made by parties or candidates; and so on. None of these issues is trivial either in the sense that the normatively appropriate answer is obvious, or in the sense that the same practice has developed almost universally across democratic countries. And matters become still more complicated if we open up the possibility of interactions between these various issues, or with other aspects of the institutional fabric such as voting rules, the structure of representation, and so on. Indeed, it is not even obvious how we should go about addressing these matters. Two ingredients seem essential however: a reasonably clear statement of the model of democratic politics to be used as the test bed within which to conduct the relevant thought experiments, and a reasonably clear statement of the relevant normative criteria. Unfortunately, neither ingredient is readily available or widely agreed upon. The first aim of this brief essay is to say something about the appropriate ingredients to use in constructing particular arguments concerned with the funding of democratic politics or, indeed, any other aspect of the design of democratic institutions. Only then will we return to the specific issue of anonymity in political donations.

II. SOME BASIC INGREDIENTS

We have already mentioned two basic ingredients: an appropriate normative criterion and a benchmark model of democratic political behavior. We will say a little about each in turn.

It is clear that political institutions are not, and should not be, judged solely by their ability to deter or avoid corruption. The central task of political institutions is to play their part in improving social outcomes. Corruption is certainly one way in which institutions may fail, but concentrating on one potential failure is unlikely to lead to good overall design. The point is simple enough and should be familiar as an application of the general theory of the second best. If there are many criteria that aggregate in some way to indicate the overall value of a particular set of political institutions, and if one of these criteria is (the avoidance of) corruption—defined in some specific way—then it will in general be the case that the optimal amount of corruption will be nonzero. Furthermore, it cannot be assumed that a reduction in corruption is necessarily a good thing.

We will say nothing very specific here about the precise nature of the overall normative criterion, whether it be some utilitarian social welfare function or some other conception of the good. The only points that seem important at the synoptic level are, first, that the normative criterion employed should be broadly consistent with the idea of democracy as such—so that it should take seriously the idea of serving the interests *of* the people and seek to do so by means of a political system that embodies the idea of government *by* the people, and second, that the normative criterion employed should be sensitive to the wide variety of ways in which the political system impacts *on* the people so that, as already noted, (the avoidance of) corruption is seen as just one aspect of the good, which may be traded off against other aspects in an overall evaluation.

Although Ayres is not explicit about the underlying model of political behavior he has in mind, it seems that his model of politics is a variant of the model associated with "rational actor political theory." The central emphasis on political deals and on the role of informational conditions in determining whether (rational) individuals will enter into deals is sufficient to make a strong connection with the rational actor model. At the same time, there are a number of indications that the model in question is not the standard economists' model in which all agents— whether potential voters, potential candidates or potential donors—are both rational and motivated by a relatively narrow view of their self-interest. References to "independent deliberation and reason-giving," and such observations as "At times, representatives should take positions that are not merely aggregations of their constituents' preferences"[3] display both a degree of unease with the standard rational actor model and a tendency toward what we might term a "deliberative democracy" model.[4] The simple point that we wish to emphasize is that without some reasonably explicit and coherent account of the underlying model of political behavior by candidates, voters, and donors, it is not possible to analyze the impact of alternative institutional arrangements satisfactorily. And the analysis that one gets depends quite crucially on the details of the model employed.

The problem is that the rational actor model and the deliberative democracy model offer very different diagnoses of the central problems of democratic politics: those models, therefore, point to very different cures.[5] In the rational actor framework, the central problems are those of aggregation and agency: how to design an institutional structure that aggregates interests appropriately and also ensures that political agents are appropriately constrained to enact the relevant policies. In the deliberative democracy model, the central problem facing the design of political institutions is the creation of an environment that encourages reasoned public debate—and this against the background assumption that individuals are motivated, at least in appropriate institutional settings, to seek out policies that are in the public interest (in some particular sense of that phrase). Voting may play a role in deliberative procedures, but that role need not be central. Certainly, the electoral process will not bear interpretation as a simple aggregation of private interests—though it may be interpreted along the lines of the Condorcet jury theorems in which voting plays the role of amplifying the enlightenment of the individual jurors and reducing the probability of mistakes.

The most fundamental difference between the two models clearly lies in the motivational structure that they assume of individuals. The standard "public choice" model takes individuals to be essentially self-interested and construes the political problem as constructing social choices out of individual values, and then implementing those choices through individual (self-interested) agents. The deliberative model, by contrast, assumes more socially or morally motivated individuals, and identifies the political problem as essentially one of attempting to reach consensus on what a more or less commonly shared morality requires.

It is appropriate at this point that we say something about our own position on this issue.[6] We take as our point of departure the rational actor model but depart from that model in several respects. First, and most fundamentally, we believe that the basic desires that serve as motivational triggers for rational agents include a desire to act as morality requires. Our rational agents are open, at least potentially, to moral argument; and moral reasons will count among their motives for action. But the desire to act as morality requires is only one desire among many, including the normal range of self-interested desires. In making our agents open to moral argument we do not wish to make them moral angels. In this sense, we seek quite explicitly to occupy a position somewhere between the standard rational actor model and the full model of deliberative democracy.

Our approach has other distinctive features. We take seriously the criticism of instrumental, self-interested voting that gives rise to the "paradox of voting."[7] The basic problem here is that self-interested and rational individuals almost never have a private, instrumental incentive to vote in large-scale elections. Since the probability that their vote will be decisive is vanishingly small, voting is literally "inconsequential." An additional, related problem is that of rational ignorance, the idea that self-interested and rational individuals will almost never have a private, instrumental incentive to gather information relative to political decision making, so that any votes they may cast may be expected to be ill-informed. Our reaction to these problems is to argue that voting in large-scale political elections is more appropriately conceived as an expressive rather than an instrumental act. Since voting is inconsequential, rational citizens will take the low-cost opportunity of expressing their support for this or that party, candidate, or position rather than consulting a private-interest calculus.

An important point here is that expressions of support cannot necessarily be assumed to correlate well with interests. To reuse an example, in a situation in which the real choice is between war and a negotiated settlement to a dispute, and on the assumption that a negotiated settlement is in everyone's interests, we might still expect some—perhaps even a majority—to vote for war. All that is required is that (some) individuals sense that their individual votes are effectively irrelevant, and choose to use their vote to express their nationalistic pride. Of course, the expression of support might also yield better—that is, more moral—outcomes than any simple aggregation of interests in some other cases. Our point is simply that the logic of the failure of the instrumental account of voting points to expressive voting, which in turn points to a very different understanding of the potential advantages and disadvantages of the electoral process.

Combining these elements of a more moral motivational structure and an expressive account of voting, we obtain the bare outline of a model of representative democracy. The model includes some aspects of the deliberative democracy tradition insofar as it admits moral argument as a relevant part of the political process but retains much of the structure of the rational choice theoretic account of politics. The model offers a basis for institutional analysis that recognizes that political institutions do more than simply aggregate interests and provide instrumental incentives. In this sense, our model is broadly consistent with Ayres's concerns and style of analysis, though since Ayres's discussion leaves his precise conception of the details of agent motivation somewhat shadowy, it would be misleading to cast our model as the one that Ayres seems to have in mind.

III. THE ANALOGY WITH THE SECRET BALLOT

An important part of Ayres's rhetorical force derives from an appeal to the analogy with the secret ballot. Specifically, Ayres suggests that the example of the secret ballot provides an insight into the more general case for secrecy/anonymity as an appropriate part of political institutions. We are, ourselves, by no means opposed to argument by analogy, but we think this particular analogy can cut several ways. We are interested in particular in the question as to how Ayres's appeal to the authority of the secrecy property fits with his general picture of politics and the understanding of voting that is implied. As we see it, what is at stake here is a tension between the narrow interpretation of the rational actor model and the more expressive/deliberative model of politics.[8] As we have already suggested, the rational actor model views voting as the revelation of essentially private interests in a process designed to aggregate those interests. It might seem that the secret ballot is an institutional arrangement well suited to this model since it allows individuals to reveal their preferences without fear or favor, and may also serve to moderate any strategic influences that arise from information on the voting behavior of others. Call this the anticorruption view. This view may be questioned from within the rational actor model, but let it stand for the moment. How does this fit with Ayres's "deliberative" picture of politics? On the face of things, poorly. One would think that any deliberative model of democracy would be inclined to see voting as an integral part of the process of deliberation. The very essence of the deliberative idea is that individual citizens should engage in public debate, giving reasons for their political views that are intended to be influential in the political decision making of their fellow citizens. Similarly, an important aspect of an expressive account of voting seems to be that voting provides the opportunity to express opinion in public in a credible manner—to publicly declare allegiance to some ideal or principle, for example.[9] But in this case, the idea of secret voting seems curiously out of step with the main thrust of the model. Secret voting breaks the most obvious connection between argument and vote, and undermines the reliability of the vote as a serious and responsible political input. If individuals are not held responsible for their vote, at least to the extent of being called upon to defend their stated opinion, it is difficult to see how the full discursive ideal is being taken seriously. Any model that tries to combine rational and deliberative elements will therefore face a trade-off between the anticorruption argument for secret ballots and the expressive/deliberative argument for open and responsible political debate. Neither argument is clearly superior in terms of the overall normative criterion of improving political outcomes as seen from the perspective of citizens. But what does seem clear is that secrecy and discussion belong in rather different camps.

We would suggest that a similar trade-off is present in relation to the institutional arrangements for campaign financing. Even if the anticorruption argument taken by itself points toward secrecy as an appropriate norm, the culture of candor that goes with disclosure is also an input into creating a more deliberative and discursive form of democracy. In fact, there is a particular wrinkle to the use of secrecy in the campaign contribution case that gives special force to this observation. Although both the secret ballot and Ayres's scheme involve the constructive use of secrecy, only Ayres's scheme is parasitic on the prevalence of *deception*. Ayres's argument depends on the claim that unverifiable statements are worthless, and on its being common knowledge that this is so. As Ayres conceives it, there are likely to be plenty of claims by those who request political favors that campaign contributions have been made. But no rational candidate will believe any such claim; there will be no trust without verification. This is part and parcel of the traditional economistic approach to rational behavior. But again we would suggest that this approach is not well suited to any political environment in which genuine trust—that is, acceptance without verification—is supposed to be in play. And such trust seems a necessary feature of many forms of representative democracy and particularly of those forms in which discussion as such is conceived to play a critical role.[10]

Suppose, for example, that some potential contributors *are* trustworthy, and suppose that trustworthy donors would find it offensive to be treated as untrustworthy. In this setting, it is easy to see that trustworthy people may refrain from making donations if their claims to have made donations are not believed. If this is so, there may be good reason for the candidates to act as if those who claim to have made contributions are telling the truth—that is, to trust everyone regardless of verification. This might well be the overall contribution-maximizing strategy for candidates, at least in the short run. Then Ayres's scheme might operate perversely to reward the liars among the putative donors, since they can now gain political favors at no cost. Of course, in the longer run, Ayres's presumption of universal mistrust may come to be justified as the liars profit and come to dominate. We will then have established a politics in which truly all men are liars (except where it is instrumentally rational for them to tell the truth). But the norm of anonymity will have been instrumental in bringing that state about, whereas a more open norm, designed in recognition of the possibility of genuine trust, might offer a better prospect of trustworthy conduct.

In this sense, there is an important difference between secret voting and campaign contributor anonymity. The secret ballot depends on, and encourages, a culture of privacy. Each can respond to questions about voting behavior with the quip "It's none of your business." But Ayres's scheme depends on and encourages a culture of widespread *mistrust*. A candidate's response to claims of financial support must be "I don't believe you." One might be prepared to tolerate a demand for privacy (with appropriate reluctance), without wanting to promote a culture of cynicism.

IV. Financing Elections

Let us at this point set the matter of analogies aside, and look directly at the question of campaign contributions and the work—for good or ill—that they do in electoral politics. Within the rational actor context, repeated elections play the dual role of identifying the chosen policy *and* of disciplining otherwise untrustworthy agents. In the simplest possible version of the rational actor model—that characterized by the median voter theorem—electoral competition performs both these roles "perfectly." The logic of the median voter theorem is that, whatever the motivations of the candidates themselves (or their sponsors), the competition for votes will drive candidates to adopt the policy associated with the median voter: any other policy platform will lose. In this simple textbook model, political contributions could have no real impact, so there is little prospect for an argument for their regulation. The real puzzle in such a model is why campaign contributions would ever be made at all.

Of course, once we depart from the simplest model, campaign contributions can have a real effect in influencing outcomes—so that there may be some grounds for regulating campaign contributions in some way. However, the nature of the role campaign contributions play and therefore the nature of any argument for regulating such donations will depend on the precise nature of the departure from the simplest model of electoral competition. It is at least possible that the role played by campaign contribution actually improves political outcome—so that rather than "perverting" the political process, campaign contributions may form a valuable part of that process. One such possibility is explored by Rietz and colleagues.[11] The basic idea in that paper is that making a campaign contribution is a costly and therefore credible way of signaling support for one or another candidate, and that such signals may provide valuable information to other voters in determining their voting behavior. Campaign contributions, in this sense, allow citizens to "put their money where their mouth is" and so escape the problem that political argument might be dismissed as "cheap talk." Other models are, of course, possible. Our point is not that this or that model is appropriate but, rather, the more fundamental point that campaign contributions could conceivably have some positive role to play, so that it is not appropriate to assume that *any* impact on political outcomes is evidence of corruption.

Part of the difficulty in evaluating Ayres's case for secrecy is that he tends to cast the definition of "corruption" pretty broadly. Following Cass Sunstein's insistence on a clear demarcation between "*market processes of purchase and sale on the one hand, and political processes of voting and reason-giving on the other*" (as quoted in Ayres, 23), Ayres seems disposed to consider *any* element of political exchange (as, for example, in logrolling) and/or the intrusion of *any* element of private interest, as opposed to more conventionally political/ideological reasons for political support, as an instance of "corruption." Such a broad definition fails to distinguish between practices that almost everyone would regard as depraved—such as direct clandestine payments of cash to a political decision maker in return for determination of policy in the donor's favor—and practices that many might feel are, if not entirely admirable, at least well short of the worst that can be imagined. Using invitations to a White House dinner as a means of raising funds for the Democratic Party may be decidedly tacky and less than one ought to expect from one's president, but it is not on a par with giving huge defense contracts to the tender offering the largest cash bribe. In other words, if we are to model *all* transfers between political representatives/candidates and external agents in quid pro quo terms, we need to be reasonably precise about the nature of both the quid and the quo in that transaction if an appropriately nuanced evaluation of such transfers is to be secured. And this would be so even if minimization of corruption were the only normatively relevant game in town. If some quid pro quo arrangements are much more objectionable than others, we have to be careful that we do not regulate the less objectionable forms out of existence at the cost of encouraging more objectionable forms. We should be careful about outlawing a practice that is merely dubious or whose effects we only suspect, if doing so risks increasing a practice that may be much more objectionable.

To focus the discussion here a little, consider a matrix of possibilities. To simplify, we consider just two categories of quid (rows) and three of quo (columns). Consider the quo dimension first. At one extreme, we can conceive of direct policy determination by the "donor": policy making is effectively up for auction to the highest bidder. At a more modest level, the donor may acquire policy influence—perhaps by means of privileged access, the opportunity to offer comment, relevant information, and/or advice. In this case, there may not even be any particular presumption of sympathy on the political agent's part: the candidate/politician simply makes herself available to hear the argument the donor seeks to make. It may even be that any such argument will itself have to pass a general "public interest" test if it is to be ultimately effective. Presumably, the donor believes that this privileged access will lead to policy influence in at least some cases, but, from the normative perspective, it is by no means obvious that this policy influence is necessarily a bad thing. The access that the contribution makes possible may serve to secure the public interest. The third and final type of quo that may be relevant arises when the benefit to donors takes the form of "incidental services" of the kind that political agents routinely provide for constituents—from assistance in getting visas, to the rental of the White House dining room for one's daughter's wedding, to the simple prestige of being seen (and photographed) with prominent politicians or the acquisition of a knighthood. Much of the practice here may be in poor taste and some of that practice may, in the long run, be corrosive of the esteem in which public office is held, but it is not obviously deeply sinister and may not have any effect on policy at all—even of the most indirect kind.

To assess how anxious about campaign contribution regulation we ought to be, we would need to know just where in this spectrum of these possibilities, actual practice lies. On this question, Ayres neither offers evidence himself nor refers to relevant literature. We simply don't know how much influence on actual policy determination a million dollars of campaign contribution buys; nor do we know what other factors are relevant in affecting that degree of influence. Rather, we are left to induce from the *fact* of the contributions that the donors must see themselves as getting their money's worth; and we are asked to base our suspicions accordingly.

A MATRIX OF POSSIBILITIES

		Quo		
		Policy Auction	Privileged Access	Incidental Services
Quid	Cash	1	2	3
	Campaign Support	4	5	6

It is worth stressing that there is at least one kind of quo within the range labeled "privileged access," where donor anonymity will not be effective in reducing campaign contributions or their impact on policy. Suppose that candidate C chooses her policy platform to maximize the probability of her election, and that this involves being sensitive to the fund-raising potential of different policies. Suppose also that potential donor D makes a contribution to candidate C's campaign funds if C's policies are in D's interests. Here, D is effectively "buying" an increased probability of C's victory, and C is "selling" policies to attract potential donors. But C's awareness of D's identity is immaterial for the rationality of D's decision to donate, and may be equally immaterial for C's decision as to which policy to espouse. Even in the presence of full anonymity, C can be aware that espousing certain kinds of policies—ones that give a substantial benefit to particular salient interests, perhaps—is conducive to larger campaign contributions, and can tailor her policy platform accordingly. We might say that the political trade or contract between candidate and donors is implicit rather than explicit, yet the same effects on policy platforms arise in this case as might arise under full disclosure. Indeed, because such implicit transactions are not *publicly* accessible, there may not be the same general mistrust of such contributions, or any real possibility of electoral backlash over such implicit political exchanges. But whether anonymity here supports such forms of "corruption" or not, there does seem to be the potential for a form of corruption that is immune from Ayres's proposed cure. Ayres would doubtless, and correctly, point to the free-rider aspects of any potential donor's decision problem if the benefits of C's election are spread across many people. But this argument does not depend on the distinction between anonymity and disclosure. The free-rider problem may arise, and arise equally, whether anonymity applies or not, so that the shift from a norm of disclosure to a norm of anonymity might have no significant effect at all. Indeed, if disclosure helps to *solve* free-rider problems among teams of donors, then anonymity will simply serve to discriminate in favor of the most concentrated interests.

Consider now the quid side of the transaction, the rows in our matrix of possibilities. The spirit of Ayres's discussion and much other treatment of campaign contributions is that the precise form of campaign contributions is largely irrelevant. This conclusion arises from the fact that candidates are modeled as a homogeneous set of simple utility maximizers for whom money income and the benefits from holding office are fully substitutable in the utility function. From the candidate's point of view, campaign contributions, of whatever form, are a close substitute for cash payments. Or so the argument goes. We would argue, however, that the form or "currency" in which benefits are received is far from insignificant. To see this, suppose that different candidates differ in their motivational structure, with some displaying more venal motivations and some displaying more "public-interestedness." Consider a comparison between two extremes. In one case a cash payment of $10,000 is offered that might be appropriated as income by the candidate; in the other case, the offer is made in terms of campaign support services—printing pamphlets, paying for TV time, or whatever—valued at $10,000. This second form of reward is such that it will be more attractive, *ceteris paribus,* to the relatively virtuous candidate—the one who values office highly relative to cash. The preference for office may reflect a value for office for its own sake, or because office provides an opportunity to "do good," or because of the public esteem that office offers. In all cases, the candidate who looks to politics as a way of making money will be screened out in favor of those candidates with other motivations. And for those who distrust the venal in politics, this must surely be an attractive feature.

In overview, then, our matrix of possibilities identifies six cases ranging from one extreme (case 1) in which cash bribes are rewarded by the direct determination of policy, to the opposite extreme (case 6) in which in-kind campaign support is exchanged for incidental benefits such as enhanced prestige. And we have suggested that in five of these six cases there may be some genuine claim that the practice has at least some merit. Only in case 1 does the normative argument seem clearly to indicate a genuine corruption of the political process. Of course, the mere enumeration of six cases does not imply that they are of equal importance, and it might be that case 1 is the overwhelmingly relevant case. But we doubt it. We think that the apparent salience of case 1 is more a product of the narrow interpretation of the rational choice approach to politics.

And there is the further consideration that larger campaign contributions may themselves be conducive to a more vibrant, engaged, and informed electorate. In a context where individuals may have rather weak incentives to inform themselves about either the attributes of candidates or the policies those candidates endorse, campaign contributions may perform the important function of ensuring that political messages are packaged in a way that voters will find accessible and attractive to attend to. After all, if campaign expenditures influence the probability of being elected at all, they must influence (potential) voters in some way—either in persuading them to alter their votes or to exercise their votes. Much political advertising might strike academic commentators as rather uninformative or less than ideally "discursive," but it is difficult to see how one could coherently be contemptuous of political advertising without being at least somewhat contemptuous of the electorate's capacity to be influenced by such advertising, and hence of the whole process of popular democracy. If on the other hand, one thought that campaign expenditures do some positive work in informing the public, then there is a cost to any proposal that seeks to reduce such expenditures—a cost that ought to be factored into any proper normative calculus. American practice has happened to hit upon a quasi-voluntary mechanism for meeting the considerable cost of providing relevant political information to voters, and of doing so in a way that provides incentives to make this information attractive and accessible to voters. This mechanism may not be ideal; it may involve some effect on policy platforms that draws those platforms away from those that a full application of the public interest norm would require. Even then, however, that cost may be one that it is reasonable to pay. And that is more likely to be one's conclusion if one believes that voter ignorance and voter apathy are significant problems.

V. PRACTICALITIES

Finally, we turn to some of the practical details that may be relevant to any choice between disclosure and anonymity. Ayres argues that a system of full anonymity is practicable and goes into some detail as to how such a regime might be organized. At the same time, it is clear that most discussion of the reform of political funding takes the opposite view. In the UK context, for example, the recent inquiry into the funding of political parties[12] dismisses the use of blind trusts (which have been used and advocated by the Labour Party prior to this inquiry) or other mechanisms attempting to institutionalize anonymity. It might be that this dismissal depends on other institutional differences between the UK and the United States. For example, almost all political donations in the UK are made to political parties rather than to individual candidates; corporate donations are both legal and commonplace in the UK; and so on. It is easy to see that differences of this type will matter. If corporate donations are allowed, for example, one might easily accept that shareholders have a right to decide (or at least monitor) such contributions and such monitoring requires at least some degree of openness.

A further practical doubt concerns the viability of the contributions-booth approach proposed by Ayres. The issue is this: if *anyone* knows the identity of donors (and the size of their donations), there will be considerable pressure in the system (from the press, as well as from politicians and donors themselves) for that information to leak out. Those charged with operating the contributions booth will bear the brunt of this pressure. And however they behave, there will always be the suspicion that some information does leak, not least since it would be impossible to prove the absence of a leak. Of course, one might refine the proposal still further so that all contributions had to be made in cash or other untraceable form so that literally no one other than the donor has information on identity. But this highlights another problem. Put crudely, what prevents the operators of the contributions booth from simply taking the money rather than passing it on to the candidate or party that it was intended for? If all political agents are to be modeled in the rational choice tradition as venal utility maximizers, the contributions-booth operators must also be modeled in this way, and anything that prevents information on donors and donations from becoming public also prevents any monitoring or auditing of their operation. These two practical problems seem to crosscut in a way that seriously undermines the possibility of an anonymous system. True anonymity would result in no donations reaching their intended target and, recognizing this, donors would be unwilling to make donations; the resultant equilibrium would be the degenerate one in which no donations are made. But then the question of how to finance politics has been avoided rather than answered.

It is worth noting, too, that Ayres sees the chief virtue of his scheme to be that of reducing the *number* of large-scale contributors. The campaign arena may, however, be one in which there is some *safety* in numbers: a situation in which there are a hundred notable givers may be more desirable than a situation in which there is only a handful, even if there is some doubt as to who constitute that handful. It is surprising, moreover, in the United States context, that Ayres does not give more attention to the problem of extremely rich individuals buying political influence by standing for office themselves (or through members of their families) and using their personal wealth to finance campaigns in a way that other less-well-off candidates could never match in the absence of campaign support from external sources. And, of course, there is the familiar point that reduced campaign expenditures would differentially favor incumbents because incumbents derive name recognition and general salience by means of the free mechanisms of ordinary media coverage.

VI. Finale

Ayres's proposal of an institutional regime of anonymity in relation to campaign contributions seems to us to be interesting but ultimately unpersuasive. The proposal is interesting because it challenges an orthodox belief in openness, a belief that is held more as an article of faith than as the result of clear analysis of the alternatives. All too often in institutional discussion, the burden of proof is decisive and that burden is itself decided by familiarity. Ayres does a positive service by opening up for consideration a possibility that mere familiarity effectively closes off. Ayres's appeal to the analogy with the secret ballot is rhetorically powerful in this connection precisely because he is able to mobilize a no less common prejudice in favor of secrecy. But this analogy may serve no less to raise reasonable doubts about the secrecy of voting as to encourage secrecy in the campaign contribution case. In any event, the analogy is far from perfect: as we see it, the secret ballot encourages "privacy" in the voting case; in the campaign contribution case, donor anonymity encourages deception

But our judgment of Ayres's argument does not depend on the strength or otherwise of any analogy. In our view, Ayres's discussion is unpersuasive because his arguments are insufficiently general. In particular, there is too little attention to the specification of the democratic context within which his recommendations are to have effect. To be sure, there is a limit on what one can reasonably expect of an author in a single paper. But, as we have tried to show, Ayres's case for anonymity depends on a whole range of matters, including among others, whether politics is best characterized by universal distrust, so that only verifiable claims are believed, or on partial trust where nonverifiable claims have at least some credibility; on what exactly the motives for giving campaign contributions are; on how broadly one understands "corruption" and whether the minimization of corruption, however exactly understood, is *the* appropriate single objective for the design of political institutions; and on what it is exactly that people do when they vote and therefore on the authority of the *vox populi* in various contexts. These are all large questions and, we think, unsettled ones. To say that they should all be settled *before* the Ayres scheme can be properly evaluated is undoubtedly a counsel of despair. But when those questions are treated in the most plausible first-cut way, the balance of considerations does not appear to favor the regulatory regime that Ayres proposes.

NOTES

1. In some cases the distinction between a corrupt bribe and a legitimate payment may hinge upon whether the action or service purchased is illegal, or on whether the intention is fraudulent (i.e., based on some deception). But if the action/service purchased is legal and there is no deception, the difference between a corrupt bribe and a legitimate payment is by no means obvious

2. Clearly, we do not wish to imply that there are only two approaches to questions of institutional design. Each of the two styles we identify is capable of supporting a wide variety of approaches. For discussion of approaches to institutional design, see R. Goodin, ed., *The Theory of Institutional Design* (Cambridge: Cambridge University Press, 1996), which also provides excellent references to the related literature. G. Brennan and A. Hamlin, *Democratic Devices and Desires* (Cambridge: Cambridge University Press, 2000), attempts both to iterate between the styles identified here and to develop a particular approach.

3. Ian Ayres, "Disclosure v. Anonymity in Campaign Finance," this volume, 27.

4. For an overview of the deliberative democracy literature and relevant references, see J. Bohman, "The Coming of Age of Deliberative Democracy," *Journal of Political Philosophy* 6 (1998): 400–425.

5. Of course, there are other models of democracy offering further diagnoses and cures. We concentrate on the two identified models for clarity and because they seem to us to be particularly relevant.

6. Our views are laid out and defended much more fully in Brennan and Hamlin, *Democratic Devices and Desires,* although the institutional structures discussed in detail do not include campaign financing.

7. For detailed discussion, see G. Brennan and L. Lomasky, *Democracy and Decision* (Cambridge: Cambridge University Press, 1993); and G. Brennan and A. Hamlin, "Expressive Voting and Electoral Equilibrium," *Public Choice* 95 (1998): 149–75.

8. For more detailed discussion of a proposal to render voting public, see G. Brennan and P. Pettit, "Unveiling the Vote," *British Journal of Political Science* 20 (1990): 311–33, and references therein.

9. Of course, this is not an essential part of an expressive account because self-expression may be sufficient.

10. For a discussion of trust, see Brennan and Hamlin, *Democratic Devices and Desires,* chapter 3 and references therein; and especially M. Hollis, *Trust within Reason* (Cambridge: Cambridge University Press, 1998).

11. T. Reitz, R. Myerson, and R. Weber, "Campaign Finance Levels as Coordinating Signals in Three-Way, Experimental Elections," *Economics and Politics* 10 (1998): 185–218.

12. *The Funding of Political Parties in the United Kingdom,* Fifth Report of the Committee on Standards in Public Life, Chairman Lord Neill (London: HMSO, 1998).

3

INSTITUTING DELIBERATIVE
DEMOCRACY

JOHN FEREJOHN

Introduction

I[1] take it for granted that we live in an imperfectly deliberative democracy. We recognize, in many of our public decision-making practices, the norm that statutes and administrative actions ought to be the result of deliberative consideration of alternatives according to public values. We also believe that public decisions ought to be responsive in some way to the diverse views of the common good held by citizens. We also believe that everyone, directly or indirectly, is equally entitled to enter into the discussions that produce such decisions and to have has views respected and taken seriously into account in whatever public decision is reached. We lament that people don't take much part in public life and don't seem to feel obligated to do so. In this sense, there seems a widespread commitment to deliberative norms, even if there is less agreement as to what such norms require of us.

Some theorists go further than this to suggest that democratic deliberation entails a commitment to public reasoning whereby participants "regard one another as equals; they aim to defend and criticize institutions and programs in terms of considerations that others have reason to accept, given . . . that those others are reasonable; and they are prepared to cooperate in accordance

with the results of such discussion."[2] The attraction of this understanding of deliberative democracy is that it promises to produce
policies that are based on a wide range of information and perspectives within society and to offer a reasonable account to every
person, which that person would be willing to accept after suitable deliberation, as to why it is that some action of hers is to be
constrained by the coercive force of the state. In this respect, deliberation over public action is expected both to produce policies
that reflect public views and to encourage citizens—at least those
who involve themselves in deliberation—to refine and enlarge
their views of what policies should be pursued.

But whether or not deliberative democracy requires a full commitment to public reasoning of this kind, it surely requires at least
some minimal procedural assurances of the kind outlined above. I
would think that the more demanding requirements of public reasoning might need to be embodied in deliberative norms rather
than imposed as institutional requirements, whereas many of the
procedural assurances can be made by designing and deploying
suitable institutions. Thus, the question in this paper is how much
of the full-blown deliberative ideal can be accomplished or encouraged by suitably designed institutions. None of this is intended
to disparage the idea that there may be a need as well for the development of a deliberative ethics. But just what shape that ethical
system would need to take will depend on what it is that institutions
cannot reliably do.

Part of the reason that the deliberative ideal is often honored
in the breach rather than in the observance is that there is little
agreement as to what it entails. No modern proponent of deliberative democracy believes that full and adequate deliberation requires that each person is entitled to have her views satisfied as a
precondition for any collective decision. Instead, deliberative
theorists ask only that decision making "aim" for consensus in
the sense of trying to take everyone's views into account. For
these theorists, however, consensus is not a precondition for social decision but is, instead, an aspiration or "regulative" aim. If,
for whatever reason, an actual consensus cannot be found for
some urgent decision, most theorists recognize the need to resort to some form of majority rule or, perhaps, to some other
kind of authoritative decision process. The resort to authority in

the absence of agreement is, however, seen as a failure of deliberation and there would be an ensuing need to justify the both the decision taken and the appropriateness of the particular decision procedure that was employed.[3]

Put this way, deliberative democracy might seem a pretty tepid ideal since it requires only that we sincerely try to reach consensus among all citizens but settles for the use of authoritative procedures in the event a consensus cannot be found. More stringent deliberative requirements have taken three forms. Some theorists have suggested that much public discussion and deliberation can take place outside formal governmental processes in groups and associations of people with presumably relatively homogeneous preferences.[4] "Decentered" public decision making in such settings might find consensus easier to achieve and the deliberative ideal more attainable.[5] Others, following Rawls's early work, have restricted the call for deliberation to a few basic kinds of decisions—those concerning the basic structure of society—that need to be addressed only rarely and without temporal urgency. For such decisions, people may be expected to have less diverse views (they are made in a constitutional setting and they are expected to shape public action into the indefinite future) and, in any case, there may be less need to resort to the imposition of coercive solutions to these problems.

More controversially, some deliberativists have argued that public decisions should not necessarily be responsive to whatever views people happen to hold, only to considered or reasonable views that have (or would) survive public discussion and deliberation. The intuition is that while real people may believe all kinds of strange things, or may on many issues have no views at all, these actual views (or nonviews) would be refined in a well-structured public discourse, and public decisions ought to be responsive to these postdeliberative views.

There seem to be two different ways to understand the views that need to be taken into account in public decision making. Public decision might be required to respond only to *reasonable* views about public action, where a view is considered reasonable in virtue of its substantive content. Rawls, and Gutmann and Thompson argue that the idea of the reasonable embodies some particular substantive commitments—such as a willingness to seek terms of fair cooperation (reciprocity). Alternatively, we might think that public decisions should be responsive to *reasoned* or *considered* views—those views or preferences that survive a well-ordered deliberative procedure (one that gives everyone a real opportunity to engage in the deliberative process). While these two ideas seem to point in different directions, many writers appear to believe that they will, as a matter of fact, converge and that only (a small number of) substantively reasonable views will withstand well-structured public deliberation. In this paper I shall title this belief the sociological hypothesis (SH). If it is true, the gap between procedural and substantive views of deliberation seems bridgeably small since good procedures will reliably encourage people to adopt reasonable views and appropriate deliberative norms and preferences. If it is not true, then we need to find nonprocedural means to encourage people to adopt reasonable views.

There are of course some questions as to whether deliberative democracy is really a suitable aspiration or critical ideal for governmental processes. The first objection is philosophical: there may simply be too much profound value disagreement, even among the reasonable views and even concerning basic constitutional issues, to permit the formation of the kind of consensus that deliberative democrats aim at. This disagreement might in fact be found even in highly decentralized social settings and it may concern issues surrounding the basic structure of society as much as more superficial disagreements. Second, there are questions of intelligence, ability and motivation. Even if consensus could, in principle, be reached among the reasonable views, is there good reason to think that imperfect decision making institutions peopled with imperfect decision makers could actually find or construct such consensual policies? Third, there are questions of psychology and sociology: even if good policies could be found, is there reason to believe that citizens would generally come to adopt one among the reasonable views as their own and therefore be able and willing to accept the (reasonable) justifications for public actions offered to them? It seems to me, as it has to others, that the deepest problem for deliberative democracy is the first, the problem of pluralism, because the severity of the other obstacles is reduced where there is a high level of fundamental agreement among citizens. It is to these issues that we turn.

The argument is developed as follows. First, I argue that any attractive form of deliberative democracy must have the capacity to make nonconsensual decisions. Second, I show that in circumstances of deep pluralism, decisive institutions must operate to aggregate incompatible views and cannot be understood as accomplishing only epistemic or constructive tasks. Building on this claim, I then explore some issues of the design of the institutional context of deliberative processes. Such contexts, I argue, shape the behavior of well-motivated deliberators and therefore the content of deliberation itself. Finally, I argue that the deliberative ideal need not presuppose that there is no deliberative division of labor and that even if deliberation is to some extent an institutionally specialized activity, there are reasons to hope that suitably structured public deliberation can be educational in the right way.

I. Deliberation and Decision

Nowadays, the deliberative democratic ideal is expected to apply to a pluralistic society. In such a society, people would be expected to have divergent interests and diverse perspectives, and, most significantly, would not be expected to exhibit wide substantive agreement on any particular conception of the good but would be committed only to living with one another on mutually agreeable terms and working out common projects from their own divergent perspectives. Their commitment to deliberation would require that public decisions be chosen based on actual public deliberations, that everyone have effective access to the deliberative forum, that every citizen be capable of giving and being moved by good reasons, and that everyone accept the obligations that follow from the deliberate choice of a public action.

The diversity of a plural society suggests that what is in the common interest would have to take account of the actual diversity of interests and views within society but that, even after full deliberation, there will often be no complete agreement as to what is the best course of action. Thus, the fact of pluralism forces a recognition that sometimes decisions will have to be taken prior to the formation of a deliberative consensus and such decisions will stand in special need of justification to those whose views were rejected or ignored. It is this fact—that in a pluralistic society, nonconsensual decisions are sometimes needed—that requires that (nonunanimous) decision-making institutions be in place to make and enforce decisions when a full consensus cannot be reached. Failure to provide nonconsensual decision-making procedures confers an unjustifiable advantage on the status quo—whatever it happens to be—and diminishes the incentive of those advantaged in the status quo to engage with others deliberatively.

Some theorists believe that the need for nonconsensual decisions can be minimized by encouraging public deliberation and decisions to take place throughout civil society and there is much value to this proposal. Indeed, one can scarcely envision, much less endorse, an organization of public life in which a centralized state had to bear the burden of all public decision making. But it is important to remember that minorities within smaller political units and associations lack the protections of publicity and formality that are available to those in larger associations. Decentered public decision making can be an invitation to local tyranny by permitting powerful local factions, minorities or majorities, to rule unchecked. Moreover, most associations in civil societies contain or affect people whose exposure is not the result of voluntary choice, such as children or neighbors, and who are poorly placed to object to informally chosen actions that take place in obscure venues. Thus one can have faith in such a solution only where associational life is made up of people with relatively homogeneous views and where decisions made in such settings do not greatly affect third parties.[6] Such circumstances seem rare enough that we think that wherever deliberation is to take place, the need for nonconsensual procedures is practically unavoidable.

Indeed, the need for (coercive) institutions would arise even in homogeneous associations in light of the coordination and collective action problems that would occur even in such settings. Taxes must be levied and criminals subjected to correction even here. Moreover, the need to organize and conduct deliberation in an orderly fashion will, even in a homogeneous society, sometimes require the use of coercion. So the problem of justification, while perhaps more visible in plural societies, is not restricted to them.

At least three kinds of institutions need to be considered: decision-making institutions (electoral rules, rules for legislative decision, and specifications of which officials can act in the absence of agreement), enforcement institutions (aimed at interpreting and applying public decisions and ensuring that they are actually carried out), and deliberative institutions (aimed at establishing conditions for effective deliberation). It is possible, in some cases where people have sufficiently well formed expectations, that informal institutions or norms might take the place of more formal ones. People might be able to "agree" (in the sense of having convergent expectations) on the circumstances in which a decision is needed prior to the formation of a deliberative consensus and, in such a case, be willing to be bound by a majority decision. But the fact of this "agreement" does not obviate the coercion that takes place when some are required to accept a course of action with which they cannot agree. Public action without deliberative consensus is action taken without the willing agreement of some even if those whose agreement was not secured choose not to press a complaint. The same consideration appears to apply to the other kinds of institutions: whether they are formal or informal, they seem equally to be source of coercion (and require justification for that reason).

Of course, in modern plural societies, it is hardly to be hoped that informal norms will suffice so, most likely, there will have to be formal institutions with well-specified rules, and the conditions under which these institutions are employed will have to be commonly known. It is also to be expected, under modern conditions, that these institutions would exhibit a pretty extensive division of labor, with some officials of the state specializing in formulating potential public decisions, others specializing in enforcement, and others maintaining the conditions under which genuine deliberation can meaningfully take place. When such specialized institutions are required, there is a need to ensure that they operate well—in the sense of achieving their purposes—and that in their operation they do not produce intolerable side effects. In particular there is a need to ensure that specialized institutions are adequately accountable and responsive.

These concerns, while applicable to institutions in general, apply with special force in the case of the decision-making institutions of a deliberative democracy. Such institutions will be employed in a consequential manner when deliberation fails to produce consensus. When there is no deliberative consensus and a decision nevertheless is needed, legislatures must vote or executives issue orders. Such authoritative decisions occur, that is, in circumstances where they have not (yet) been fully justified in the sense of being accepted by each of the citizens from her own vantage point, and they require special attention to providing further justification. Such justification must aim to explain why it was that a decision was needed prior to the formation of a deliberative consensus, why the institution that made the decision was entitled to do so, and why the particular decision that was taken was warranted.

II. Two Models of Democracy: Aggregation versus Deliberation

The traditional deliberative model, which aims to find the best course of public action—an epistemic task—is sometimes contrasted to an aggregative model of democracy, which is said to take the preferences of individuals as given and simply aggregate these preferences into collective preferences—thereby constituting the public choice. Some modern deliberativists—denying the pure epistemic conception in favor of a constructivist interpretation of the common good—press this contrast as well. Individual preferences, on the aggregative interpretation, are to be accorded respect because they represent the individual's own judgements about what would be best for her.[7] And as is well known, with sufficient preference diversity, the aggregative model will generally produce arbitrary collective choices—choices that appear to be impossible to justify on any reasonable account of the what the public good requires because they depend completely on substantively irrelevant features of the aggregation procedure. This unattractive aspect of the aggregative model has made appealing an approach to democratic choice that sees democracy as aiming at some more or less process-independent conception of the public good. But the attraction of deliberative democracy, on this view, turns on the plausibility of there being, either prior to or as a product of the process of deliberation, some reasonable candidate for what this public good is. And, the plausibility of this belief is threatened by the acceptance of pluralism.

Recently, deliberative theorists have tried to come to grips with this issue in various ways. One way to is to follow Rawls in arguing that the pluralism that must be taken account of is limited to those views that are reasonable conceptions of the good.[8] Only those views which are reasonable are candidates for serious consideration. For example, in their recent book, Gutmann and Thompson suggest that we need not aim at finding an agreement with religious views that reject the idea that children are to be educated in a way that suits them for participation in a pluralistic deliberative society.[9] Another approach is to limit the range of public action to the kinds of things that might be agreed to, given the level of social diversity (this might be accomplished by refusing to decide in the absence of deliberative consensus). This austere approach would seem to limit the capacity of a people to deal with a changing social and technological environment. A third method is to employ the deliberative process itself to define or constitute the public good by identifying the public good as the outcome of a well-functioning deliberative procedure.

In various ways, each of these responses to reasonable pluralism can be (and has been) criticized. It seems hard to defend the practice of limiting the preferences that need to be taken account of; at the very least we would need a quite a strong theory of "reasonability" to do the job. Why can't people demand justifications that actually satisfy them, given the beliefs and preferences they actually have? By what authority are they required to alter their actual views in some way so as to make them worthy of being taken account of in public deliberation? Deliberativists see such alteration as instances of desirable public education or opinion transformation, whereas liberal thinkers are more skeptical. I assume that there is a defensible middle ground—one that says that we need not take full account of just any preference or view a person happens to have but that we must also be skeptical of any principle that requires that individuals move very far from the considered views that they actually have. This line is

particularly troubling for those deliberativists who envision deliberation taking place among representatives of the people. In
such a conception ordinary people who are not participants in
the discussions may lack the information necessary to enable
them to learn and alter their views.

It seems almost as difficult a course to limit the range of action
of the state in a way that prevents people from carrying out projects that are common to most of them. If there was a very wide
range of reasonable views, a public deliberation process aimed at
getting consensus might, in the name of producing legitimate
policies, restrict itself to a very limited range of projects. This
would be another way of building an unjustifiable status-quo bias
into the deliberative requirement. One would hope, of course,
that holders of reasonable views would alter their policy preferences in the course of deliberation in such a way as to permit desirable public action. Whether such a happy result can ordinarily
be expected is not, however, clear, especially since the option of
inaction will usually favor the interests of some views over others.

Finally, as many have argued, it seems incoherent and arbitrary simply to define the public good as the result of whatever institutional decision process happens to be in place. This is especially so when it is noticed that apparently ephemeral changes in
decision-making institutions or procedures can produce substantially different public decisions. It is hardly to be believed that
the best course of action would be unstable in this manner.

It is not surprising that there is no completely satisfactory
treatment of pluralism by deliberativists because, from a formal
perspective, the recognition of pluralism reintroduces the problems of the aggregative model into the deliberative context. The
interpretation of the "preferences" to be aggregated is now, of
course, changed to correspond to postdeliberative views about
what the polity should do. But, as long as there is sufficient post-
deliberation preference diversity, the results of aggregation will
be arbitrary in the same way that nondeliberative processes are.
Moreover, such postdeliberative diversity is virtually assured by
the assumption of reasonable pluralism. Whether "reasonable" is
given a procedural or substantive interpretation, under virtually
any circumstances postdeliberative views will be heterogeneous
and will therefore entail some version of the arbitrariness results

of social choice theory. Thus, it appears that even in a deliberative democracy, pluralism can produce morally arbitrary results.

But should we be concerned about this as long as the preferences that go into the social decision are formed in the right kind of deliberative circumstances? If postdeliberative preferences incorporate reasonable views of the good, isn't there some sort of guarantee that the resulting policy, while perhaps arbitrary, will at least be one that is justifiable on substantive grounds (from within one or more of the reasonable theories)? While this question is not yet well enough formulated to give a completely satisfactory answer, the existing theoretical results give little reason to believe that this will be the case. For example, the "chaos" results produced by McKelvey and others,[10] however they are modified in later treatments, suggest that with only a small amount of preference diversity a very wide range of policies can be produced. When applying these results to postdeliberative preferences, each move along a majoritarian path is now ratified by a majority in terms of its considered preferences. In that sense, there is no smuggled venality or self-regardingness in the argument. One can, of course argue (as do Coleman and Ferejohn[11]) that actual political processes would not work in so shortsighted a fashion, but this response only limits, rather than eliminates, the substantive arbitrariness of the outcomes.

Alternatively, one might suppose that deliberation will generally reduce pluralism in preferences on the grounds that deliberation will tend to eliminate disagreements based on misunderstanding and trigger empathy and altruistic feelings. By producing social cohesion not only by persuasion but also by means of emotional bonding, postdeliberative preferences might be systematically less likely to produce arbitrary policy choices. There is, as yet, very little reason to believe that this claim is true. Deliberation may as easily help participants to get clear on what it is they really want to do, taking into account other reasonable views, and to see more clearly how their judgments as to the best course of action differ from those of others. But continued argument with these now clearly perceived adversaries may work to diminish empathy and altruistic feelings. Even if people embrace deliberative norms that require the giving of reasons that other reasonable people can accept, deliberation may permit them to calibrate their agreements in such a way that others are given reasons that they can "just barely" accept. This seems especially likely in a society in which the diversity of reasonable public views is substantial.[12]

Finally, as has been suggested, perhaps we should not regard as problematic the fact that outcomes are procedure dependent so long as people are free to choose the decision procedures themselves. But, as William Riker argued long ago, this answer only pushes the problem back one level.[13] As long as people choose procedures in light of the outcomes the procedures tend to produce, their choice of procedures will be similarly arbitrary, even if this choice is made by actors employing their postdeliberative preferences. Of course, people may not choose their institutions in this way but may instead choose institutions that are attractive for reasons unrelated to their likely performance. For example, we may choose institutions that give everyone equal votes and equal access to agenda, even if these institutions tend to produce decisions that depart substantially from any particular substantive conception of justice or equality.

The point is that the deliberative ideal will have to be embedded, to some extent, in institutions that aggregate diverse preferences into collective decisions. It seems clear that however these institutions are designed, and however well they operate, they cannot *guarantee* that the resulting decisions are good even if people take full advantage of their deliberative opportunities and obligations. But it does seem possible that institutions can be designed in ways that improve the quality of deliberations and resulting collective decisions relative to what they would otherwise exhibit. And, in any case, decisions that emerge from such an open process might very well enjoy a kind of legitimacy that is partially independent of the content or effects of the decisions themselves.

Making progress in this direction demands that we try to develop a better understanding of how the ideal of deliberative democracy can be embodied in democratic institutions. Deliberative democracy requires institutions to organize and regulate deliberation, to make authoritative decisions (or at least to recognize when they have been made), and to implement and enforce these decisions. Institutionally embodied, deliberative democracy requires the use and threat of coercion no less than other governmental arrangements, even though the purpose for which these coercive elements are arranged is to aim at getting the right answers to questions of political morality by means of achieving democratic agreement. These institutional requirements, while permitting deliberation, may also set limits on just how far we can go in attaining the deliberative ideal. It is important to know whether there are such limits, as I believe, and to begin to trace them.

My goal in the next sections of this paper is to begin to evaluate these institutional questions. I hope to show that there are some difficult practical trade-offs that need to be faced if we are to make progress in improving deliberative democracy by means of institutional reforms and that there are real limits to how far we can go by simply reforming institutions. I try to explore some of these limits, at least qualitatively. Going further will require more attention to what we might call democratic ethics—norms that aim to regulate how people behave in deliberating, deciding, interpreting, criticizing, and carrying out public courses of action—not a subject to which I try to contribute here, except to speculate in passing, on what form such an ethics might usefully take.

III. Institutions and Deliberation

We can approach the question of the design of deliberative institutions in at least two ways. We might evaluate institutions in light of their structural features—without regard for the consequences of their operation. Thus, majority rule is attractive because it gives each citizen an equal vote, does not contain a bias toward any particular choice (such as remaining at the status quo), and is decisive in the sense that it takes only a bare majority to make a collective decision. In this sense majority rule seems to be structurally or procedurally fair. Of course, as is by now well understood, to ensure structural fairness we need to worry about more than the equality of vote distribution, so attention must be paid to equality of access to the agenda. In any case, we can imagine procedurally fair decision procedures that are sensitive to this issue as well. The problem with this approach to institutional

design is that it is not clear that procedurally fair decision procedures will actually work to produce substantively fair outcomes.
Indeed, work in social choice theory suggests that such a result
probably cannot be established for any conception of substantive
fairness.

For this reason, I take a more consequentialist approach to ana-
lyzing institutions. This does not mean that we should abandon
considerations of procedural fairness altogether but suggests that
we need to take account of other features of institutions as well.
The particular feature I focus on here is one that seems necessary
for people to be able to refine their preferences during the course
of deliberation. Deliberation takes place within an institutional
nexus, and if we are to expect citizens to transform or refine their
beliefs in public discourse, they must have reasonable grounds for
anticipating the consequences of the choices they must make during the deliberative process. Unless they can, in effect, anticipate
the consequences of choosing particular alternatives, it is hard to
see how they can reliably form preferences for these alternatives.
Working backwards, this entails figuring out, at the stage of deliberation, how decisions will be implemented once they are made;
how they will be made after they are discussed; and, finally, how
they will be discussed. I argue that each of these issues must be addressed institutionally, so that citizens can know, at least roughly,
how their institutions work in order that they can work to refine
their views while deliberating with others.

Enforcement Institutions

Most models of deliberative democracy presume that everyone
intends to play her part in implementing whatever collective decision is deliberatively arrived at. This is what is required of those
who are sincerely committed to taking part in a deliberative process. Indeed, this is one of the great virtues of deliberative democracy. If public decisions are actually of a kind that can be endorsed by anyone holding a reasonable view of the public good,
and if communication processes are in place that successfully ensure that most citizens hold such views, public decisions can be
seen as jointly made. Each person can plausibly see such decisions as, in some sense, her own, even if she didn't actually partic-

ipate in their making. In that sense, each person can see herself as responsible for doing her part in giving the decision its full (jointly intended) effect.

But, as I suggested earlier, the presumption that individuals will feel committed to doing their part is not sufficient for the successful operation of a well functioning deliberative democracy. For one thing some decisions will be taken without a deliberative consensus and may require those who disagree in principled ways with the decision to play a part in carrying it out. In such cases, if the disagreement is sufficiently profound, it will not be clear to everyone that such a decision will be actually carried out or carried out without protest or other harmful side effects.

Second, when a collective decision is made, it is rarely certain just what is required of each individual in order to implement the decision. Typically, even if there is a consensus on what should be done, problems of coordination and collective action will remain that must be resolved if a collective decision is to be made effective. Third, public decisions are typically made at a level of generality that requires interpretation before the decision can be applied to particular cases. Such interpretations inevitably have an irreducibly creative aspect and cannot be fully anticipated at the time the public decision is made. This implies that different (perhaps justified) beliefs as to how public decisions would be applied will induce in participants different deliberative preferences. In this sense, deliberative preferences depend on expectations about interpretive practices. For these reasons, the sincere commitment of all citizens to do their part to implement a public decision will not generally be sufficient to allow participants to foresee the consequences of decisions they take collectively, and lacking this ability, citizens will not generally be able to form fully deliberative preferences among courses of action.

While the problem of enforcement of deliberative agreements is probably intractable at a theoretical level, it might be possible to ameliorate its effects somewhat in practice by establishing stable and predictable institutions to interpret and enforce public actions. To the extent that the police and the judges reliably enforce public legislation in principled ways that can be foreseen at the deliberative stage, citizens will be able to make fairly stable judgments about alternative courses of public action. But, the existence of such reliable enforcement mechanisms probably requires that they operate in a way that is substantially autonomous from public opinion, especially the opinion of that part of the public that lost out in the decision. Such autonomy in turn has far-reaching consequences: first, it raises the possibility that policy making will not be securely anchored in deliberative public choice; and second, it lessens the responsibility of each participant to play a part in carrying out the results of such collective actions.

Decision-Making Institutions

I assume that while deliberating about a potential social action, everyone knows that if consensus cannot be reached, a decision will be reached by voting or some other authoritative decision procedure. In this sense, deliberation takes place in the shadow of this decision procedure, whatever it is. Because of this, the structure of decision procedure—which we shall take to be a voting rule—might affect the process of deliberation itself. Suppose, for example that a deeply plural society makes its difficult decisions by simple majority rule. Everyone will know, at the deliberative stage, that there is no real need to get everyone's support—a simple majority is all that is necessary in the end. In this setting, alternatives might then be chosen to reflect the majoritarian features of the democratic process rather than the deliberative aim to attain the agreement of all reasonable views. In this sense, the structure of the decision process might make it unlikely that deliberation, even by well-motivated participants, will result in the sharing of socially valuable information. This can be seen in the structure of jury decision making

Suppose there is a five-person jury that must decide the guilt (G) or innocence (I) of the accused and that all the jurors are well motivated in sense that each seeks to find the best possible judgement based on all available information.[14] Assume that all the jurors believe before hearing any evidence that the accused is equally likely to be guilty or innocent and that, at the trial, each receives a signal of the guilt or innocence of the accused, which is correlated with the actual guilt or innocence of the accused. In particular, assume that if the accused is guilty, the signal received by each juror indicates guilt two-thirds of the time, and similarly if the accused is innocent. Assume further that these signals are independent, so that each juror has valuable information to contribute to the collective decision. Finally, let's assume that each juror regards it as three times as bad to convict an innocent person as to acquit a guilty one.[15]

Following deliberation over the trial evidence, the jury will decide the question by a vote taken by secret ballot. Under common (criminal) jury rules, a unanimous judgment is required to reach a guilty verdict. The use of a secret ballot is designed to exclude inappropriate forms of influence from affecting the decision. It is clear in this case that a well-functioning deliberative process would induce each juror to reveal her information during either the deliberation or voting stage, so that the collective decision will take all relevant data into account.

Suppose now that deliberations have already occurred and that the jurors have not, for whatever reason, fully revealed their observations during this process, and the jury is now proceeding to take a vote. Remember, we have assumed that jurors care only about getting to the truth of the matter and are therefore consequentialist in choosing how to vote in order to get the right decision. A rational and consequentialist juror would decide how to vote by focusing only on those circumstances where her vote would actually have an effect on the outcome—after all, her vote would not matter in any other circumstance. Would rational jurors, motivated only to get the right collective decision, vote in a way that reflects their private observations? Would they, in a word, truthfully reveal their private information?

To answer this question, assume that all jurors are voting truthfully and that a particular juror has received an observation suggesting that the accused is innocent. She knows, in view of the voting rule, that her vote will be decisive only if all the other jurors have voted that the accused is guilty, that is, her vote will be decisive only if all the other jurors have received information that the accused is guilty. If she were to vote not guilty, that would be the collective decision, even though everyone else voted the other way. Now, the probability that the other jurors could all have received a guilty signal when the defendant is innocent is obviously very small, so our (well-motivated voter) would not vote for a not-guilty verdict in this circumstance because, in this circumstance, she "knows" that she is the only juror who received the signal that the accused is not guilty. In this sense, juror decision making will be strategic.

The same phenomenon occurs with any other voting rule. Assume that the jury uses majority rule and note that a voter is pivotal only in case the other jurors have reached a tie. For truthful voting to be an equilibrium, the juror would have to be willing to vote truthfully in this circumstance. But note that if the other voters are tied and our juror has received a guilty signal, she would conclude that the defendant is guilty with probability two-thirds. Voting to convict, while getting the right outcome with highest probability, will lead to a one-third chance of convicting an innocent person. Voting to acquit, while running a higher risk of acquitting a guilty person, leads to a preferable decision (because it is much worse to convict the innocent than to acquit the guilty). Indeed, Austen-Smith and Banks show that except in very special cases, in any equilibrium some jurors must rationally vote insincerely or strategically. In this sense, jury decision making will be "strategic" at the stage of voting even though jurors are concerned only to get the right answer, and because of this strategizing, jury decisions will fail to aggregate available information.

But then, in view of the incapacity of voting to fully transmit available information, can't well-motivated voters find a way to reveal their sample information during the deliberative stage? This doesn't appear to be likely either.[16] Suppose the voter is someone who has a prior belief, before making an observation, that the accused is guilty—so likely, for example, that she would think the accused guilty even if she had received the information of all twelve jurors that he was innocent—but whose (private) observation suggests that the accused is not guilty. If such a voter were to reveal her observation, it might prevent the jury from reaching what she is convinced is the correct conclusion (that the accused is guilty). The problem here is that this juror has prior beliefs that make it very likely that the accused is guilty, and this will give her a reason to conceal her observation from the others. Thus, if this reasoning is right, deliberation as well as voting will be strategic in jury processes, however well motivated jurors are to reach the truth.

Recent work by Andrew McLennan suggests that things may not be quite so bleak as this argument suggests. He shows that even in circumstances in which fully revealing observations is not consistent with rational decision making, rational voting may reveal enough information to get right answers with very high probability.[17] Thus even if, in equilibrium, jurors do not always reveal their observations, the collective decision may nevertheless approximate the outcome that would have occurred if they had. In any case, while the results in this area of research are quite new and, as is often the case of game theoretic applications, fairly sensitive to details of model specification, it seems clear that the institutional setting within which deliberation takes place can introduce complex incentives to strategize even among well-motivated voters.

One response to this issue is to assert that these results show only that well-motivated consequentialist voters face strategic difficulties in deliberating. However, an appropriate deliberative ethics would rule out consequentialist reasoning in this context and replace it with an injunction always to reveal all information during the deliberative process. Then, once all information was revealed, some appropriate institution or calculating device could be employed that would indicate the best decision, and then everyone would vote to implement it. In the case of the unanimity-rule jury, the four guilty signals and one innocent signal would have indicated the accused was so likely guilty that a guilty verdict was best, and then all the jurors would vote guilty. In the case of the majority-rule jury, the collective judgment would be in favor of a not-guilty verdict, and everyone would vote for this outcome after all available information was revealed. In this case, the voting stage is not invoked when deliberative reasons run out but instead formally ratifies deliberative decisions.

While this is a promising suggestion in some respects, it is not clear how attractive it would be in circumstances of deep pluralism. In such settings, even if all information were revealed, deep and intractable disagreement would remain—that is what such pluralism implies—so we could not necessarily expect all to concur in judgment. This suggests that unlike the jury situation, it is futile to hope that any way of pooling the revealed information would be anything other than an arbitrary combination of incompatible reasonable views. But if this is true, what is the point of an injunction to reveal all information? It seems that such an ethical injunction would be attractive only when the group is deciding about courses of action on which all reasonable views could be expected to concur. Such action courses would seem to be candidates of an overlapping consensus. But on other issues—those on which reasonable views may differ—it is hard to see what the ethical injunction to reveal all information would accomplish.

Deliberative Institutions

I argued above that deliberation takes place against a background of common understandings about what will occur following the formation of, or the failure to form, a deliberative consensus. Deliberation, at least once the polity approaches a point of making a decision, requires a system for regulating discussions to ensure that discussions occur in an orderly or rulelike fashion. Deliberative institutions have the purpose of regulating the conditions under which deliberation can successfully take place. Such regulation is required to ensure that information is widely available about the agenda for decision; to determine who is entitled to speak to which issues; to establish what decisions are possible on each issue; to specify how proposals may be modified; and to ensure that the deliberative process is sufficiently transparent for reasoned persuasion to take place. Regulation may also be needed to structure the agenda for discussion and, if necessary, for amendment, to discourage dilatory tactics, and to fix the context within which reasons may be given. Regulation is also required to ensure that coercive threats, force, and bribery are restrained.

There are good reasons to believe that regulations of this kind can have substantial effects on the content of public deliberation. There is a substantial literature in positive political theory that shows how seemingly small changes in deliberative institutions—such as changes in agenda-formation rules—can have the effect of altering what will be said and what will be decided. It should be emphasized that these effects are not confined to weird or pathological examples but arise in quite common circumstances. The general principle is that no matter what voting rule is being used, outcomes will reflect the order in which proposals are considered.

An especially interesting example of a regulatory rule affecting deliberation is the requirement that if a vote must be taken, it should (or should not) proceed by secret ballot. Here the contrast will be familiar. If a secret ballot is required (in the event that a vote is needed) people have a diminished incentive to reveal the fact that they disagree with an expressed sentiment. They may choose, instead, to simply wait until a vote takes place and then vote for an option for which they offered no argument. Such phenomena are common and occasionally, in some faculty meetings, lead to embarrassment, such as the failure of proposals against which no one has presented an argument. By reducing the incentive to argue controversial positions, the use of secret ballot may appear to diminish the information content and value of public deliberation.

However, one reason for having secret ballots may be to encourage the revelation of information that would otherwise remain private. The secret ballot is sometimes (perhaps usually) adopted to permit people to express controversial views that they would be afraid to express in public speech. For example, when the Democrats in the House of Representatives decided, a quarter century ago, to elect committee chairs by secret ballot, the purpose was plainly to reduce the fear that committee chairs would retaliate against those who (unsuccessfully) opposed their reelection. Indeed, immediately after the secret ballot was introduced, three (very conservative) committee chairs were toppled (and the remaining conservatives began to respond to the legislative demands of their more liberal Democratic colleagues). In this case, the introduction of a secret ballot seems to have permitted the expression of views that would otherwise have been repressed. It is difficult to say that deliberation—giving reasons to which at least a majority could agree—actually increased in this case. No one stood up to make speeches opposing the committee chairs. But, even if the reasons for the public action remained unexpressed, their content was probably commonly understood and the resulting action might plausibly be said to have been related to reasons in an appropriate way.

Someone could object that the justification for secret ballots in this case arises from the warranted fear that power will be exercised against those expressing unpopular views. What really should be done in this case is to prohibit the strong from intimidating the weak, so that the weak may feel free to speak. Whether this is really possible in circumstances of deep disagreement and high stakes, I cannot say. But the same point may be made in a more mundane fashion in circumstances where intimidation is not at issue. Here we may draw on the extensive literature on agendas and agenda formation. There is little need to mention that the choice of agenda rules can privilege some outcomes over others and that, for this reason, the choice of an agenda for decision will affect the contents of deliberation. The general point is that the choice of deliberative institutions is not neutral with respect to the substance of deliberation.

IV. DELIBERATION AND REPRESENTATION

It is unrealistic to think that most people would actually be inclined to, or able to, participate very much in public deliberation even in a decentralized public sphere, and so the construction and expression of reasonable views must usually be accomplished by representatives or delegates of the people. If deliberation aims only at consensus among reasonable views, and not necessarily consensus among all persons, one could expect decisions by representatives to produce adequately responsive policies insofar as all the reasonable views are on display in the representative body. One would, of course, need to design the electoral process to ensure that representation works to produce a fuller range of alternative public views within the legislature (perhaps by adopting a version of proportional representation and embracing term limits or rotation in office). And we would also need to design the rules of the legislative process to encourage considered views to converge on the reasonable ones during the process of deliberation. In other words, we would want to ensure that, within the legislature at least, the sociological hypothesis was true.

But, even if such a convergence could be assured, legislative policies would not necessarily appear to be justified to those who remained outside the legislature and who, not having actually deliberated, may continue to hold unreasoned or unreasonable views as to what should be done. The deliberative ideal with representative government seems much better suited, therefore, to producing good policies than to producing citizens with reasonable views. Indeed, one might think that the best result of deliberation within the legislature is that the legislature adopt good policies (based on consideration of all reasonable views and evidence) and that legislators accept and endorse these decisions, but that their revised preferences separate them from their constituents. If we accept that most citizens cannot or will not take part in policy making or debate, deliberative democrats need to find other ways to engage their views, so as to encourage processes by which most citizens will come to have reasonable preferences, ones that would lead them to accept good reasons and endorse good policies. We would like, that is, to ensure that a broad form of the sociological hypothesis holds within society at large. This requires that legislative deliberation and communication be conducted in such a way that people outside the legislature tend to adopt reasonable views.

This suggests that deliberative democrats must conceive of the relation between government and citizens, in modern circumstances, as having an important tutelary aspect in which people who have not taken an active part of the deliberative process nevertheless come to adopt reasonable views. Is this kind of relationship consistent with genuinely democratic rule? I think it can be if it is true that even people who are not actively engaged in collective deliberation are or can be engaged in the active reconsideration of their own views in light of new information they receive. Such people are not mere spectators whose views can be shaped by politicians or powerful interests but are active and shrewd observers and analysts of the political work around them; they are driven to form and reform their beliefs in light of received information. One (admittedly speculative) idea is to build on the ideas of Gilligan and Krehbiel on confirmatory signaling;[18] they argue that internally diverse legislatures have more signaling (communicative) capacity to outsiders (say to the public) than less diverse ones. Fostering more openly argumentative practices in which the plurality of perspectives among officials and their opponents is in plain public view, such as the British practice of the question period, might work to make public debate among representation more informative to citizens.

I think recent developments in the deliberative norms that operate within the U.S. Supreme Court help to illustrate the possibilities of this approach. There has been an increasing tendency for justices to write concurring opinions rather than signing onto a single rationale for a Court decision. Some writers have deplored this development as corrosive of legal values such as predictability and stability. But from the present point of view, the rise of concurrences may be seen as an attempt to provide distinct rationales for a decision that can appeal to those who hold conflicting conceptions of the good. The production of such separate and partly inconsistent opinions may, plausibly, have the effect of making a decision appear to be appealing to people who otherwise might disagree at quite fundamental levels. Concurrences can also have the effect of signaling the presence of conflicting viewpoints on the Court and, as Gilligan and Krehbiel argue, this has the effect of enhancing the communicative capacity of Court opinions. Admittedly, the Court is not designed to be a representative institution, but historically it appears that there are usually various conflicting viewpoints sitting at any particular time.

Reforming electoral institutions to ensure a broader representation of views within legislatures would work in the same direction. True, the effects of such reforms might be relatively weak, but they point to ways of making the public decision process more communicative for ordinary citizens, without officials needing to assume a didactic position toward the populace. More and broader political competition would, by itself, make public deliberation more informative to nonparticipants.

V. Discussion

From the perspective of the ideal of deliberative democracy, actual public decision-making processes can be defective in at least two ways. First, they might be insufficiently democratic. Actual processes might not in fact be open (directly or indirectly) to the views held by all citizens, either because of the refusal to hear or engage the views that some people hold or because

many people lack effective means to enter into public deliberations or to make their views convincing to others. Decisions are
frequently made by public officials in nontransparent situations
often influenced by the wealthy and powerful, without the opportunity for critical input from those with divergent perspectives. Second, institutions can be inadequately deliberative in
that decisions are not based on reasons of the kind that can be
endorsed by all citizens, or even if they are, no real attempt is
made to produce those reasons as part of coming to a decision.
The sense that current institutions are defective in both these
senses has, in our history, often fueled reform impulses aimed at
opening up governmental processes to wider popular input
and, less directly, encouraging that public decisions be based on
public reasons in an acceptable way.

The usual explanations for the failure to approach the deliberative ideal—why it is not even attractive as a critical standard—
are that it is internally incoherent or that it is somehow unsuited
to the conditions of modern society. Deliberation might, for example, be elitist and therefore inherently undemocratic, or democratic rule might be necessarily nondeliberative, in some basic
sense, so that aiming to have deliberative democracy would be to
aim at a nonentity. Alternatively, perhaps modern government is
simply too large and specialized to permit citizens to engage in
deliberation equal terms.

These complaints, while perhaps containing some truth, have
not been the focus of this essay. I assume not that deliberative
democracy is attainable but that current institutional practices
can be improved by making them more democratic and more deliberative. On some views of democracy, deliberation and democracy pull apart from each other. Deliberative institutions, like
courts, aim at justice, whereas democratic institutions aim to construct compromises that are acceptable to suitably constituted
majorities. Courts, on this view, should produce predictable and
consistent patterns of decisions, driven by reasons of certain
kinds, and be insulated from popular impulses to do otherwise.
Legislative and executive institutions, on the other hand, are appropriately more responsive to public and popular direction
whether or not that direction is consistent and predictable.

Seeking to bridge this divide, some have urged that the political branches behave in a more deliberative fashion by basing their decisions on public reasons, reasons that could be accepted by all, rather than by designing policies to maintain power by satisfying interest-group demands. Others have wanted courts to make more room for democratic impulses, either by deferring to legislative judgments or by adopting jurisprudential doctrines that are open to wider deliberative input. But, there is reason to doubt that these paths are open. Would the public put up with having its opinions, no matter how poorly formed, ignored by its elected representatives? Would litigants accept judicial decisions based only on judgments of good policy? Madison and Montesquieu may have been right in noting the powerful arguments in favor of giving separate institutional embodiment to legislation, administration, and judging.

At a theoretical level, the tension between deliberation and democracy might be real and intractable, but at a more practical level—beginning with a very imperfect set of deliberative democratic institutions—it may be possible to increase deliberative capacities of political institutions while also making them more democratic. Whether this really is possible depends on the way in which the deliberative and democratic aspects interact when institutionally embodied. It is possible that making an institution more democratic—more open to a wider range of inputs from citizens—would undercut its deliberative capacities. The converse supposition seems possible too.

One of the virtues of the current discussions of democratic deliberation is that they may help us to develop institutional reforms that are likely to ameliorate defects in current decision-making processes. I take this to be largely a question of institutional design, though it is also clear that the issue might also be approached by looking at what public norms, expectations, and practices we should try to adopt and maintain, if our aim is to improve the deliberative aspects of our democracy. I have nothing negative to say about an approach aimed at finding better deliberative norms or practices and instilling them in leaders as well as the broader public; indeed, I think such inquiry is equally necessary. But I think it is unwise to place too much weight on the likelihood of achieving improvements in democratic practice solely through the ethical transformation of citizens. Some ethical transformation will, no doubt, be necessary but it seems wise to try to facilitate it by embedding individuals within institutional structures that encourage and support deliberative activities under democratic conditions.

Institutionalizing deliberative democracy is a demanding task but, arguably, it is one that we have as a nation been embarked upon for more than two centuries. It is well to remember that the parade of failed reforms is long. Progressive efforts to regulate political parties with the aim of making them more democratic have often worked, directly or indirectly, to discourage voter participation and to increase the alienation of citizens from the public-agenda-formation process. These reforms have encouraged many people and groups to define their interests ever more narrowly and to press their claims with increasing single-mindedness. Arguably these reforms have produced, simultaneously, a reduced institutional capacity to craft compromises and much less willingness to moderate claims on the public. For similar reasons, recent efforts to regulate campaign finance have probably worked to increase the separation of voters from their elected officials and increased the influence of economic and other interest groups.

Previous democratic reforms also have often failed to take sufficient account of the fact that much that affects our public life is governed by nonpublic events and actions, economic, physical, or social, and deliberation doesn't promise to have much leverage on the "nonpublic" events that may influence our lives greatly. Instilling deliberative norms and practices in government may slow public decision processes so much as to impair our collective capacity to deal with economic and social change. Many of the reforms of the Progressive period seem, in retrospect, to have had the effect of emasculating government capabilities and permitting unjustifiable social and economic conditions to persist and develop. For this reason, I think it is vital that democratic reform preserve the capacity of government to act decisively on important occasions. If it is to permit the people to have maximal control over the conditions in which they live, democracy no matter how deliberative, will always require authoritative decisions and the institutional structures by which to make and enforce them. Institutional reformers forget this fact at our peril.

NOTES

1. Carolyn S. G. Munro Professor of Political Science and Senior Fellow of the Hoover Institution, Stanford University. Visiting Professor of Politics, New York University School of Law.

2. Joshua Cohen, "Procedure and Substance in Deliberative Democracy," in Seyla Benhabib, ed., *Democracy and Difference* (Princeton: Princeton University Press, 1996), 100.

3. "At some point and on some issues, however, deliberation will not lead to agreement. . . . At this point, when conflict remains after good deliberation, a democracy has two choices—to remain at the status quo or to act, by coercing some to go along with others." Jane Mansbridge, "Using Power/Fighting Power," in Seyla Benhabib, ed., *Democracy and Difference* (Princeton: Princeton University Press, 1996), 47.

4. Ibid., 21–30.

5. Economists should recognize the affinity of this idea to those of Charles Teibout, who recommended decentralizing public decisions, as far as possible, to localities so that people would be encouraged to migrate to places that produce public policies they like. Insofar as people sort themselves into homogeneous jurisdictions, it makes little difference which decision-making procedures are used, and unanimity rule, whether embodied institutionally or as a normative expectation, may be employed (leaving aside strategic considerations).

6. Insofar as these conditions of local homogeneity hold, however, the informational advantages of deliberation are attenuated since people would have little need to confront novel viewpoints and try to accommodate them.

7. I should point out that this subjectivist interpretation of preference is by no means mandated by the formalism of the aggregative view. Alternatively, one could construe preferences as judgments held by an individual, indicating how alternative courses of public action are evaluated. This "values"-based interpretation is suggested briefly in Kenneth Arrow, *Social Choice and Individual Values* (New Haven: Yale University Press, 1963).

8. John Rawls, *Political Liberalism* (Cambridge: Harvard University Press, 1993).

9. Amy Gutmann and Dennis Thompson, *Democracy and Disagreement* (Cambridge: Harvard University Press, 1996).

10. Richard D. McKelvey, "Intransitivities in Multidimensional Voting Models and Some Implications for Agenda Control," *Journal of Economic Theory* 12 (1976): 472–82. Linda Cohen, "Cyclic Sets in Multidimen-

sional Voting Models," *Journal of Economic Theory* 20 (1979): 1–12. Norman J. Shofield, *Social Choice and Democracy* (Berlin: Springer, 1985).

11. John Ferejohn and Jules Coleman, "Democracy and Social Choice," *Ethics* 97 (1986): 6–25.

12. It may be objected that this claim illicitly smuggles a bargaining conception of politics into the deliberativist model, a conception that deliberativists have been at pains to criticize. I agree. But this form of bargaining—bargaining among reasonable views—appears to meet the stringent requirements that Joshua Cohen imposes on deliberative politics and seems pretty hard to eliminate completely. After all, everyone with a reasonable view is being offered reasons that she can accept. To insist that she can reasonably hold out for a better deal is simply to give her a veto over public policy that seems arbitrary.

13. William Riker, *Liberalism against Populism: A Confrontation between the Theory of Democracy and the Theory of Social Choice* (San Francisco: Freeman, 1982).

14. All that is necessary for this argument is that the jury be sufficiently large, and it is convenient for the argument that it have an odd number of members. Also, the fact that a jury is deciding whether a defendant is guilty or not is inessential. It could just as well be deciding on whether or not to take a course of action. What is important to applying this argument to a more legislative setting is that there is a truth of the matter, based on all the information, as to which course of action is best.

15. This discussion is motivated by the work of Austen-Smith and Banks, which showed that truthful revelation of private information through voting is almost never consistent with rationality. David Austen-Smith and Jeffery S. Banks, "Information Aggregation, Rationality, and the Condorcet Jury Theorem," *American Political Science Review* 90 (March 1996): 34–45. See also, Tim Fedderson and Wolfgang Pesendorfer, "Convicting the Innocent: The Inferiority of Unanimous Jury Verdicts," *American Political Science Review* 92 (March 1998): 23–35.

16. Peter Coughlan has shown that the phenomenon illustrated above is not robust to the introduction of deliberation in the following sense: if jurors are permitted to reveal their private information prior to voting, there is an equilibrium in which jurors reveal truthfully during the deliberation stage and are believed, and each well-motivated voter takes all the information fully into account and the jury votes unanimously for the optimal decision. But if voters have divergent prior beliefs, it appears that some jurors will always be unwilling to reveal what they know, and jury decisions will be in this sense suboptimal. There is little work so far on models with divergent prior beliefs so the discussion here remains speculative. See Peter Coughlan, "In Defense of Unanimous Jury Verdicts: Mistrials,

Communication, and Sincerity," Social Science Working Paper 1012, California Institute of Technology (1997).

17. Andrew McLennan, "Consequences of the Condorcet Jury Theorem for Beneficial Information Aggregation by Rational Agents," *American Political Science Review* 92 (June 1998): 413–18.

18. Thomas W. Gillian and Keith Krehbiel, "Asymmetric Information and Legislative Rules with a Heterogeneous Committee," *American Journal of Political Science* 33 (1989): 459–90.

4

DEMOCRACY, ELECTORAL
AND CONTESTATORY

PHILIP PETTIT

I have argued elsewhere that the ideal of democratization—the ideal of bringing government under the control of the governed—has two dimensions.[1] It represents both the familiar ideal of giving people electoral control over government and the usually unarticulated ideal of giving them contestatory control as well: giving them the sort of control that comes from the ability to contest government decisions effectively.

This essay approaches the two-dimensional conception of democracy from a new angle. I begin with some propositions about the normative role of democracy (section 1). I argue that democracy can play this role only so far as it operates in two distinct dimensions, electoral and contestatory (section 2). And then I try to show two things: first, that the institutions found in polities that we are happy to describe as democratic display those two dimensions (section 3); and, second, that the two-dimensional conception can help us in thinking about how those institutions might be reformed so as to serve democracy better (section 4). The first argument is an attempt to show that the two-dimensional conception is fairly true to established ways of conceiving of democracy; it does not represent a new-fangled idea. The second is a complementary attempt to show that nevertheless there is point to articulating that conception; it enables us to take a critical view of actual democratic practice. The essay concludes with some general observations on the emerging conception of democracy (section 5).

In earlier work I made a case for a two-dimensional conception of democracy, and I looked at the likely shape of such a democracy, starting from the requirements of the distinctively republican ideal of freedom as nondomination. I make no republican assumptions in the current essay. The points that I argue are defended on relatively—though only relatively—ecumenical grounds.

I. The Normative Role of Democracy

Perhaps because it is inherently vague, the concept of democracy is easy to characterize. It is that of a system of government—a set of rules under which government is selected and operates—whereby the governed people enjoy control over the governing authorities. The concept is vague because it does not, in itself, tell us what kind of control, and how much control, the people ought to have over the authorities. Also it does not tell us anything about which are the controlled authorities and who belongs to the controlling people. Different conceptions of democracy offer specifications of such indeterminacies in the abstract concept; the two-dimensional conception to be outlined here provides one example of how that may be done.

Even with the points of indeterminacy unresolved, however, most of us will agree that democracy, or at least democracy as it ought to be, is a desirable system of government. Certainly we will agree that it scores decisively over familiar alternatives such as a dictatorship, or a one-party system, or a system run by professional elites. But if we think that democracy is superior to such alternative systems, then that is presumably because we think that it serves the role of a system of government better. Whatever other virtues we may see in democracy—and I say nothing here on those virtues—we would hardly favor democracy over alternatives, if we did not think that it serves that role better than those alternatives. So what, then, is the role that a system of government ought to play? What is the role that we think democracy can play better than alternatives?

In approaching this question, we might take our start from the various themes sounded in the extensive literature on democracy: that the democratic system gives voice to the will of the people; that it protects people best from government; that it ensures a sort of equality between citizens; and so on. I prefer to approach it afresh, however, working from four presumptions about government that fit fairly well with common thought, or at least with common thought in more or less egalitarian, secular cultures. These presumptions tell us in the broadest terms what brief we should expect government to discharge and they thereby direct us to a story about the normative role of a system of government, in particular a democratic system of government; the role of the system will be precisely to ensure that government discharges that brief.

Four Presumptions about Government

The presumptions I start from are these:

1. If government is desirable from the point of view of a given population, then members of that population must have certain interests in common; in the event that there are no common interests, there will be no desirable purpose for government to serve. More on common interests in a moment.

2. In most cases, common interests will be matters that people are capable of recognizing as common interests in the course of discussion and reflection. They will represent common, recognizable interests, as we can put it, not just common interests, period.

3. Government ought to be orientated toward the satisfaction of the common, recognizable interests of the people governed. It ought to do whatever it can to advance the common good, as it used to be put.

4. Not only ought government to be orientated toward the satisfaction of people's common, recognizable interests; those are the only factors that it ought to take its ultimate guidance from. Government ought to countenance no other master.

Common Interests

We turn to the discussion of those presumptions in a moment but, on the face of it, they are hard to resist. Or at least they are hard to resist, if we assume that the notion of common interests is well defined: that is, that there really are matters that deserve to be described in such terms. What then makes something a matter of common interest? How is the concept of common interest to be specified? In asking that question, I do not presuppose that we can come to theoretical agreement on a very specific list of common interests, or even on what might be described as a specific conception of common interests; I believe, as will become clear, that such a list and such a conception is just what we should want democratic practice itself to identify. All I presuppose is that there is an abstract specification or definition or concept of common interests on which we can agree.

Here, then, is the definition or concept that I favor. A certain good will represent a common interest of a population, I say, just so far as cooperatively avowable considerations support its collective provision. What are cooperatively avowable considerations? They are considerations such that were the population holding discussions about what it ought to cooperate in collectively providing, then they could not be dismissed as irrelevant.[2] They are those considerations to which no participant in a cooperative scheme could deny relevance or weight under ordinary standards of conversational practice. They are not selfish or sectional considerations, for example, not considerations that some parties to the discussion would have to see as calls for special treatment and, in particular, as calls that they had no particular reason to heed.

This way of defining common interests is broadly contractualist in spirit; it owes much in particular to the interpretation of Rawlsian contractualism developed in the work of T. M. Scanlon and Brian Barry.[3] It rejects the idea that common interests are to be defined as those private interests that happen to be shared by everyone in a community; as Robert Goodin argues, such a least-common-denominator definition would make common interests so elusive and unstable as to be of no normative significance.[4] Without departing too far from our sense of what makes for a genuine interest, and what makes for an interest's being really common—so at least, it seems to me—the definition offers us a firmer and potentially more useful way of thinking about common interests.

The concept is built on the basis of two assumptions, neither of which is particularly troublesome. First, that there really is a distinction between cooperatively avowable and cooperatively unavowable considerations. And second, that there is a fact of the matter as to what these support. The first assumption is borne out by the relative ease with which conversational practice polices the distinction between what in a given context are relevant reasons and what irrelevant. The second may seem to run afoul of the possibility that while cooperatively avowable considerations may offer support for certain initiatives, they are liable to offer equally strong support for rival sets of initiatives: typically, sets of initiatives that would benefit different groups differently. But this possibility need not be an insurmountable problem.

The reason is that in many situations there will always be a further cooperatively avowable consideration available: viz, that everyone is worse off not agreeing at all than agreeing on one or another of the rival schemes and that some measure ought to be adopted, therefore, to break the tie. The situations where people will take this view are those situations of compromise where no one feels that his or her position is wholly undermined by the failure to get his or her preferred solution. The measure adopted for resolving a stalemate in such a situation of compromise may be to toss a coin, for example; or to go to adjudication of some kind; or of course to put the issue to a majority vote in the electorate or parliament.

On the view to be developed here, democratic practice should serve to give a detailed specification of common interests in roughly the sense just defined. Indeed such practice may be required, as in the voting case, to break what would otherwise be stalemates and so to determine, not just discover, what will count in some cases as common interests. But it may be useful if, anticipating democratic practice, I say a little on what goods are likely to constitute common interests. This will help to generate a more vivid sense of the category of things I have in mind. And it may serve to motivate the definition I prefer, so far as the things envisaged do intuitively count as common interests.

The standard view of common interests, and it is supported by the contractualist approach taken here, directs us to procedural and institutional arrangements for solving familiar game-theory predicaments.[5] The coordination predicament, where everyone prefers that all choose the same alternative—drive on the right or the left—and is otherwise indifferent between alternatives. Or the compromise predicament, where everyone prefers that all choose the same alternative—say, that all operate under certain rules of ownership and transfer—but among the different alternatives, they divide on which should be the option selected.[6] Or the assurance predicament, where everyone prefers that all choose a certain alternative but no one wants to choose it in the absence of an assurance that others are going to do so too. Or the exchange predicament, where everyone prefers that all take a certain course rather than all doing anything else but where everyone prefers not to have to take that course himself or herself; each prefers to exploit or free ride on the efforts of others.[7]

Many such predicaments may lend themselves to spontaneous resolution in the course of social evolution.[8] But where they are unresolved or not satisfactorily resolved, cooperatively avowable considerations will surely argue that collective action should be taken to provide a resolution. Thus those procedural and institutional arrangements that allow for the resolution of such predicaments are likely to count as common interests. And so of course are those substantive goods that are attained as a result of the resolution: external defense, internal harmony, and the like.

But common interests, on the definition adopted here, may also prove to require redistributive measures. Redistribution may be in the common interest because everyone wants to be protected against a certain sort of difficulty—say, medical or legal or financial—and only those currently in such difficulty benefit. Or it may be in the common interest because while everyone wants a certain sort of good—say, to be able fully to enjoy membership in his or her cultural group[9]—providing that good may require spending more resources on some persons than on others. Or it may be in the common interest because certain disadvantaged groups cannot be expected to cooperate without compensation for certain disadvantages that they suffer. The fact that a group has certain interests in common does not presuppose that members already enjoy similar economic standing or identical cultural affiliations; it is wholly consistent with economic, social, and indeed ethnic diversity.[10]

Back to the Four Presumptions

So much by way of explaining the notion of common interests. The first presumption is that if it is desirable to have a certain population governed as a single group, then members must have certain interests in common; there must be certain things whose collective provision is supported by the sorts of consideration avowable in the spirit of cooperation. It may prove, of course, that few if any goods are matters of common interest for a given population; it may be that cooperatively avowable considerations generate a lot of ties, for example, and that divisions run so deep that no side is willing to compromise. In such a case it will not be desirable for that population to be subjected to a single government, though it may well be desirable for different groups to organize themselves around territorially distinct centers of government.

The second presumption registers that people are not merely centers where interests exist and can be satisfied. For any interests they have in common, people are generally capable of recognizing and endorsing those interests, if indeed they are not already aware of them.[11] They are not merely passive bearers of common interests; they are active, discursive creatures who are in principle capable of perceiving whatever interests they have in common.

The third and fourth presumptions draw fairly uncontentious moral lessons from the twin facts that if shared government is desirable, there will be common interests on the part of the people governed, and that the people served will be generally capable in such cases of recognizing and endorsing the common interests in question.

The third presumption draws the lesson that government should be orientated toward the satisfaction of people's common, recognizable interests. It holds out the satisfaction of such interests as a natural goal for government to pursue. We assume that government is in place. And we assume that there are common, recognizable interests on the part of the population. What could be more natural, then, than to suggest that government should be orientated toward the satisfaction of such interests?

The fact that government is oriented toward the satisfaction of such interests need not mean, of course, that it takes entirely into its own hands the provision of the goods in question. It may be in some cases that the collective provision of those goods is best achieved by means of community rather than government action. And if that is so, then a government orientation toward the satisfaction of common, recognizable interests would presumably require it only to facilitate such community action, say, by protecting rights required for such action or even by providing resources that make it more effective.

The fourth presumption says that not only should a government be orientated toward the satisfaction of its people's common, recognizable interests, that is the only ultimate goal that it ought to embrace and pursue; it is the only factor that ought to be allowed to shape the formation and implementation of policy. This presumption is reasonable in light of the fact that whatever government does, it does on a coercive basis; at the least, it does it with the help of taxes levied on its people. That government should be restricted to the service of people's common, recognizable interests probably counts, indeed, as itself a matter of common, recognizable interest.

What is involved in restricting government to the service of people's common, recognizable interests? It means that government policy formation and policy implementation must be shaped only by factors such that it is in people's common interest that they play a shaping role. The forms of policy adopted or the modes of implementation favored may happen to advantage some over others. What is important, however, is that though they give advantage to some in this way, the forms and modes in question materialize under a pattern of policy making that is in the common interest of the community. Suppose that policy is made under the head of a common, recognizable interest in having basic scientific research conducted in the society. What is important in the forming and implementing of research policy is that decision making take place without regard to the sectional interests of this or that group, or the personal preferences of this or that individual; it must take place, so far as possible, on the impersonal basis of what is best for the promotion of the research required.

This fourth presumption is not excessively restrictive. While it rules out the factional state that favors special groups, for example, it does not rule out the state that advances the interests of some without any cost to the interests of others; there may be a common interest in government's exploiting opportunities for such Pareto improvements. While it rules out the paternalistic state that pays no attention to whether people endorse the interests it tries to satisfy, it allows government to generate debate on whether such and such hitherto unrecognized interests should indeed be endorsed. And while it rules out the perfectionist state that tries to advance certain causes, irrespective of the recognizable interests of its population, the fact is that many such causes are likely to connect with its people's interests in a way that can readily be made salient.

The fourth presumption is not often articulated but it comes close to the surface in the principle ascribed to Bentham by John Stuart Mill: "Everybody to count for one, nobody for more than one." The most striking effect of the presumption is to ensure that no one's interest should weigh more heavily than another's in determining what government does: no one should count for more than one. Were it the case that only common, recognizable interests had a controlling role in relation to government, after all, it would follow that government treated people as equals. Thus the presumption may be at the source of the many claims that democracy gives expression to the value of equality, awarding each voter the same political resources.[12]

The Role of a System of Government

We can summarize the upshot of our four presumptions in the thesis that government should advance all and only the common, recognizable interests of its people. And with that thesis in hand, we can return now to the question of what is the role of a system of government. What is the role such that we democrats must think that the democratic system of government—the democratic set of rules for how government should be selected and

operate—does or can play it better than alternatives like a dictatorship, a one-party regime, or a bureaucratic elitism?

The answer suggested by our presumptions is that the role of
a governmental system is to constrain government—to guide it
and to check it—so that it tracks all and only the common, recognizable interests of the governed. Those of us who are democrats will want to say, then, that a democracy—a set of rules that
puts the selection and operation of government under the ultimate control of the governed—can serve better than alternatives to constrain government in this way. We will want to make
against alternatives the sort of point that Tom Paine made about
the rule of a single prince: "It means arbitrary power in an individual person; in the exercise of which, *himself*, and not the *res-
publica*, is the object."[13]

Given this vision of the role that a democratic system of government is supposed to play, and to play better than alternatives,
the question arises as to how it can best hope to achieve this. We
have taken democracy so far to be nothing more specific than a
system of government under which those who are governed enjoy
a certain control over those who govern them. We can now ask
about what specific forms a democratic system should take if it is
to discharge this task as well as possible. We shall be concerned
with that question for the remainder of the paper.

II. The Two Dimensions That Democracy Needs

Authoring and Editing

The normative role of democracy, as characterized in the previous section, has a dual aspect. First, democracy has to orient government to all the common, recognizable interests of its people.
And, second, it has to orient it only to such common, recognizable interests; it has to neutralize the impact of other influences.
The first requires, in positive mode, that democratic institutions
make it possible to search out and authorize policies whose implementation promises to advance common, recognizable interests. The second requires, negatively, that equally democratic institutions make it possible to scrutinize the policies identified,
and the other factors that influence how policies materialize, to

try to weed out those that do not answer to common, recognizable interests.

Democratic institutions must have a positive search-and-identify dimension, then, and a negative scrutinize-and-disallow dimension. They must conform to what Daniel Dennett calls a generate-and-test heuristic.[14] The search-and-authorize dimension—the generative mechanism—will help to ensure that all policies whose implementation might advance common, recognizable interests get a hearing. And the scrutinize-and-disallow dimension—the testing mechanism—will help to ensure that only policies and modes of policy making that really answer to common, recognizable interests survive and have influence. The first dimension will guard against false negatives by allowing every possible common-interest policy into consideration. The second dimension will guard against false positives by subjecting the policies adopted and their mode of implementation to a rigorous testing and filtering procedure.

The two-dimensional structure envisaged has analogues in a variety of areas, most obviously in the area of natural evolution. Natural mutation ensures that in the course of evolution, many variant genes and organisms make their appearance. Natural selection ensures that only those that are adaptive—only those that promote the inclusive fitness of the gene—survive and spread. The two-dimensional structure required in the political case will have to operate on parallel lines. There will need to be an institutionalized means of guaranteeing a generous supply of candidates for consideration as common, recognizable interests of the sort that government ought to take into account. And there will have to be an institutionalized means of ensuring—or at least of raising the probability—that only those policies and those modes of implementing policies that do genuinely answer to common, recognizable interests survive to have influence in the corridors of power.

A second exemplar of the two-dimensional structure required in democratic institutions is provided by the way in which control is exercised over the text that appears in a newspaper or journal. The original text is actually provided by the respective authors of the pieces, be they journalists or outsiders who submit pieces for publication. But the text that finally appears is determined by the hand of the editor or editors; they select from submissions and, with any piece accepted, they require abbreviated or otherwise amended versions. The authors determine all the candidates for publication that come the way of the newspaper or journal. But only the candidates that satisfy the editors ever get to be actually published.

By analogy with this case, what democratic institutions have to do is, first, to establish an authorial dimension of control—control by ordinary people—for searching out and generating a rich supply of presumptive common-interest policies; and second, to establish an editorial dimension of control—again, control by ordinary people—for rigorously scrutinizing and eliminating those candidate policies and those modes of policy implementation that do not advance common, recognizable interests. The lesson of the two-dimensional structure is that people will have to be able to determine both the general policies that government considers and the policies and modes of policy implementation that are allowed to shape the things that government finally does.

Can we be any more specific at this abstract stage about the institutions likely to be required by these two dimensions of democratic control? I think we can. The model of author and editor gives a particularly useful basis for considering the sorts of institutions that democracy is likely to require.

The Authorial Dimension

How are the people to be authors of those candidate common interests that get to be articulated in politics? Such an authorial role has to be implemented, clearly, by electoral institutions whereby policies and policy-making agencies are thoroughly discussed and are chosen from among a range of alternatives; in particular, from among a range of alternatives that anyone in principle can help to determine. It is only by recourse to electoral means that we can hope to ensure a generous supply of candidates for consideration as matters of common, recognizable interest.

But an electoral mandate will not identify the policies adopted and implemented as expressing, beyond all possible doubt, matters of common, recognizable interest; it will not ensure a thorough scrutiny and editing of the policies that come to the surface, for elections operate on the basis of something less than unanimity and, notoriously, it is possible that an electorally backed policy will express only the common, recognizable interest of a majority or plurality of voters. And that problem apart, electoral control leaves those in government with a capacity, as they implement policy, to give influence to factors such that it is not in people's common, recognizable interest that they be effective.

This second problem is probably more serious than the first. The reason is that elections do have a mechanism for dealing with the first. In elections where parties compete with one another, the fact that a policy adopted by one party is actually inimical to the interests of some minority—if indeed it is a fact—gives rival parties a reason to draw attention to that fact and to lessen thereby the support that the offending party receives. Those parties may persuade some supporters who do not belong to the relevant majority to change their votes, they may shame majority supporters into changing their allegiance, or they may shame the party itself into changing its policy. But this mechanism is not as powerful as we might like, and of course it still leaves the second problem mentioned in play.

Even if electoral institutions offer a reliable means of producing a generous supply of candidates for matters of common interest, then—even if they reduce the risk of false negatives—still they do not incorporate a reliable means of ensuring that only matters of common, recognizable interest shape what happens in and at the hands of government. The authorial control that they would give ordinary people—and the limited editorial guarantee that they would provide—needs to be complemented by a fuller measure of editorial control.

The Editorial Dimension

How might such editorial control be implemented? The control in question cannot be exercised collectively, in the manner of electoral, authorial control; whatever problems arose in the first dimension will recur in the second. The editorial control that democracy requires—the control designed to ensure, ideally, that only matters of common, recognizable interest have an influence on government—has got to be exercised by individuals or groups at a noncollective level.

How much can we say about the mode of noncollective, editorial control that democracy might incorporate? There are three points that can be registered, it seems to me, with a reasonable degree of confidence.

First Point: the Impossibility of a Veto System

The first point to be registered is that while editorial control must operate at noncollective levels, it cannot plausibly take the form of a veto. Not an individual veto. And not the group-level veto envisaged in some past arrangements: for example, in the veto that the tribunes of the plebs could exercise in republican Rome or in the veto given to the assembly of the people in James Harrington's republican vision of *Oceana*.[15]

The reason that no such veto can work is this. Matters of common, recognizable interest can often be advanced in different ways, where one way is more costly for this group, a second more costly for that, and where the different groups therefore will prefer different approaches. It may be a matter of common, recognizable interest that the tax system should be made more efficient, that a new power station should be constructed, or that various antipollution measures should be implemented. But any way of advancing such a cause is bound to hurt some more than others. There will always be a minority who are negatively affected by any improvement in the tax system, a minority who live in the vicinity of a new, much-needed power station, and a minority who depend for their livelihood on industries hard hit by important antipollution legislation.

If people had an individual power of veto then every such initiative could easily be stymied—certainly it would become more difficult to realize—as persons each tried to push the relative costs of the initiative elsewhere. And by parity of reasoning, many an initiative of this kind could become difficult to access if different groups within the society had a power of veto; where groups were differently affected, the worst hit would be likely to block the initiative in the hope of inducing others to bear the costs. There might be a possibility of resolving stalemates by bargaining, of course, but that can be no consolation in the present context, for bargaining would scarcely serve to guard against false positives.

Second Point: The Possibility of Contestation

The second point to be registered is that short of the veto, there is still an important power of challenge that might be invested in individuals or groups. This becomes salient by analogy with the power of challenge—challenge as distinct from veto—that some real-life editors enjoy. Take the sort of journal, or even newspaper, that is run on fairly cooperative lines: say, because it is actually owned by those who write for it and work on it. With such a publication, the editors may not be given the right to veto outright any piece authored by one of the writers. But clearly they can still exercise a great deal of editorial control. Instead of vetoing a piece they do not like, they can contest its publication before a meeting of the owners or before a meeting of a board appointed by the owners. They can argue that the journal or newspaper in question has such and such standards, or such and such a role, and that the piece in question does not fit. And they can expect to succeed in this sort of challenge whenever they make what is accepted as a good case.

Short of giving individual people or groups of people a power of veto over government, it might be possible to give them a power of contestation on parallel lines to the case just envisaged. All we have to assume is that where there are electorally supported policies or modes of policy implementation that do not promise to promote common, recognizable interests, then: first, this is capable of being established in debate and argument; second, it is possible to have bodies set up—perhaps under an electorally approved arrangement—that can be relied on to give a fair hearing and discussion to the different arguments and to pass compelling judgments; third, the judgments of such bodies can be given suitable authority in relation to the decision making of government; and fourth, it can be a matter of common belief in the society that this is the case, so that minorities need not be fated to distrust the bodies.

The element in these assumptions that is likely to be challenged is the claim made in the second, and presupposed in the fourth, that it is possible for certain bodies to be impartial on matters where the population is divided. It may be said that since the bodies imagined are likely to reflect the society as a whole, there is little reason to think that they will not divide on the same lines as the electorate or the elected representatives; thus they may be expected to support whatever the electors or representatives proposed.

But this objection supposes that members of such a body are bound to make a judgment dictated by whatever interest may be thought to have influenced electors and representatives. And that is clearly not so. They will be asked to judge on the factual issue of whether the policy as identified and implemented is supported by common, recognizable interests and only by such interests. For example, they may be asked to judge on whether the change to the tax system is dictated only by the common interest in making the system more efficient, and not in part by the interest of an effective coalition in pushing the relative costs of change onto a minority. The question will be the factual one as to whether the change proposed does indeed make a good claim to be in the common interest, so that the negative effect on the minority can be regarded as just an unhappy accident.

It requires a determined cynicism—and a cynicism that is apparently not shared in democratic electorates[16]—to believe that faced with deciding such a factual issue, any body that is representative of the society as a whole will divide on the same interest-bound lines that are taken to have divided electors or representatives. But even if we are cynical, there is an important reason that such a body should prove impartial, and should be generally expected to prove impartial. This is that in a society where divisions remain relatively civil, the members of such a body will stand to win the good opinion of most of their fellows only so far as they are seen to discharge their allotted brief. We may assume, as the established tradition has it, that people care a lot about the opinion that others have of them.[17] And we may expect that it will be possible to organize relevant bodies in such a way that this desire for esteem will provide motivation enough for members to act impartially.

Third Point: Introducing Contestability

We have seen that while the editorial dimension of democratic control cannot require a veto, it may operate effectively under a regime where government decisions are always contestable. But the prospect of a contestatory regime may not be all that attractive; it may seem to hold out the specter of endless disputation and a chronic inability to get things done. The third point I want to make at this stage, however, should dissipate that specter. It is that there are ways of achieving the control that democratic contestability would give to ordinary people, short of allowing a society to get bogged down in never-ending contestations.

Consider the way in which things are likely to evolve with the editors of our imagined journal or newspaper. A regime of frequent contestation, involving regular challenges before the editorial board, would be very likely to prove both time-consuming and inefficient; many of the challenges would be of the same sort, for example, and would be routinely upheld. We can readily envisage steps being taken, then, to reduce the contestatory load. There are two steps, in particular, that spring to mind.

The first would be for the editors and editorial board to agree on the conclusiveness of certain grounds for challenge, on the need for submissions to be prepared for consideration according to certain guidelines, on the expectation that no contributor be in the pay of certain interests, and perhaps even on specific constraints that any published piece ought to meet, and to lay out these points of agreement in the form of procedures that writers can take for their guidance. The procedures might rule out the publication of any material of an offensive kind, for example; they might require that an advance outline of every submission be cleared in advance; they might stipulate that contributors should declare any personal interests in the matter on which they are writing; and the like. The promulgation of such a policy would involve the preemptive acceptance of certain contestations, in the sense that it would have the effect of removing certain submissions—or at least reducing the incidence of certain submissions—that would be contested, and successfully contested, by the editors. It would create procedural resources designed to facilitate the contestation that actually occurs.

The second step that the editors and editorial board might take in order to make a contestability regime effective would be to allow room for *ex ante* as well as *ex post* contestation. Instead of allowing only the contestation whereby the editors challenge a finished submission before the editorial board they might allow editors to have a say at an earlier stage by inviting authors to seek editorial input and advice whenever they are worried about the possibility of objection. They might introduce consultative as well as procedural resources in support of *ex post*, appellate contestation.

Not only would procedural and consultative resourcing reduce the need for appellate contestation by the editors. Such resourcing would also facilitate whatever contestation occurs at the appellate stage, for if the editors can argue that a given piece offends against clearly stated editorial procedures or that it breaches an agreement made in consultation with the authors, that will strengthen the contestatory case that they can make against it. Procedural and consultative measures should serve at once to reduce the need for, and enhance the effectiveness of, appellate contestation.

Moving back now to the political world, it should be obvious that there is room for giving people resources of contestation at three levels. It is possible to give people procedural and consultative resources as well as the appellate resources originally considered.

The consultative resources envisaged would require a recognition by those in government of the need to have input from various groups on its intended directions and initiatives, and an institutionalized means of eliciting such input and giving it a role in decision making. The procedural resources would come with the imposition of a variety of constraints on governmental decision making. As authors for our imagined publication are required to satisfy stated editorial policy, so governmental decision makers might be required to satisfy a variety of constitutional and other constraints. In particular, they might be required to satisfy constraints such that any breach of a constraint, even prior to its imposition, would have made a plausible case for contesting the offending decision or law.

Putting procedural and consultative resources in place ought to reduce the need for appellate contestation, as in the case of the publication imagined. But, as in that analogous case, it ought also to improve the effectiveness of such appellate contestation as continues to occur, for if people can argue that government is in breach of a procedural constraint or if they can show that it is going against something agreed in consultation with one or another public group, then that ought to make an appeal against a government decision or law all the more effective.

One final remark. I mentioned above that electoral institutions may serve a secondary editorial role in guarding against some false positives—I gave the example of electoral competition and challenge—as well their primary, authorial role in guarding against false negatives. I should also mention that the sorts of contestatory measures envisaged here may equally serve a secondary authorial role, as well as their primary, editorial brief. The processes of consultation, just to take one example, may obviously serve to draw attention to hitherto unperceived matters of common interest, as well as serving to test candidates already in place. For simplicity's sake, I will not comment further on the dual role of the two sorts of institutions but it should be recognized that I do simplify things when I suggest one-one linkages between electoral institutions and the authorial role and between nonelectoral institutions and the editorial function.

III. ABSTRACT REQUIREMENTS, ACTUAL INSTITUTIONS

How far do democratic institutions incorporate the two-dimensional structure that democracy ideally requires? How far do they have an authorial channel for raising the probability that all common, recognizable interests get a hearing and an editorial channel for making it likely that only such interests are influential? How far do they serve to guard against false negatives, on the one hand—that is, failures to recognize certain matters of common, recognizable interest—and false positives, on the other: failures to weed out factors other than matters of common, recognizable interest from the realm of policy making? Only if we have some sense of how actual institutions behave in this way can we gain a perspective on how they might be improved, if indeed improvement is feasible.

The Meaning of Democratic Institutions

Democratic institutions may be understood in a narrow or a broad sense. Narrowly construed, they are those institutions that are part of a system of democratic election. Broadly construed, they are all those institutions that we would expect to find in any regime worthy of being described as a democracy; they are institutions such that we would be loath to describe a country that did not have them as a democracy, or at least as a democracy in the established, Western sense of the term. These latter institutions will include democratic electoral institutions, of course, but they will also include institutions that provide for a rule of law, the independence of the courts, the impeachability of public officials, a free press, and so on. Most of us would balk at describing as democratic a country that gave no place to such measures, even if the authorities were elected in a more or less democratic way.

In asking how democratic institutions measure up to the abstract ideal of a two-dimensional democracy, I shall take these to comprise both electoral and nonelectoral institutions. I consider briefly how well democratic electoral institutions fit with our two-dimensional model, and then at some greater length how well democratic nonelectoral institutions do so.

The Role and Limitation of Electoral Institutions

The electoral procedures that we associate with real-world democracy allow for the periodic, popular election of certain authorities, at the least, the legislators. They ensure both that the periods between elections are not very long and that the elections are popular in the sense that all competent adults have electoral rights—they can stand for election and they can vote in elections—and are able to make their voting decisions without undue pressure.[18] And in most cases they leave open the possibility that the very rules under which those in government are selected, as well as the rules under which they operate, can themselves be put to the electoral test: they can be amended by the elected politicians themselves or by the people in a referendum.

Under these electoral institutions, the governed people have an important authorial role in relation to political decision making. They choose the personnel who will author the laws and decisions to be introduced by government or who, at the least, will supervise their authorship by bureaucratic officials. In this way they are the indirect authors of whatever policies those personnel put forward in office.

That the people are the indirect, electoral authors of such policies suggests in itself that the policies endorsed will generally be worth considering as candidates for matters of recognizable interest. It would certainly be surprising if none of the policies collectively authored by the people had a connection with common interests. But in any case democratic electoral institutions are designed in other respects to reinforce this effect and to make popular elections a plausible means of generating a rich supply of candidates for matters of common interest.

The reason, roughly, is this. Those who stand for political office will have an incentive to enhance their chances of election and reelection by promoting any cause that can attract general support. And any cause that answers to a common, recognizable interest will attract general support. Thus those who stand may be expected to be on the lookout for matters of common, recognizable interest that they can espouse. Most presumptively common-interest policies will be shared by all parties, of course, and will not surface much in electoral discussion. But the parties will have a keen interest in identifying any novel matters of common interest that can give them an electoral advantage over their competitors. And so there should be relatively little danger of politicians and people failing to detect various matters of common, recognizable interest. False negatives should not be a major problem.

These comments are, of necessity, rather brief and under argued. The point is not to provide a detailed defense of democratic electoral institutions, as we know them. Rather, it is to show that under such institutions people are enabled, however imperfectly, to play the first, authoring role required by the two-dimensional ideal of democracy.

But if democracy encompassed nothing more than electoral institutions, then however well it did in generating a rich supply of candidates for matters of common interest—for avoiding false negatives—it would be ill equipped to guarantee the avoidance of false positives. It might seem to guard against the adoption of policies for the furtherance of goods that do not answer in any way to the interests of the people or that do not answer to recognizable interests. But it would offer relatively inadequate protection against the adoption of policies that represent majority interests alone. And it would do little or nothing to guard against the influence of hostile factors in the specification and implementation of policy.

It takes only a majority, or even a plurality, of votes to be elected. And so there is a permanent possibility that this or that minority—stable or issue-based—will be overlooked in the electoral process. Electoral competition, as already noted, may be held to diminish this problem, as parties seek to criticize one another's policies. But this competitive factor is scarcely a substantive protection, particularly with the policies that the major parties share—these will constitute the bulk of their policies—and that do not come up for discussion at the time of elections.

Apart from this majoritarian worry, the second and more important problem, as we have already stressed, is that the people are only the indirect authors of the policies that are put up as candidates for matters of common interest. This means electoral control still allows governmental policy making to be influenced by factors such that it is not in the common, recognizable interest of people that they have an influence. Policies are specified in detail and implemented by the successful party or parties in government and, ultimately, by the public service that those in government try to oversee. Thus it is possible that in the specification and implementation of common-interest policies, for example, those in government will not be guided just by common interests. The implementation of policies may be designed to serve a particular electoral, bureaucratic, or just personal advantage. And policies that appear to represent common interests in the indeterminate rhetoric of an election may materialize in the fine print of legislation and regulation as policies that serve only the ends of this or that special-interest lobby.

This latter development is particularly possible, of course, if the elected government is in the debt of such a lobby for its support in the course of the electoral campaign or indeed for its support over the term of government. The organization or association in question may be able to damage the government through adverse media publicity, for example, or through taking actions—say, closing down operations in electorally sensitive locations—that reflect badly on government.

Nonelectoral Institutions

The nonelectoral institutions associated with democracy can be represented as attempts to respond to this problem, putting in place measures designed to increase protection against false positives and to try to ensure that only the common interests of the people dictate what government does, both in policy formation and in policy implementation. We saw in the previous section that measures for guarding against false positives—measures for giving people noncollective, editorial control of government—amount to contestatory resources, and that they come in three broadly different categories: procedural, consultative, and appellate. Without stretching things unduly, we can see many of the nonelectoral institutions that are associated with democracy as providing contestatory resources in these categories. Of course, the institutions in question can often be seen in other guises too, but it will be useful for our purposes to present them as devices for testing policy formation and implementation, and so for giving people control on the editorial as well as the authorial front.

Procedural Resources

The procedural resources that democracies typically institute, to go to the first category, come in two broad kinds. On the one hand, there are procedural constraints on the content of government decisions, in particular laws. And on the other, there are procedural constraints on the process whereby decisions and laws get to be authorized.

The most important content-related constraint is embodied in the principle of limited government, as we might call it. This principle is not often spelled out in the documents of those regimes that we would be happy to describe as democratic, but it is almost always built clearly into the practice. It says, roughly, that there is a limit to the range of matters on which government

can rule. The strictest version is incorporated in the harm principle put forward in John Stuart Mill's essay "On Liberty," according to this, government is warranted in interfering in the lives of
individuals only to prevent them from harming others.[19] Less
strict versions, all of them vague in the detail of what they require, prescribe that government ought to be restricted to dealing with issues that are, broadly, in the public domain and ought
to respect the privacy of individuals.

But the principle of limited government, however understood,
does not exhaust the content-related constraints that most
democracies impose on those in power. Almost all democracies
recognize, formally or otherwise, that no laws should be passed,
no decisions taken, that offend against any of a variety of individual and group expectations. Those expectations may be encoded
in a bill of rights or implied in a founding constitution. But
equally they may just be registered informally as matters of convention such that a parliament that tried to remove them could
expect widespread resistance. Thus they may be matters of common law, so long tested and tried that no parliament would con-
template setting them aside.[20] Or they may be matters subject to
"ordini" as distinct from "leggi," in the language of Machiavelli;[21]
matters of custom or "ethos" as distinct from law or "nomos" in
the even older, equally influential language of Polybius.[22]

There are different versions of the protected expectations in
different cultures, but they are most familiar to us in Western
countries in the guise of the basic liberties and rights. For example, freedom of expression and association and movement; the
right to dispose as one wishes—more or less—of those things that
one owns under local property rules; and the right to a fair trial
in the case of criminal impeachment. We would be loath to describe as a democracy any system that denied these sorts of claims
to individual members.

So much for procedural constraints of a content-related kind
that democracies generally impose on government. Other procedural constraints restrict the process rather than the content of
governmental decision making. I have a number of familiar restrictions in mind, nothing very esoteric, and I list them here
without detailed commentary.

1. Rule of law. The law-based decisions of government have got to be general and apply to everyone, including the legislators themselves; they must be promulgated and made known in advance to those to whom they apply; they should be intelligible, consistent, and not subject to constant change; and so on.[23]

2. Separation of powers. The legislative, executive, and judicial functions should be sufficiently separate to guarantee at least two things: the independence, in most of their operations, of the courts; and the requirement that those in executive government have to get parliamentary approval—the approval of legislators—for the main initiatives they undertake.[24]

3. Deliberative democracy. The decisions of those in government should always be backed by reasons, whether the decisions be judicial, executive, or legislative in character; and the validity and relevance of the reasons offered ought to be subject to parliamentary—and, inevitably, community—debate.[25]

4. Bicameral approval. There ought to be two houses of parliament, distinct in the basis on which they are elected or in the mode of election to them; and the approval of each ought to be required in the course of most legislation, so that the different mix of interests represented by the two houses has each got to be satisfied.

5. Depoliticized decision making. Subject to the possibility of review in extreme cases, certain decisions are best left by elected governments to bodies and officers who are appointed on a statutory basis for a set period of time. These are decisions in which elected politicians are likely to have self-seeking interests, inimical to the public interest; they are best put at arm's length on the grounds that no one should be judge in his or her own case: *nemo judex in sua causa*. Examples recognized in many jurisdictions include decisions on public prosecution; decisions on redrawing electoral boundaries; decisions on interest rates; and even decisions on certain planning issues.

6. Independent accountability. There should be provision for the auditing of government accounts by an independent authority, with the reports of that authority available for debate in parliament and community.

7. Freedom of information. Subject to a time embargo in certain sensitive areas, there ought to be provision for members of the public, including the press, to access documentary information on the data and arguments that carry weight in decisions by public bodies.[26]

Without going into detail, it should be obvious that the procedural constraints just reviewed, whether content-related or process-related, are well understood as providing ordinary people with preemptive resources of contestation against government decisions. To the extent that government decisions are required to satisfy these constraints, they are less likely to reflect matters that are not truly of common interest. False positives should be a somewhat lesser problem than they might otherwise have been. So at any rate I assume.

Consultative Resources

Consultative opportunities have long been available, at least as a matter of formal right, in matters where government requires parliamentary support. Parliament can be petitioned by members of the public to act on a certain matter. Individual parliamentary representatives can be accessed by their constituents or by this or that lobby group. And parliamentary inquiries and committees can often be accessed in a more formal, often public manner. But much government is now conducted, whether we like it or not, in domains where parliamentary control is not available or parliamentary scrutiny is almost certain to be ineffective. Thus the traditional avenues of public access provide ordinary people with only very limited consultative resources.

The reason that government escapes effective parliamentary control and scrutiny is that, on pain of infeasibility, administrative decisions in contemporary democracies cannot all be implemented by means of regular legislation. They have to be taken under delegated or subordinate legislation that gets very little parliamentary scrutiny. Or they have to be left to the discretion of the relevant agency or officer.

But most contemporary democracies have developed some means whereby the public, on an individual, organizational, or associational basis, are enabled to have an input into such legislatively underexamined decision making; and these measures are often applied to decision making more generally. Thus we find that provision is made, sometimes under a statutory, legislated requirement, for the establishment of advisory, community-based bodies that administrative agencies have to consult; for the setting up of public hearings and inquiries relevant to this or that proposed venture of government; for the publication of proposals—say, in "green" or "white" papers—and the eliciting of responses from members of the public; and for the conduct of focus-group research or research of a related kind into public opinion on issues where the government intends to take action.

These initiatives, together with the traditional modes of access to parliament, represent consultative resources that are of the first importance from the point of view of preventing government from succumbing to false positives. They give concrete form to the old injunction *audi alteram partem*[27]—hear the other side—and they offer at least some prospect that government will be dissuaded from taking action in cases where the line proposed does not answer to common, recognizable interests; in particular, where it promises to treat a minority in a deleterious way.

Of course, as already noted, many government decisions, even decisions that are prompted by common, recognizable interests, will be relatively more damaging for one group than for others, and that group may be expected to protest at the consultative stage. But if its voice has been fully heard—and that may be tested in later appeals—then members of that group may feel some greater confidence that though they suffer more than others, that is just bad luck and not a result of their being treated as less than equals. They can agree that it is in the common, recognizable interest of members of the community that a power station of a certain sort be constructed, for example, and they may come to see that, though they are hurt by the decision, the best place to locate the power station is indeed in their own neighborhood.[28]

Appellate Resources

In any regime that we would be happy to describe as a democracy, it goes without saying that citizens must be able to challenge officers of government in the courts on matters of private law, as it goes without saying that officers of government may be charged with offenses against the criminal law. Like ordinary citizens, government officials and bodies are capable in proper democracies of being sued for torts, breaches of contract, breaches of trust, and the like.

But democracies go much further than this in allowing ordinary citizens to challenge those in government. They allow citizens to appeal to parliament for an inquiry into the doings of government, whether the inquiry takes the form of a parliamentary question or a full-scale investigation by a parliamentary committee. That is implicit in arrangements already described. And, over and above that, they provide citizens with a capacity to challenge a government initiative on three more or less distinct counts: for its legality under public law; for its substantive merit; and for its general propriety.[29]

To challenge government action for its legality under public law is to apply for the judicial review of the action in question.[30] The challenge may be brought under the head of a written constitution or international covenant, or on grounds that the action offended against natural justice, was not within the authority of the agent, was in some other way unreasonable, and so on. The remedy that the courts can offer in the case of a successful challenge is to quash the relevant decision of government, to order the government to perform appropriately, or to prohibit it from continuing on its current path.

The courts, in particular the high court or supreme court, are the forums in which people can challenge the government on grounds of legality. But in most democratic jurisdictions bodies of a different kind—they are often described as tribunals—provide people with the opportunity to challenge government on a different count, to do with the substantive merits of decisions taken rather than their strict legality. These tribunals are often specialized, with one tribunal dealing with land use, another with education, another with immigration, and so on. They are associated with the rise of administrative law over the past fifty years and they differ from the courts in being able to substitute their own decisions for the decisions of government that are under challenge.

Not only may people in most democracies contest government initiatives for their legality and their merit, they may also bring challenges of "maladministration"—charges of neglect, inattention, delay, arbitrariness, and so on—of a kind that the courts and the tribunals won't always be able to hear. These are brought before those complaints officers, some specialized, some not, who are generally described as "ombudsmen." Ombudsman figures are able to investigate a complaint and publish a report and, while they do not have a power to enforce a remedy, they are often effective in securing compensation, and even a change of practice on the part of government agents.

These avenues of challenge represent, from our point of view, potentially important resources of contestation. They may not all work well; indeed, it may even be that some work for ill—say, the institution of judicial review—in being overcautious and overcensorious of electoral and parliamentary choice.[31] But they do represent a an attempt to guard people against false positives, that is, to guard against those in government forming or implementing policies in a way that is not responsive just to the common, recognizable interests of their citizens. They are designed, however imperfectly, to protect people from the danger of government officials and bodies behaving in a corrupt or factional manner.

IV. Democratic Reform

At this point my essay would ideally provide a list of reforms that ought to be made in the institutions of democracy. But that is infeasible both for a shallow and a deep reason. The shallow reason is that it would take me too far afield. The deep reason is that institutional reform requires an input not just from the theoretical analysis of ideals and models but also from empirical investigation into how various ideals and models work in different situations.

Still, short of providing a manifesto for democratic reform, our discussion does provide a useful perspective on issues of reform. It furnishes us with a picture of the role that democracy ought to play: that of empowering the common, recognizable interests of ordinary people, and nothing else besides. And it gives us a view of the rationale of existing democratic institutions, electoral and nonelectoral. They can be seen as serving to guard, however imperfectly, against two dangers: on the one hand, false negatives—the failure in certain cases to recognize genuine matters of common, recognizable interest—and on the other, false positives—the empowerment of factors other than common, recognizable interests in the realm of policy making.

With this perspective in place, it should be possible to conduct a proper review of the way democratic institutions work, looking at respects in which they are capable of being improved. It may be useful to illustrate the critical power of the perspective by considering six prima facie implications for some reforms.[32] These are just prima facie, because the case for or against a given reform must always depend on empirical considerations that we do not have time here to rehearse. They do not include more or less obviously needed reforms, such as restrictions on the campaign finances of political parties. They are all of them at least mildly controversial and that, indeed, is one reason for choosing them.

The first three reforms canvassed bear on electoral institutions; the second three on nonelectoral.

1. No citizen-initiated referenda. The CIR is often hailed as a way of truly putting power in the hands of the people; it enables citizens, on getting enough signatures, to trigger a referendum. But from our point of view, the CIR has some obvious disadvantages. It facilitates voting on the basis of majority goals, passions, or ideals in a way that may allow of little or no contestation by minority groups; it invites the influence of moneyed interest groups that can spend lavishly in support of their favored line; it makes inconsistent public decisions possible, since the voting collectivity cannot be subjected to a discipline of intertemporal consistency; and it makes possible decisions that do not take account of empirical feasibility—that aim at the first-best and achieve only the third-best—since participants in a large-scale election are often expressive rather than pragmatic in the way they vote: they might well vote for banning brothels, for example, heedless of the consequences of driving prostitution underground.[33]

2. Compulsory voting. Once it is accepted that the point of elections, at least in good part, is to generate policies that are candidates for being matters of common interest, it becomes obvious that if any section of the population is systematically excluded, then this point is less likely to be achieved. It will not matter that the exclusion is voluntary, as when a significant section of the people do not bother to turn out at elections, or even to register; that would make the exclusion tolerable only for those who think that the important thing is that people have equal political resources or opportunities. And so the line taken here would argue in favor of compulsory registration and compulsory attendance at the voting booth. Only such a measure would guarantee that politicians will put forward policies and personnel designed to appeal to all sections of the community, not just to those who are more likely to vote under a voluntary system.

3. Mixing electoral systems. If we adopt the perspective appearing here, then we need not worry about which voting system best serves to give voice to the people; we may even think that that is a silly, pseudometaphysical question. But what we must readily acknowledge is that if the electoral system works in part with one voting system, in part with another—say, if a majoritarian system applies for the lower house, a more proportional system for the upper[34]—then that is all to the good. It means, on the face of it, that there is less chance that false positives, or the proponents of false positives, will be given electoral support. Whatever policies are endorsed, or personnel elected, they will have to prevail under different ways of reflecting the preferences of the people.

4. Depoliticizing more decision-making areas. There are some decisions currently in the hands of elected politicians that would be better put at arm's length, as decisions on matters like interest rates and electoral districting have been put at arm's length in many jurisdictions; otherwise they will be taken under pressures that do not answer to people's common, recognizable interests. Take decisions on sentencing levels for various criminal offenses. Any lowering of those levels, however beneficial overall—however well it serves people's common, accessible interests—will lead sooner or later to a heinous offense, as when someone commits a crime, for example, under new parole arrangements. Any

such offense will become a matter of media attention, public out-
rage, and a call on government to do something in response. And
it will then be next to impossible for politicians not to respond by
calling for a return to more severe, perhaps counterproductive,
sentencing rules.[35] In a case like this, the cause of empowering
only people's common interests, in particular their interest in
crime reduction, may require that the day-to-day decision making
be handed over to a body that is staffed by professionals and representatives of the community—subject to ultimate parliamentary control—and that makes its judgments away from the the-
ater of politics.

5. Deliberative consultation. Consultation with communities
often occurs on the basis of an invitation to those concerned to
present their problems to government. But this skews consultation toward those who are immediately and distinctively enough
affected—often negatively affected—to want to come forward.
That in turn means that the opinions presented may not be representative; that government may feel free to treat those opinions
seriously or not, depending on its independent wishes; and that
those who are consulted by government are led to be cynical
about consultation, they may be cynical about their power or
their lack of power, depending on the case in question. The remedy would seem to be the introduction of something like the deliberative poll—or, more modestly, the citizens' jury[36]—in which
a random sample of the population are selected, brought together to discuss and be informed about different views on some
set of issues, and then polled for final judgments.[37] This promises
to give a picture of the predominant view—it is hoped that because of the discussion, not a sectarian view—that people in the
community would form after due consideration.

6. Empowering community movements. At the consultative or
appellate stage, it is very difficult for an individual to garner the
information or marshal the expertise required to make a significant input. Indeed, the exercise may be jeopardized by free-rider
effects, as the individual despairs of the prospect of having any
personal impact on what happens. In this situation, the main
hope of securing democratic ends—in particular, the main hope
of ensuring that governmental policy formation and policy implementation are scrutinized for false positives—lies with the ex-

istence and activity of nongovernmental organizations: for example, an environment movement, a women's movement, a consumer movement, and so on. That being so, a democratic system ought to make provision for such movements to be able, depending on membership and the like, to claim public resourcing and to have standing in consultative and appellate forums.

I hope that these examples will show that even if the two-dimensional image of democracy is grounded in some common presumptions about how government should operate, and even if it is already reflected in the electoral and nonelectoral institutions of those countries we tend to see as democracies, still it has interesting implications for how democratic institutions should be reconceived and refashioned. Born in the old, the two-dimensional image can still give us a good way of thinking about the new.

V. The Emerging Conception of Democracy

Not only does the two-dimensional conception of democracy make sense of why we associate certain institutions, electoral and nonelectoral, with democracy. And not only does it provide a critical perspective for assessing the performance of those institutions and for exploring reforms, it also has some distinctive features that are independently worth remarking.

The first is that the democratic ideal hailed in this paper—the ideal of government's tracking all and only the common interests of the people—is not a pure procedural ideal and not a perfect procedural ideal but, rather, an imperfect procedural one.[38] If we want to give two people an equal chance of getting a cake, then a pure procedure designed to secure that result would be to toss a fair coin; there is no criterion of their having an equal chance of getting the cake that is independent of such a procedure. If we want them to divide the cake equally—given the assumption that they are each interested only in getting as much as possible for themselves—a perfect procedure for securing that result would be to impose the "I cut, you choose" rule; there is an independent criterion of their each getting a half of the cake—we could weigh their pieces—but, idealizing somewhat, the "I cut, you choose" procedure is perfectly designed to achieve that result. By contrast with such foolproof procedures for securing certain results, an imperfect procedure would differ from the pure one in supposing that we have a procedurally independent criterion or conception of the result to be achieved. And it would differ from the perfect one in failing to provide a guarantee of that result's being achieved: following it would at best increase the probability of obtaining the result. The example that Rawls gives of such a procedure is the criminal trial procedure for determining guilt.

The fact that common interests are defined independently of democratic institutions, electoral or contestatory, means that democratic procedure is not a pure procedure in relation to the goal of advancing all and only the common interests of the populace. And the fact that we can envisage democratic procedure's failing to advance that goal—the fact that we can always imagine invoking common interests to criticize what happens under such procedure—means that it is not a perfect procedure in relation to the goal. This, it seems to me, is all to the good. It means that we can never be silenced in criticism of democratic process—we can never be told that, by definition, whatever democratically happens is for the democratic best—and that, as citizens, we can continue to try to affect that process. Yet it does not point us toward any better way of determining what will advance all and only the common interests of ordinary people. Even if democratic procedure is an imperfect heuristic for identifying that target, it is manifestly the best procedure around. As we mentioned, indeed, it may even be an essential part of determining certain detailed matters of common interest, as when majority voting is used in situations of compromise to break what would otherwise be universally damaging stalemates.

The second point bears on the nature of this process. As envisaged here, it does not promise to deliver the common-interest ideal in the mechanical way that market process is held to deliver the ideal of competitive pricing. Market process is mechanical in the sense that those who are led by market pressures to price their goods at the competitive level may have no conception of what it is they are being led to do. Democratic process, as envisaged here, is not mechanical in that sense. Consider those who participate in the attempt to identify common-interest policies, or in the attempt to scrutinize candidate policies or modes of policy implementation, for how far they really are in the common interest. The picture developed here presents them as mostly involved, quite consciously, in seeking out matters of common interest. The process is dialogical or hermeneutic rather than mechanical.

The remaining observation that is worth making about the emerging conception is that it enables us to identify certain common modes of thinking as fallacious. A first fallacy it identifies is that of associating democracy exclusively with the rule of the collective people: the rule of the people en masse; in a word, people power. If the role of democracy is to empower all and only the common, recognizable interests of people, then a very bad way of pursuing that role will be to give over control of government to anything like unconstrained, majority rule. Polybius distinguished between "democratia" and "ochlocratia"[39]—other ancient writers used the terms differently—and it is not fanciful to associate "democratia" in his usage with the rule of the people operating under constitutional procedures and "ochlocratia" with the rule of the people when majority feeling or opinion can automatically prevail, in the way that it does in a mob. Those thinkers who associate democracy exclusively with the rule of the collective people—certainly those who associate it with people power—might be said to mistake it for what can properly be described in English, according to the OED, as ochlocracy.

A second fallacy identified under the perspective that emerges here consists in associating democracy with active control, whether by the collective people or by any other body. Someone controls a result actively just in case he or she exercises choice in determining that the result comes about; someone controls a result passively just in case things are arranged—whether or not at his or her own devising—so that it will conform to how he or she prefers that it be: the preferences, if not the choices, are privileged.[40] From the point of view emerging here, it would be a mistake to think that democracy exists only so far as ordinary people actively control things, for in order to empower all and only the common, recognizable interests of people—particularly, in order to empower only those interests—we will have to have recourse to procedural, consultative, and appellate measures that serve to give ordinary people passive rather than active control of what happens. If the measures work effectively, then they ensure not that ordinary people dictate what policies will be selected and applied but that the policies selected and applied will conform to people's common, recognizable interests.

It might be worth quoting, in this connection, the medieval adage to which many trace the core idea of democracy, even though it was an idea that took a long time to have democratic effects. *Quod omnes tangit ab omnibus tractari et approbari debet.* What touches all ought to be considered and approved by all. This does not say that what touches all ought to be decided by all, only that what touches all ought to elicit the considered approval of all.[41] And that is to say that what touches all ought to be controlled by all in the passive mode of control, not necessarily in the active.

A third and final fallacy that the emerging perspective leads us to identify is that of thinking that democracy lives only in the oxygen of public debate and participation. The forums in which policy formation and implementation are effectively tested for false positives are not exclusively chambers of public debate in which the people or their representatives are sovereign. They include also the more or less professionalized forums in which consultations are offered and negotiated, and appeals of various kinds heard and judged. The fact that these spaces are not governed by public will, and often not opened to the public gaze, does not mean that they are hostile to democracy. On the contrary, they may be absolutely essential to the achievement of democratic aims: in particular, to ensuring that only matters of common, recognizable interest tend to prevail in government.

Democracy is not inherently a collective matter, then; it is not inherently a matter of active control; and it is not inherently the sort of system that confines decision making to sites that are available to public scrutiny and influence. Democracy does not mean the reign of the collective, active will of the public or its representatives. It is a system, rather, in which things are organized so that while the people collectively have enough electoral power to guard against false negatives, the people noncollectively enjoy enough contestatory power to guard against false positives.[42]

NOTES

1. Philip Pettit, *Republicanism: A Theory of Freedom and Government* (Oxford: Oxford University Press, 1997), and "Republican Liberty, Contestatory Democracy," in Casiano Hacker-Cordon and Ian Shapiro, eds., *Democracy's Value* (Cambridge: Cambridge University Press, 1999). See also Ian Shapiro, "Three Ways to be a Democrat," *Political Theory* 22 (1994): 124–25, and "Elements of Democratic Justice," *Political Theory* 24 (1996): 579–619.

2. See too Jon Elster, "The Market and the Forum: Three Varieties of Political Theory," in J. Elster and A. Hillard, eds., *Foundations of Social Choice Theory* (Cambridge: Cambridge University Press, 1986), and Jürgen Habermas, *A Theory of Communicative Action*, vols. 1 and 2 (Cambridge: Polity Press, 1984, 1989).

3. John Rawls, *A Theory of Justice* (Oxford: Oxford University Press, 1971); T. M. Scanlon, "Contractualism and Utilitarianism," in A. Sen and B. Williams, eds., *Utilitarianism and Beyond* (Cambridge: Cambridge University Press, 1982); Brian Barry, *Justice as Impartiality* (Oxford: Oxford University Press, 1995); T. M. Scanlon, *What We Owe to Each Other* (Cambridge: Harvard University Press, 1998).

4. Robert E. Goodin, "Institutionalizing the Public Interest: The Defense of Deadlock and Beyond," *American Political Science Review* 90 (1996): 331–43. For background on the idea of common interest, see Brian Barry, *Political Argument* (London: Routledge, 1965).

5. Russell Hardin, *Collective Action* (Baltimore: Johns Hopkins University Press, 1982).

6. Richard Bellamy, *Liberalism and Pluralism: Towards a Politics of Compromise* (London: Routledge, 1999), and Peter Vanderschraaf, "The Informal Game Theory in Hume's Account of Convention," *Economics and Philosophy* 14 (1998): 215–47.

7. Philip Pettit, "Free Riding and Foul Dealing," *Journal of Philosophy* 83 (1986): 361–79.

8. Brian Skyrms, *Evolution of the Social Contract* (Cambridge: Cambridge University Press, 1996).

9. Will Kymlicka, *Multicultural Citizenship* (Oxford: Oxford University Press, 1995).

10. See Philip Pettit, "Minority Claims under Two Conceptions of Democracy," in D. Ivison, P. Patton, and W. Sanders, eds., *Political Theory and the Rights of Indigenous Peoples* (Cambridge: Cambridge University Press, forthcoming). Imagine a society where all are agreed on certain substantive moral or religious tenets, and where cooperatively avowable considerations would seem to support the collective reinforcement of

certain customs, including customs that do badly by some of the parties to the cooperation, say, women, or those in a certain caste. Are these to be regarded as common interests? Yes, I would say, so far as the tenets in question retain a hold on everyone. But of course the cooperatively avowable considerations that support the collective reinforcement of the customs are not robustly considerations of this kind; they will cease to be cooperatively avowable as soon as a single individual departs from the tenets in question. This being so, it is natural to think that among the common interests of a population, there is an important distinction between those that are robust common interests and those that are only fragile common interests. I make nothing further of the distinction in this essay, though it will clearly be of relevance in other debates.

11. Cass Sunstein, "Democracy and Shifting Preferences," in David Copp, Jean Hampton, and John E. Roemer, eds., *The Idea of Democracy* (Cambridge: Cambridge University Press, 1993), 196–230; John Ferejohn, "Must Preferences Be Respected in a Democracy?" in David Copp, Jean Hampton, and John R. Roemer, eds., *The Idea of Democracy* (Cambridge: Cambridge University Press, 1993), 231–41.

12. Ross Harrison, *Democracy* (London: Routledge, 1993), chapter 1; Thomas Christiano, *The Rule of the Many: Fundamental Issues in Democratic Theory* (Boulder: Westview Press, 1996), chap. 2.

13. Tom Paine, *Political Writings* (Cambridge: Cambridge University Press, 1989), 168.

14. Daniel Dennett, *Kinds of Minds: Towards an Understanding of Consciousness* (London: Weidenfel and Nicolson, 1996).

15. James Harrington, *The Commonwealth of Oceana and A System of Politics*, ed. J. G. A. Pocock (Cambridge: Cambridge University Press, 1992).

16. Tom R. Tyler, R. J. Boeckmann, H. J. Smith, and Y. Y. Huo, *Social Justice in a Diverse Society* (Boulder: Westview Press, 1997), 83.

17. Arthur O. Lovejoy, *Reflections on Human Nature* (Baltimore: Johns Hopkins Press, 1961); Philip Pettit, "*Virtus Normativa*: A Rational Choice Perspective," *Ethics* 100 (1990): 725–55; Geoffrey Brennan and Philip Pettit, "Hands Invisible and Intangible," *Synthese* 94 (1993): 191–225; Richard H. McAdams, "The Origin, Development and Regulation of Norms," *Michigan Law Review* 96:2 (1997): 338–433.

18. Adam Przeworksi, "A Minimalist Conception of Democracy: A Defense," in Casiano Hacker-Cordon and Ian Shapiro, eds., *Rethinking Democracy* (Cambridge: Cambridge University Press, forthcoming).

19. John Stuart Mill, *On Liberty*, ed. E. Rapaport (Indianapolis: Hackett, 1978); Joel Feinberg, *Harm to Others* (Oxford: Oxford University Press, 1986), 1.

20. A. V. Dicey, *An Introduction to the Law of the Constitution*, 10th ed., ed. E. C. S. Wade (London: Macmillan, 1960), 198–201.

21. Machiavelli, *The Complete Work and Others* (Durham: Duke University Press, 1965), 241.

22. Polybius, *The Histories* (Cambridge: Harvard University Press, 1954), bk. 6, 47.

23. L. L. Fuller, *The Morality of Law* (New Haven: Yale University Press, 1971); C. L. Ten, "Constitutionalism and the Rule of Law," in R. E. Goodin and P. Pettit, eds., *A Companion to Contemporary Political Philosophy* (Cambridge, Mass.: Blackwell, 1993).

24. William B. Gwyn, *The Meaning of the Separation of Powers* (The Hague: Nijhoff, 1965); M. J. C. Vile, *Constitutionalism and the Separation of Powers* (Oxford: Oxford University Press, 1967).

25. Joshua Cohen, "Deliberation and Democratic Legitimacy," in A. Hamlin and P. Pettit, eds., *The Good Polity* (New York: Blackwell, 1989), 17–34; Cass R. Sunstein, *The Partial Constitution* (Cambridge: Harvard University Press, 1993); Amy Gutmann and Dennis Thompson, *Democracy and Disagreement* (Cambridge: Harvard University Press, 1996).

26. Bernard Manin, *The Principles of Representative Government* (Cambridge: Cambridge University Press, 1997), 167–68.

27. Peter Cane, *An Introduction to Administrative Law*, 3d ed. (Oxford: Oxford University Press, 1996), 160; Quentin Skinner, *Reason and Rhetoric in the Philosophy of Hobbes* (Cambridge: Cambridge University Press, 1996), 15–16.

28. Philip Pettit, *Republicanism: A Theory of Freedom and Government* (Oxford: Oxford University Press, 1997), 198–200.

29. See for an overview, Cane, *An Introduction to Administrative Law*.

30. Ibid., 8.

31. Jeremy Waldron, *Law and Disagreement* (Oxford: Oxford University Press, 1999); and T. D. Campbell, *The Legal Theory of Ethical Positivism* (Brookfield, Vt.: Dartmouth, 1996).

32. John Uhr, *Deliberative Democracy in Australia: The Changing Place of Parliament* (Cambridge: Cambridge University Press, 1998), chap. 9.

33. Geoffrey Brennan and Loren Lomasky, *Democracy and Decision: The Pure Theory of Electoral Preference* (Oxford: Oxford University Press, 1993).

34. Samuel Issacharoff, P. S. Karlan, and R. H. Pildes, *The Law of Democracy: Legal Structure of the Political Process* (Westbury, N.Y.: Foundation Press, 1998), chap. 11.

35. Philip Pettit, "Republican Theory and Criminal Punishment," *Utilitas* 9 (1997): 59–79.

36. J. E. Kendall Stewart and A. Coote, *Citizens' Juries* (London: Institute of Public Policy Research, 1994).

37. James S. Fishkin, *The Voice of the People: Public Opinion and Democracy* (New Haven: Yale University Press, 1997).

38. My thanks to Thomas Pogge for raising this issue with me. See Brian Barry, *Political Argument* (London: Routledge, 1965), chap. 6; and Rawls, *A Theory of Justice*, 85–88.

39. Polybius, *The Histories*, bk. 6, 57.

40. Amartya Sen, "Liberty and Social Choice," *Journal of Philosophy* 80 (1983): 18–20; see also Harrison, *Democracy*, 4–5.

41. Manin, *The Principles of Representative Government*, 87–88.

42. I received useful comments when the paper was presented at a seminar in the Research School of Social Sciences, Australian National University, and I was also helped by some separate comments from Geoffrey Brennan and Bob Goodin. I benefited further from a very searching but constructive discussion of the paper at the Center for Human Values in Princeton, and I owe substantive debts to the formal commentator, Connie Rosati, and to the many who offered comments during the session and afterwards; I hope they will see their influence. Finally, I am grateful for comments received when the paper was presented to the Department of Government at Harvard. The paper was finalized in the course of a semester as Visiting Professor in Philosophy at Columbia University, and I gladly express thanks for the home away from home that Columbia provides me as a regular visiting professor.

PART II

DEMOCRACY BEYOND THE NATION-STATE

5

SELF-DETERMINATION
AND GLOBAL DEMOCRACY:
A CRITIQUE OF LIBERAL
NATIONALISM

IRIS MARION YOUNG

Like most eras, ours contains apparently opposing tendencies. On the one hand, processes of globalization challenge the ability of the nation-state to govern the affairs that most affect its citizens. On the other hand, nationalist ideas and movements have lately received renewed popular support.

Recent political theory has responded to and reflected on each of these apparently opposing sociohistorical trends. Some theorists construct moral criticisms of assumptions of state sovereignty and nationalist commitment, and argue for a more cosmopolitan conception of political community. Others argue for the moral value and legitimacy of nationalism in a form compatible with liberal democratic principles and institutions.

"Nationalism and cosmopolitanism have always gotten along well together, as paradoxical as this may seem." So says Jacques Derrida, in *The Other Heading*, his meditation on European identity and responsibility in an imploding world.[1] Derrida himself suggests one interpretation of this enigmatic sentence. European nationalisms have the peculiar form of justifying themselves as cosmopolitan. "Our Frenchness consists in that we gave to the world The Rights of Man."[2] Another interpretation he does not suggest but which is consistent with the spirit of his remark is that the logic of both nationalism and cosmopolitanism gives primacy to sameness over difference. Cosmopolitanism often expresses an abstract individualism that doubts that cultural difference does or should matter politically. Nationalism is sometimes an understandable reaction to a cosmopolitan assertion that we are all simply human, with the same basic human rights and needs. Nationalism, however, even in the liberal versions I will analyze in this essay, asserts the unity of a people over a territory in ways that often suppress differences within and wrongfully exclude and oppose differences without.

In this essay I aim to sort out some of what is right and wrong about both cosmopolitanism and nationalism, in order to develop a vision of politics for the contemporary world that includes the proper insights of each while criticizing and rejecting their problematic aspects. This account envisions global political institutions that recognize local and regional cultural and historical differentiation and self-determination. With some reconstructed concepts and arguments, I hope to make the motivations of both cosmopolitanism and nationalism get along well together.[3]

The essay has the following critical and positive elements. First, I criticize the arguments of some political theorists for a liberal version of nationalism. Thinkers such as Yael Tamir, David Miller, and Will Kymlicka are right to affirm the moral value of cultural membership as a source of the self. Efforts to distinguish a distinct kind of cultural group, nation, from other cultural groups, however, presuppose what they aim to justify. Arguments that national members have special obligations of justice they do not have to others, moreover, are problematic. In a world of global interdependence, obligations of justice extend globally. Such moral arguments challenge the legitimacy of a world order composed of independent sovereign states, a world order that economic powers and interactions are challenging practically. Assumption of the norm of independent and unified state sovereignty is also being challenged from within by groups inside states claiming special rights and autonomy. Giving adequate recognition to such group-differentiated movements against the oppression of states, I argue, requires abandoning the concept of nation and replacing it with a concept of distinct people. The idea of a people should be conceptualized in relational rather than substantive terms. Those who theorize the importance of recognizing the distinctness of peoples in politics are right to emphasize a principle of self-determination for peoples. This principle of self-determination still tends to be understood today, however, as the claim for a right to an independent state. This interpretation coheres neither with a challenge to the states system nor with the claim that all peoples should be able to exercise self-determination. Thus the idea of self-determination should also be reconceived in relational terms that cohere with openness and interdependence. The claim of global governance coupled with a principle of self-determination for peoples yields an image of federalism as a global governance principle. I end by articulating some elements of such global democracy.

I. PROBLEMS WITH LIBERAL NATIONALISM

Some political theorists are minting a new brand of nationalism, a liberal nationalism. Liberal nationalism endorses values of liberty, formal equality, constitutional law, nondiscrimination, and democratic procedures, and argues that a plausible conception of particular affiliations and obligations of national members can be compatible with these liberal values. For some years Michael Walzer has championed a position like this, though he has not called it liberal nationalism. More recently Charles Taylor, Will Kymlicka, Yael Tamir, David Miller, and Margaret Canovan have formulated versions of a liberal nationalist political theory.

Liberal nationalism would seem to sit comfortably within a more general politics of difference that argues that public discussion and policies should attend to and sometimes affirm social-group differences. In this section I will argue, however, that it is possible and necessary to distinguish a recognition of the difference and autonomy of distinct peoples from the affirmation of nationalism.

I read liberal nationalism as a response to the cosmopolitan individualism that implicitly underlies most contemporary moral and political theory. Such cosmopolitanism considers illiberal and reactionary the inclination of many people to identify with a national group and wish special ties of affiliation with it. Affirmation of nationalist sentiments and sense of obligation, some suggest, wrongly limits the freedom of those persons who do not feel the national identification or identity with a minority group.[4] The idea that nations may elevate the good of their own members above that of any and all outsiders, moreover, conflicts with a moral norm that presumes that all human beings have equal moral worth. Both liberty and good character, then, require of citizens a stance of cosmopolitan individualism. Nation ought not to define the bounds of either moral or political community.[5] A liberal constitution should affirm the rights of individuals as individuals, and states ought to be culturally neutral.

Liberal nationalism responds appropriately to the abstraction and bloodlessness of such cosmopolitan individualism. This position fails to recognize that each of us is born into a community with a given history, set of traditions, and meaning. The particular relations in this community give texture to our social affiliation, and in particular condition the value frameworks within which we develop our ability to make particular decisions, including decisions to change some of the community's practices or to leave the community. We grow up learning a particular language, or sometimes particular languages, and our linguistic particularity gives us an oral and literary history, as well as particular ways of expressing ourselves to particular others who speak the language. Because cultural group membership nurtures us and gives us many meaningful social relationships, we can be obliged to help preserve the group and ensure its well-being for the sake of those whose identities do or will partly depend on it. The depth of languages and cultural flexibility toward the future can live only if many people are deeply immersed in and love them. Human spirits must take particular form; they cannot survive with universal principles and technical formulae alone.[6]

Liberal nationalists go further than affirming the moral value of affinity with particular historical and cultural groups as a source of the self. Some believe that the existence and value of each such distinct people implies special rights and obligations. Some argue that a nation is a particular kind of cultural grouping with a unique claim to statehood. Some also argue that obligations of social justice in the form of redistributive welfare policies hold only between conationals. While I accept the liberal nationalist affirmation of the value of particular membership, I will criticize these second two widely accepted claims, which have received philosophical justification in the literature arguing for liberal nationalism. My critique will focus on David Miller's book *On Nationality*, but I will refer to texts by Kymlicka and Tamir as well.

A. *The Concept of Nation*

If a nation has special claims to statehood, then not just any cultural grouping can be a nation. Possibly tens of thousands of cultural groupings exist in the world, and most people would agree that we cannot have so many independent states. Thus the political theory of liberal nationalism takes as one of its tasks distinguishing nations from other sorts of cultural groups, often called ethnic groups. This task turns out to be difficult, however. I submit that these accounts attempting to distinguish a nation from an ethnic group tend to be circular. The criteria for distinguishing nations from other cultural groups turn out to presume an idea of independent statehood.

David Miller argues that a nation is the sort of social entity that should have its own set of political institutions and that the best way to ensure this is to advance independent statehood for the nation. A nation is best protected and nurtured if it coincides with a state, and a state is strongest and most stable it if coincides with a single nation. Where history, the geographic dispersion of nations, or scale make multinational states either necessary or more practical, this is a less desirable and less stable organization than a nation-state.[7] Will Kymlicka, on the other hand, believes that multinational states must be the norm in today's world because many nations have become intertwined territorially, historically, and economically. Yet Kymlicka also defines a nation as a special kind of group with inherent rights of self-government that other kinds of groups do not have.[8]

What is supposed to distinguish a nation, which has moral claims to self-government, from an ethnic group, which does not? Miller admits that there is no sharp dividing line between nation and ethnic group. Both are collectives of people with certain shared cultural characteristics such as language, music, a history of visual art, territorial contiguity, and so on. In both cases part of what makes the members of the group a group is the fact that its members recognize one another as members of the same group. Miller admits that nations may evolve from ethnicities.

A nation must be distinct from an ethnic group, however, according to Miller, because many nation-states today have several ethnicities within them. He offers the United States and Switzerland as two key examples.[9] More contentiously, perhaps, Miller invokes the difference between the British nation and its component groups of English, Scots, Welsh, and Northern Irish as evidence that a nation is something distinctive over and above ethnicity or cultural membership.[10] But what is this something?

Miller is careful to say that what national members share that distinguishes them from other groups ought not be thought of as biological or racial, nor is it even essential that members of a nation were all born in the same land. A key difference between *liberal* nationalism and more traditionalist and illiberal nationalisms is this insistence that a nation is not a "natural kind" but, rather, a particular social construction. Thus for Miller, what distinguishes a nation from other kinds of groups is that its members see themselves as belonging together to a community that is extended in history and active in character. The same can be said, however, about many of the groups Miller clearly thinks of as ethnicities or subnational groups, such as African Americans or French Nova Scotians or Fijians of Indian descent. A nation is further characterized, he says, by a connection to a particular territory. This trait, too, while perhaps necessary to the concept of a nation for Miller, cannot be sufficient because it is true of many groups he wants to classify as ethnicities or subnational groups, such as Welsh, Walloons, or Chicanos. There is only one characteristic left that in Miller's concept of nation seems decisively to distinguish a nation from these other kinds of cultural groups with which the idea of nation is closely aligned. A nation is marked off from other communities, he says, by its distinct *public culture*. A public culture is different from private culture. Private culture consists in the tastes, preferences, and specific practices of a group—its recipes, its love of particular sports, the way members of the group typically spend their Sundays. A public culture is a collective's sense of rights and citizen responsibilities as defined by political rules that are the product of a long history of public debate.[11] The one characteristic that most distinguishes the concept of nation from ethnicity, that is, presupposes the existence of distinct and common political institutions within which public discourse takes place among a broad community of strangers and is extended over generations.

Will Kymlicka also distinguishes a nation conceptually from an ethnic group, and for similar reasons. On his account, a nation is a special kind of cultural group with inherent rights of self-government that no other sort of cultural group has. For him a nation is "a historical community, more or less institutionally complete, occupying a given territory or homeland, sharing a distinct language or culture."[12] Because a nation is institutionally complete, and has resided in its own territory for generations, it has a right to self-government. Many nations, such as indigenous nations in North America, have been conquered by other groups who unjustly rule over them and do not recognize their right to self-government. To the extent that the self-governing rights of historic nations are not recognized, they ought to be. Because the history of so many nations has become intertwined or overlapping in territories, state institutions, and economic interdependence, most states today are or should become multinational states whose constitutions grant specific autonomy to their component nations. While this is usually the most just and practical way to recognize the claims of nations, multinational states are inherently unstable because each of the component nations has a tendency to separate from the others.

As it is for Miller, for Kymlicka, the reason to draw a clear distinction between a nation and an ethnic group is to determine which groups have rights of self-government and which do not. For him the concept of nation is an either-or concept. Either a group is a historical community, living in its historic homeland, sharing a distinct language and culture, or it is a cultural group whose members have left their homeland voluntarily to make a new life within another nation. The concept of nation thus dominates the logic of the distinction between nation and ethnic group, as the hegemonic unity of a society that justifies both separate government and the expectation that newcomers will integrate.

This either-or concept of nation, however, does not accommodate well to the actual diversity of peoples. Many people of African descent in the United States, or many of Indian descent in Africa, were forced to migrate, and due to a history of exclusion they maintain a certain degree of distinctness as peoples today. Many other groups worldwide do not fit well into Kymlicka's two-part division of nation versus ethnic groups. Where, for example, are Gypsies? What about Hutus and Tutsies or Khlosa and Swaze? I will argue shortly that in order to accommodate such realities, the distinctness of peoples should be conceptualized in terms of degree rather than kind.

Kymlicka's use of the concept of nation also tends to be circular, I suggest. A distinction among kinds of groups is supposed to give moral foundation to a right of self-government. Implicit in Kymlicka's definition of a nation as a "historical community, more or less institutionally complete, occupying a given territory or homeland . . ." is the assumption that this particular kind of group either is today or once was an independent polity. Like Miller, I suggest, Kymlicka tends to presuppose political community as part of the concept of nation but then uses this concept of nation to justify judging that some groups but not others have legitimate claim to be distinct polities.

Such circularity is unavoidable, I think, because the idea of nation cannot name a distinct kind of cultural group. All efforts to distinguish a nation from an ethnic group seem to presuppose that a nation is a *political* community and that an ethnic group is not. The idea of a nation entails the idea of a group of people who not only share cultural characteristics and recognize each other as a group but also have, once had, or aspire to have distinct, unified, and independent institutions of political governance. As a number of writers have pointed out, the idea of a nation emerged with the building of modern state forms in Europe.[13] This means, as I have been suggesting, that the concept of nation actually presupposes the concept of sovereign state. For this reason, it cannot be used as an independent criterion to justify claims to sovereign independence.

Such use, however, is the primary political function of the idea of nation. A nation is supposed to be a kind of cultural group distinct in character from other kinds of groups that share language, location, history, and artistic and everyday life traditions. That special character is supposed to justify a unique moral claim to political self-determination. There is no way to distinguish a nation from other kinds of cultural groups, however, without smuggling political self-organization into the idea of nation. Since most people in the world would rather be able to think of themselves as self-governing than governed by others, and since being taken as a nation gives a group a stronger claim to self-government, most groups want recognition as nations. Much energy, negotiation time, and blood is spent on struggle over the boundary between the merely ethnic and the national. This boundary, I have been arguing, is entirely a *political construct* that does not correspond to the cultural character of the contesting groups, their longevity, or degree of cohesion. I will argue below that recognizing the mystifying or ideology character of the idea of nation entails rethinking the meaning, justification, and implications of claims for political self-determination. Before turning to that positive argument, I will examine another common argument for liberal nationalism, the welfare argument.

B. *The Welfare Argument*

Several philosophers argue that nationalism has positive value because it promotes social justice. The argument, as I understand it, goes as follows. In large, industrial, capitalist societies, promoting social justice requires strong welfare-state policies that meet needs and provide services. Such welfare state policies require redistributive measures whereby some citizens contribute more than others for the sake of the less advantaged. The sense of justice according to which citizens are willing to contribute to and support such welfare state policies, however, depends on particularist affiliations of common culture and a sense of belonging. Yael Tamir puts it this way:

> The "others" whose welfare we ought to consider are those we care about, those who are relevant to our associative identity. Communal solidarity creates a feeling, or an illusion, of closeness and shared fate, which is the precondition of distributive justice. It endows particularistic relations with moral power, supporting the claim that "charity begins at home."[14]

If we look at the history of the formation of welfare states, it is claimed, we find this condition confirmed. Welfare states emerged and remain strong in those societies that had or were able to build a single strong national identity. Nationalism provides the political "engine" that makes the state strong enough to mobilize political resources to enact welfare policies and to enforce them.[15] The achievement of the modern state is universalist in the sense that nationalist movements and commitments motivate individuals to expand their sense of obligation beyond the members of their family, clan, or village to strangers with whom they identify as belonging to the same cultural and historical community. The appeal of nation as "imagined community," then, enables the sense of justice to extend to relatively distant strangers.[16]

I find the welfare argument for liberal nationalism problematic in two respects. Because it endorses the claim that citizens have obligations of justice only to those whom they identify as conationals, this argument can be used to endorse the preservation of privilege and exclusion from benefits that many people find unjust. In making that obligation contingent upon sentiment, moreover, this line of reasoning makes for bad moral argument.

The liberal nationalist construction of national obligation explicitly endorses external exclusions. It does not claim that citizens in a particular nation have no obligations at all to people outside their borders; they have obligations of respect, hospitality, and the defense of human rights. Obligations specifically of distributive justice and attention to the welfare and capabilities of others to live satisfying, productive lives, however, do not extend beyond borders. Each nation is obliged to take care of its own, and to the extent that the leaders of a nation-state fail in discharging those obligations, outsiders have no obligation to take them up, though they may of course decide to help out of a sense of beneficence.

Not only does the welfare argument of liberal nationalism explicitly allow for external exclusion, it opens the door to internal inclusion. The argument that obligations of justice extend only to those with whom citizens identify as belonging to a common national culture and history can legitimate rejection of redistributive policies perceived to benefit groups with whom many citizens do not identify. White Anglo Americans appear increasingly reluctant to support redistributive policies, partly because many of them wrongly believe that these policies primarily benefit African Americans and Latinos, with whom they do not feel such strong ties of common culture and shared history. The feelings of redistributive solidarity for which many Europeans have long been admired are coming under significant strain today in those societies with significant numbers of non-European immigrants, such as those of Turkish, North African, or South Asian origin.[17] This resistance to redistribution seems especially strong when some of those who would benefit from redistributive policies not only are culturally different from others in the society but refuse to assimilate to a dominant national culture, and even claim self-determination for their people. Some New Zealanders of European descent question redistributive welfare policies to Maori, who themselves assert a right of self-determination in the context of New Zealand society. The position that obligations of justice extend only to conationals justifies anti-immigration politics and policies. On this argument, restrictions on immigration are justified not only to preserve a national culture[18] but also to preserve or enlarge redistributive policies from which citizens withdraw support when they perceive immigrants benefiting from them.[19]

The argument that nationalism is a positive value because it motivates citizens to support redistributive policies, moreover, is philosophically problematic. It makes obligation contingent on sentiment. It might be true today that the willingness of citizens to be taxed to pay for public services and redistribution depends on nationalist sentiment. It might also be true (though I have my doubts) that the origins of the welfare state lie in the ties of national identification European states built and appealed to in the nineteenth century. These are contingent empirical claims about historical and contemporary motivational supports for welfare policies. They do not show that national identification is a *necessary* condition of welfare state policies, and they certainly cannot provide a *moral* argument for nationalism.

Arguments that people have obligations of justice to others cannot depend on their having feelings of identification with those others. At best, feelings of identification can sometimes explain why some people sometimes recognize the obligations they have (or believe they have obligations they do not have). In fact, we most often need to make arguments that some people have obligations of justice to others when those with the obligations fail to recognize them; and people often deny their obligations because they feel no affinity for those others or positively dislike them. Moral arguments for obligations of justice must rest on more objective and normative grounds than feelings of familiarity or cultural affinity.

Writers such as Charles Beitz and Thomas Pogge give more objective criteria for determining the scope of people across whom obligations of justice extend. Wherever people act with a set of institutions that connect them to one another by commerce, communication, or the consequences of policies, such that systemic interdependencies generate benefits and burdens that would not exist without those institutional relationships, then the people within that set of interdependent institutions stand in relations of justice.[20]

Onora O'Neill states a similar objective test. The scope of persons to whom agents have obligations of justice extends to all those whose action the agent presupposes as a background or condition for her own action. The scope of justice includes all those to whom an agent is connected through socially contextualized causal relationships. An agent stands in relations with others where obligations of justice hold when her actions can affect them, or when their actions can affect her even if indirectly through the mediation of the actions of others. In O'Neill's view, this entails a global scope of justice today.[21] If I jump into my car each morning on the assumption that cheap gasoline will continue to be readily available to me on the street corner a few blocks away, then principles and obligations of justice apply to my relations with all those people, from the oil workers in Venezuela to the buyers and brokers who organize the oil industry, to all the others whose actions contribute to the institutions of production, refinement, trade, and transportation that get the gasoline to my car. We all together act within a constellation of interdependent institutions to which principles of justice ought to apply. To the extent that injustices exist within this institutional web, those who benefit from the injustices have obligations to those who are harmed, and their national membership or mutual identification is irrelevant to assessing such obligations. Later I will return to this argument about the scope of justice to support a moral critique of the system of states' sovereignty and envision an alternative system of global governance.

II. The Distinctness of Peoples

Efforts to defend a specific positive value to the idea of nation and distinguish nations from other types of cultural groups fail, I have argued. Claims that the scope of justice extends only to conationals, moreover, and that nationalism is valuable because it motivates redistributive policies are philosophically and politically suspect. These critiques appear to lead us back to the cosmopolitan individualism to which I said that liberal nationalism is an appropriate reaction. If the scope of distributive and institutional justice extends to all those persons with whom we are in institutional relations, and if the distinction between nation and other sorts of cultural affinity groups is relatively arbitrary, then from a moral point of view we are all simply individuals with human rights and their correlative obligations. While persons should be free to associate with one another as they choose, the facts and feelings of membership have no specific moral implications.

This is not the conclusion I draw, however, from this critique of liberal nationalism. The opposition that liberal nationalism expresses to cosmopolitan individualism contains a core of truth. A great many people think of themselves as belonging to a people or peoples whose distinct history, language, values, and practices have helped shape who they are. These usually involuntary affiliations provide not only a background for action but also many of the cultural, moral, and material resources for interpreting the world. People often cherish these group affinities, and insist on recognition and support for their efforts to pursue their group-based way of life without being dominated, discriminated against, or exploited by others. Claims about the global scope of justice and the importance of individual rights do not speak to these powerful, and I believe often legitimate, group-specific claims for recognition and self-determination.

Is it possible to affirm positive claims of group affinity, distinctiveness, and self-determination without accepting the concepts and sentiments of nationalism? It must be, I suggest, for at least the following reason. The claims of many distinct peoples for recognition and self-determination are often thwarted by international acceptance of a unique claim of supposed nations to self-determination in the form of independent sovereign statehood. The claims of indigenous peoples are central for me, but the claims of many other distinct peoples often go unheard within a ruling paradigm of nation-states. While I reject the concept of nation as a specific kind of cultural group, I shall argue that the idea of distinct peoples is appropriate and legitimate. A political theory of distinct peoples relies on a relational social ontology instead of the substantial logic typical of nationalism. In accordance with such a relational logic, moreover, the concept of self-determination should be rethought along lines of autonomy and participation rather than exclusion.

A. Relational Ontology of Distinct People

Both in political theory and in ordinary discourse, "nation" usually appears as an all-or-nothing concept, in two respects. Most generally, a nation is supposed to be a special kind of group with specific political claims that other groups do not have. On this construction, either a group counts as a nation, in which case it has right to self-government, or it is merely an ethnic or religious group, in which case it does not. Second, nationalist ideologies tend to define their groups in either/or terms. They conceptualize the nation as strictly bounded between insiders and outsiders, and seek to define attributes of national identity or character that all members share. Claiming such an essence to the nation sometimes oppresses individuals within who do not conform to these national norms, and sometimes oppresses outsiders against whom national members set themselves in opposition.

If political theorists wish to respond to the complexities of cultural differentiation and recognize legitimate claims of justice, I suggest that we would do better to use a concept of distinct people, rather than nation, and to see distinctness as a matter of degree than of kind. No longer do we need to make a specious distinction between nation and ethnic group, but we can nevertheless follow the observation that some peoples are distinct from others to a greater degree and in more respects.[22]

People experience themselves as sharing affinity with some and as distinct from others in many possible respects: language, historical connection with a territory, self-understanding as having a shared history, religious practice, artistic conventions and meanings, a dialogic consciousness of dwelling together distinctly, being segregated and stereotyped by a dominant group, and so on. Some groups are distinct from one another in only some of these ways, and others are distinct from one another in all these respects. The Scots are distinct from the English in respect to historical religious affiliation, history, and territory. Where language once was a major distinction between the peoples, this distinction has lessened, though it is still present to a degree. When they think of themselves in relation to Russians or Chinese, however, I suspect that most Scots think of themselves as more like the English than not.

Replacing the idea of nation with that of distinct people, then, relies on a relational rather than substantial social ontology. A relational conception of difference does not posit a social group as having an essential nature composed of a set of attributes defining only that group. Rather, a social group exists and is defined as a specific group only in interactive relations with others. Social group identities emerge from the encounter and interaction among people who experience some differences in their ways of life and forms of association, even if they regard themselves as belonging to the same society. A group will not regard itself as having a distinct language, for example, unless its members encounter another group whose speech they do not understand. In a relational conceptualization, what constitutes a social group is less internal to the attributes of its members and more a function of the relations in which it stands to others. On this view, social difference may be stronger or weaker, and it may be more or less salient, depending on the point of view of comparison. A relational conception of group difference does not need to force all persons associated with the group under the same attributes. Group members may differ in many ways, including how strongly they bear affinity with others of the group. A relational approach, moreover, does not designate clear conceptual and practical borders that distinguish one group decisively from others, and distinguish its members decisively. Conceiving group differentiation as a function of relationship, comparison, and interaction, then, allows for overlap, interspersal, and interdependence among groups and their members.[23]

There are thousands of groups in the world today who consider themselves distinct peoples—whose members share cultural characteristics and histories by which they consider themselves distinguished from others, and who recognize one another as in the same distinct group. Some of those who consider themselves distinct peoples in the world today are generally considered what are called nations; many are not so considered but would like to be; some do not claim such a degree of distinctness but nevertheless make political claims against the state under whose jurisdiction they find themselves or on international bodies. Since the concept of nation, as I have argued, is implicitly linked to statehood, and since the international system resists the recognition of new states, many who legitimately consider themselves distinct peoples do not receive the regional and/or international recognition they deserve. Many are culturally, economically, or politically dominated by other peoples within a nation-state, and for this reason they struggle for self-determination. If we abandon the idea of nation along with its association with independent statehood, then distinct peoples can be more easily recognized in their distinctness, because the political consequences of this recognition remain to be worked out.[24] Distinct peoples have prima facie claims to self-determination. A critique of nationalism and attention to the relational distinctness of people, however, leads to a reconceptualization of the meaning of self-determination. Before proposing such a reconceptualization, it is important to explore arguments against the primary mode of self-determination now recognized in international relations, namely, the centered sovereignty characteristic of the states system.

III. Moral Challenges to Sovereignty

I have argued that the concept of nation presupposes the concept of an independent sovereign state. More often than not, nationalism embodies a claim of a people to have a single and unified state of their own, through which that people can claim a right of self-determination over a territory that entails a right of noninterference by all other actors. Such a concept of unified, centered, and independent state sovereignty, however, is coming under question today, both theoretically and practically.[25] In this section I review many of these criticisms of a concept of unified and independent sovereignty. External challenges to such claims of state sovereignty build on the cosmopolitan arguments I cited earlier to the effect that globalization makes peoples interdependent and thereby brings them together under the scope of justice. Internal challenges attend to the fact that most states in the world today have jurisdiction over a plurality of peoples who claim recognition and special rights.

I distinguish the concept of sovereignty from that of *state* institutions. States are public authorities that regulate the activities of those within their jurisdictions through legal and administrative institutions backed by the power to sanction. While only states can be unified sovereigns with no authority above them, they need not be, and many strong state institutions currently exist at a jurisdictional level smaller than sovereign states. State institutions are capable of being subject to review or override without losing their status as states. They can share jurisdiction with other states, and their jurisdiction need not encompass all the activities in a territory. The critique of sovereignty that follows should not be understood as a critique of state institutions as such. There are good reasons to preserve state institutions, and indeed, I shall argue, to extend the functioning of state institutions to a more global level.

A *sovereign* state wields central and final authority over all the legal and political matters within a determinate and strictly bounded territory.[26] Sovereignty entails a clear distinction between inside and outside. Within a sovereign state there are often partial and lesser governments and jurisdictions, but the sovereign government exercises a higher and final authority over them. The sovereignty of the state is partially constituted by the states outside it, moreover, states that recognize it as a legitimate sovereign state. This recognition entails a principle of nonintervention; for a state to have final authority implies that no other state and no transnational body has the authority to interfere with its actions and policies.[27]

Some writers claim that states today no longer have sovereignty in the sense I define here, and perhaps never did. It is questionable, that is, whether states today really exercise centrally coordinated power that is systematically connected over domains of government, and that they exercise it as a final authority. State power today, some claim, is in fact much more fragmentary and limited than the commitment to sovereignty would have one believe.[28] Whatever the factual situation of state powers, however, the *idea* of sovereignty still carries much weight among political leaders and scholars, both regarding the relation of states to internal organization and jurisdictions, and international relations. Many today continue to believe that states *ought* to be sovereign, and that to the degree that their sovereignty is under challenge or in a process of fragmentation, that steps should be taken to reinforce a system of strong sovereign states. Others disagree, and promote either internal devolution or the external evolution of transnational authorities. I shall argue that a principle of state sovereignty lacks moral legitimacy, both regarding external and internal affairs.

A. *External Challenges*

Considerations of global justice call into question the legitimacy of claims by states that they alone have the right to attend to affairs within their borders and have no obligations to peoples outside their borders. I discussed earlier the arguments of Charles Beitz, Thomas Pogge, and Onora O'Neill, among others, that there are no privileged grounds for limiting the scope of evaluations of justice to relations between people within nation states. Moral evaluation of social relations in terms of justice and injustice apply wherever social institutions connect people in a causal web. The scope and complexity of economic, communication, and many other institutions in the world today constitute a sufficiently tight web of constraint and interdependence today that we must speak of a global *society*.[29] Principles of justice apply to relations among persons, organizations, and state institutions in diverse reaches of global society. These claims of justice constitute a double challenge to the moral boundaries of states. Agents outside states have some claim to judge and regulate the activities of states over affairs within their jurisdictions, on the one hand; states and their members, on the other hand, have obligations to people outside their borders. Considerations of economic regulation, human rights intervention, environmental protection, and migration are among those that raise profound issues of justice that challenge sovereignty in this double way.

The principle of sovereignty gives to states the right and power to regulate for the benefit of their own members. States ought positively to pursue economic gain for their own citizens at the expense of other people in the world if necessary, so long as they do not forcefully invade and conquer the territories of other sovereign states. They have the right to exclude persons from entry into their territory in order to preserve the privileged access their members have to resources and benefits there. States or their citizens owe no general obligation to others outside, whatever their needs or level of relative deprivation. Any efforts states or their members make to help needy people elsewhere in the world are superogatory.

Several moral arguments can be offered against this view of the right of nonintervention in states' policies and their right to be indifferent to the circumstances of those outside their borders. Charles Beitz questions the moral right of states to keep for themselves all the benefits derived from the natural resources that happen to lie within their borders. Resources such as fertile land, economically valuable minerals, and so on are by no means evenly distributed around the globe. Because the placement of resources is morally arbitrary, no state is entitled to treat them as its private property to be used only for its own benefit. Because certain resources are necessary for the productive capacity of all societies, they must be considered a global common. Their use and the benefits of their use should thus be globally regulated under a cooperative framework of global justice.[30]

The global-resources argument is one example of a challenge to the sovereignty claim that outside agents have no claim to regulate the actions of states over activities that take place within their jurisdiction. The state of production, finance and communications in the world has evolved in such a way that many actions and policies internal to a state nevertheless sometimes have profound effects on others in the world. A moral challenge to a principle of nonintervention has come most obviously from environmental concern. States' internal forestry policies, their kind and level of industrial pollution regulation, and similar policies produce consequences for the air quality and climate of many outside their borders. Economic and communicative interdependence, moreover, generate certain international moral claims over other kinds of internal policies. Financial policies of the German or Japanese states, for example, can seriously affect the stability of many other economies. Such interdependencies as these call for some form of international regulatory scheme that aims for stable and just cooperation.

Many argue, furthermore, that current distributive inequality across the globe raises questions of justice that require a globally enforced redistributive regime. The fact that some peoples live in wasteful affluence while many more in other parts of the world suffer from serious deprivation itself stands as prima facie grounds for global redistribution. But these facts of distributive inequality alone do not make a very strong case for global economic regulation. More important is the history of dependence and exploitation between the now poor and now rich regions of the world, and the continuance of institutional structures that perpetuate and even help enlarge global privilege and deprivation. Some scholars argue that the current wealth of Europe and North America compared to societies of Africa, Latin America, and South Asia is due to a significant degree to the colonial relations among these regions that looted for three centuries. While the poorer regions of the world today are composed of independent states with the same formal sovereignty rights as any other states, some argue that the colonial economic relations between North and South persist.[31] The economies of the South depend on capital investment controlled from the North, and most of the profits return to the North. Their workers are often too poorly paid by multinationals or their local contractors to feed their families, and farmers and miners of the South obtain very unfavorable prices on a global resource market. Such deprivation has forced most governments of the Southern Hemisphere into severe debt to northern banks and to international finance agencies such as the World Bank. This indebtedness severely restricts the effective sovereignty of southern states because mighty financial institutions have the power to control those states' internal economic policies, all for the sake of preserving the existing system of international trade and finance and the benefits it brings primarily to some in the North.

The issue is not simply distributive inequality, that some people in some parts of the world are seriously deprived while others in other parts of the world live very well. Rather, the global institutional context sets different regions in relations of dependence and exploitation with others, and this institutional system reproduces and arguably widens the distributive inequalities. Redress of unjust deprivation and regulation of the global economy for the sake of promoting greater justice thus calls for institutional change, and not merely a one-time or periodic transfer of wealth from richer to poorer people.

B. Internal Challenges

Internally, the idea of sovereignty entails that a state has ultimate authority to regulate all the activities taking place within a specific territorial jurisdiction. This often seems to mean, by implication, that the same form of law, regulation, and administration ought to apply to all the peoples and locales within the territory. Both these aspects of internal sovereignty are morally questionable, however, because they do not sufficiently recognize and accommodate the rights and needs of national and cultural minorities. Political recognition for distinct peoples entails that they are able to practice their culture and that they can affirm their own public culture in which to express and affirm their distinctness. To the degree that peoples are distinct, moreover, they have prima facie rights of self-governance. These points entail that peoples who dwell with others within a wider polity nevertheless limit the sovereignty of that wider polity over their activities.[32] The limitation of sovereign authority of a wider polity over groups and locales may vary in kind or degree, from local or group-based autonomy over nearly all affairs to self-governance over only a small range of issues, such as family law or the management and utilization of particular resources. As those examples indicate, moreover, local self-determination may vary according to whether it is legislative or administrative or both. Despite the strong claims of most states to be sovereign over all the activities in their particular territories, the sovereign power of many states today is already limited or restricted in many ways that recognize or accommodate national, cultural, and religious differences within their claimed jurisdictions.[33]

Many of these challenges come from indigenous peoples. Most of the world's indigenous peoples claim rights of self-determination against the states that claim sovereign authority over them. These claims are difficult or impossible for states organized in the existing states system to accommodate because they involve claims about the rights to use land and resources, and the right to develop governance practices continuous with precolonial indigenous practices, which are often at odds with the more formal and bureaucratic governance systems of modern European law. The struggles of most indigenous peoples for culture rights and self-determination reveal asymmetries between the indigenous peoples' societies and the European societies that colonized them. This cultural and institutional clash continues to provoke many states to repress and oppress the indigenous people. Despite unjust conquest and continued oppression, however, few indigenous peoples seek sovereignty for themselves in the sense of the formation of an independent internationally recognized state with ultimate authority over all matters within a determinately bounded territory. Most indigenous peoples seek significantly greater and more secure self-determination within the framework of a wider polity.[34]

Despite the locality of their claims, indigenous people have forged a global social movement that has achieved significant success in the past two decades in gaining recognition for the legitimacy of their claims. In some regions of the world, they have had some successes in motivating some social and political changes to accommodate their needs and interests. Properly recognizing the claims of indigenous peoples today, however, requires challenging the international system of sovereign states. Indigenous peoples worldwide have long been aware of the incompatibility of their claims to justice with the concept of state sovereignty that predominates in international relations. Especially in the past two decades they have organized across different parts of the world and have succeeded to some extent in having the uniqueness of their claims recognized by international bodies such as the World Court or the United Nations. Their social movements have prompted some reforms in the policies of some states that claim to have jurisdiction over them. Despite these successes, many nation-states continue to repress indigenous movements. Their accommodation to indigenous demands for self-determination require a degree of institutional change that most states are unwilling to allow, especially if other states in the international system are not doing so. Thus indigenous peoples' movements are both a source of ideas and action beyond the system of sovereign states, and at the same time show the limits of that system.[35]

I dwell on the situation and claims of indigenous peoples because they fundamentally challenge the world order of sovereign states. Nevertheless, there are many other peoples who claim to be oppressed or lack sufficient recognition by the states that the international system recognizes as having jurisdiction over them. Many of these peoples claim a right of self-determination in the sense of wanting a sovereign state of their own. Such claims often create serious conflict, however, especially when different groups seek sovereignty over the same or overlapping territories. Other groups do not claim sovereignty in this sense, either because they are dispersed geographically or because their claims to autonomy do not encompass all governance issues. Whatever the status of the claims resisting alleged domination, I suggest that most are poorly addressed by a concept of self-determination that equates it with central and final sovereignty.

IV. Rethinking Self-Determination

At least since the early twentieth century the right of self-determination for peoples has been interpreted as a right for distinct peoples to have a sovereign state of their own with a single contiguous territory enclosed by unambiguous borders. This right of sovereignty entails a principle of nonintervention; a state that is sovereign over a territory and a people has final authority over that territory and people, and no outside state or agent has legitimate claim to interfere with the decisions and actions of that authority. Because this interpretation of a principle of self-determination is so absolute, exclusive, and territorially based, it tends to imply a coincidence of one distinct people for each state. Because distinct peoples are also territorially interspersed, however, that logical implication of a principle of self-determination for a people has often generated violent conflict. This inside-outside noninterference concept of self-determination for peoples was probably always inadequate, but today it is dangerously so.

This concept of self-determination interprets freedom as noninterference. On this model, self-determination means that a people or government has the authority to exercise complete control over what goes on inside its jurisdiction, and no outside agent has the right to make claims upon or interfere with what the self-determining agent does. Reciprocally, the self-determining people have no claim on what others do with respect to issues within their jurisdictions, and no right to interfere in the business of the others. Just as it denies rights of interference by outsiders in a jurisdiction, this concept entails that each self-determining entity has no inherent obligations with respect to outsiders.

Freedom as noninterference assumes that agents, whether individual or collective, are independent of one another except insofar as they choose to exchange and contract. The arguments that I have made above about the scope of justice and global interdependence of peoples, however, challenges such an assumption of the independence of nations or states. Thus a theory of self-determination for peoples should recognize that peoples are interdependent, and for this reason that noninterference is too simple an interpretation of self-determination.[36]

Much feminist theory has criticized a rigid idea of independence as inappropriate for a moral theory of autonomy, and proposes to substitute a relational understanding of autonomy that recognizes the constitution of agents by interaction with others and their interdependencies.[37]

The idea of relational autonomy takes account of the interdependence of agents and their embeddedness in relationships at the same time that it continues to value individual choices. In this concept, all agents are owed equal respect as autonomous agents, which means that they are able to choose their ends and have capacity and support to pursue those ends. An adequate conception of autonomy should promote the capacity of agents to pursue their own ends in the context of relationships in which others may do the same. While this concept of autonomy entails a presumption of noninterference, it does not imply a social scheme in which atomized agents simply mind their own business and leave one another alone. Instead, it entails recognizing that agents are related in many ways they have not chosen, by virtue of economic interaction, history, proximity, or the unintended consequences of action. In these relationships agents are able either to thwart one another or support one another. Relational autonomy consists partly, then, in the structuring of relationships so that they support the maximal pursuit of agent ends.

In his reinterpretation of ideas of classical republicanism, Philip Pettit offers a similar criticism of the idea of freedom as noninterference.[38] Interference means that one agent blocks or redirects the action of another agent in a way that worsens that agent's choice situation by changing the range of options. On Pettit's account, noninterference, while related to freedom, is not equivalent to it. Instead, freedom should be understood as nondomination. An agent dominates another when he or she has power over that other and is thus able to interfere with the other *arbitrarily*. Interference is arbitrary when it is chosen or rejected without consideration of the interests or opinions of those affected. An agent may dominate another, however, without ever interfering with that person. Domination consists in standing in a set of relations that makes an agent *able* to interfere arbitrarily with the actions of others.

Real freedom means the absence of such relations of domination. Pettit argues that institutions should promote and preserve nondomination for everyone. To do so, they must have regulations that sometimes interfere with actions in order to restrict dominative power and promote cooperation. Interference is not arbitrary if its purpose is to minimize domination, and if it is done in a way that takes the interests and voices of affected parties into account. Like the feminist concept of relational autonomy, then, the concept of freedom as nondomination refers to a set of social relations. "Non-domination is the position that someone enjoys when they live in the presence of other people and when, by virtue of social design, none of those others dominates them."[39]

I propose that a principle of self-determination for peoples should be interpreted along lines of relational autonomy or non-domination rather than simply as independence or noninterference. On such an interpretation, self-determination for peoples means that they have a right to their own governance institutions through which they decide on their goals and interpret their way of life. Other people ought not to constrain, dominate, or interfere with those decisions and interpretations for the sake of their own ends, or according to their judgment of what way of life is best, or in order to subordinate a people to a larger "nation" unit. Peoples, that is, ought to be free from domination. Because a people stands in interdependent relations with others, however, a people cannot ignore the claims and interests of those others when their actions potentially affect them. Insofar as outsiders are affected by the activities of self-determining people, those others have a legitimate claim to have their interests and needs taken into account even though they are outside the government jurisdiction. Conversely, outsiders should recognize that when they themselves affect a people, the latter can legitimately claim that they should have their interests taken into account insofar as they may be adversely affected. Insofar as their activities affect one another, peoples are in relationship and ought to negotiate the terms and effects of the relationship.

Self-determining peoples morally cannot do whatever they want without interference from others. Their territorial, economic, or communicative relationships with others generate conflicts and collective problems that oblige them to acknowledge the legitimate interests of others as well as promote their own. Pettit argues that states can legitimately interfere with the actions of individuals in order to foster institutions that minimize domination. A similar argument applies to actions and relations of collectivities. In a densely interdependent world, peoples require political institutions that lay down procedures for coordinating actions, resolving conflicts, and negotiating relationships.

The self-determination of people, then, has the following elements. First, self-determination means a presumption of noninterference. A people has the prima facie right to set its own governance procedures and make its own decisions about its activities, without interference from others. Second, insofar as the activities of a group may adversely affect others or generate conflict, self-determination entails the right of those others to make claims on the group, negotiate the terms of their relationships, and mutually adjust the terms' effects. Third, a world of self-determining peoples thus requires recognized and settled institutions and procedures through which peoples negotiate, adjudicate conflicts, and enforce agreements. Self-determination does not imply independence but, rather, that peoples dwell together within political institutions that minimize domination among peoples. It would take another essay to address the question of just what form such intergovernmental political institutions should take; some forms of federalism do and should apply. Finally, the self-determining peoples require that the peoples have the right to participate *as peoples* in designing and implementing intergovernmental institutions aimed at minimizing domination.

I have argued for a principle of self-determination understood as relational autonomy in the context of nondomination, instead of a principle of self-determination understood simply as noninterference. This argument applies as much to large nation-states as to small indigenous or "ethnic" groups. Those entities that today are considered self-determining independent states in principle ought to have no more right of noninterference than should smaller groups. Self-determination for those entities now called sovereign states should mean nondomination. While this means a presumption of noninterference, outsiders may have a claim on their activities.

Thus the interpretation of self-determination as nondomination ultimately implies limiting the rights of existing nation-states and setting these into different, more cooperatively regulated relationships. Just as promoting freedom for individuals involves regulating international relations to prevent the domination of peoples.

V. GLOBAL DEMOCRACY

The argument in this paper has taken apparently divergent turns between cosmopolitanism and the recognition of difference. Many problems that cause conflict and require cooperation to solve, such as war, environmental degradation, and global distributive justice, require global regulatory institutions to solve. At the same time, I have agreed with those political theorists who argue that affiliation with cultural and historically differentiated peoples provides a basis for meaning and value in people's lives, and for this reason the distinctness of people should be publicly and politically recognized. The principles and movements of multiculturalism within and across states today challenge traditional ideas of the unity of nation-states and uniformity of the application of their regulations.

From this dual argument I conclude something similar to several others recently writing about these issues: peace and justice in the world today require a transformation in governance institutions that is both more encompassing than existing nation-states and at the same time devolves and decentralizes authority to units of a smaller and more diverse character than many existing nation-states.[40] In this concluding section I sketch some principles for envisioning such transformed institutions of global democratic regulation.

I imagine a global system of regulatory regimes to which locales and regions relate in a federated system. These regimes lay down rules regarding that small but vital set of issues around which peace and justice call for global cooperation. I envision seven such regulatory regimes, though the number could be larger or smaller, and the jurisdictions defined differently: (1) peace and security; (2) environment; (3) trade and finance; (4) investment and capital utilization; (5) communications and transportation; (6) human rights, including labor standards and welfare rights; and (7) citizenship and migration. I imagine that each regulatory regime has a functional jurisdiction separate from those of the others, each with its own regulatory function. Each provides a thin set of general rules that specify ways that individuals, organizations, and governments are obliged to take account of the interests and circumstances of one another. By distinguishing regimes functionally, such a global governance system deterritorializes some aspects of sovereignty.[41]

Each of these issue areas already has an evolving regime of international law and organization on which to build in order to create a global regime with greater enforcement strength and resources for carrying out its purpose. For the most part, however, only the activities of states are subject to regulation under those treaty regimes. An important aspect of decentering governance through global regulatory regimes would consist in making at least some of the activities of nonstate organizations, such as municipalities, private for-profit and no-profit corporations, and individuals, directly addressed in global regulation, with regional and local governments as tools of implementation.

Within the context of global regulatory regimes, everyday governance ought to be primarily local. What defines a locale may vary in accordance with the way people affiliate, their history, priorities, and relationship with others. Locales consist in first-level autonomous units of governance. Some might be defined as self-determining peoples. While rooted in place, these might not be associated with a single contiguous territory. The Ojibwa people could count as a self-determining local unit, for example, even if some of the members are dispersed territorially. Many locales ought to be heterogeneous and multicultural, however. Thus metropolitan regions are a primary candidate for self-determining units. Such autonomous governance units should be institutionalized as *open*, both in a territorial and jurisdictional sense. Autonomous peoples or communities may overlap in territories, and their governance needs to recognize the situations and problems they share with others, as well as how their actions may affect the conditions of action of other units.

Local units, in this vision, are autonomous in the sense that their members construct their own institutions of governance as they choose, within the limits of global regulation. The global level of governance is "thin," in the sense that it lays down only rather general principles. Local jurisdictions "thicken" them into administrable programs and rules by interpreting and applying them according to their own procedures, priorities, and cultural understandings.[42]

A major purpose of global regulatory regimes, in the model I imagine, is to protect local units and their members from domination. Self-determination understood as nondomination, you will recall, does not mean only a presumption of noninterference for the autonomous unit. Even more important, it means that autonomous units are embedded in institutionalized relationships that protect them from dominative threats. Some local units are more vulnerable than others to such threats. Global regulatory regimes should aim to minimize domination both of individuals and of self-determining locales. To the extent that peoples and locales have often experienced domination by neighboring peoples or nation-states that have claimed jurisdiction over them, one purpose of global regulation is to protect such vulnerable peoples and locales. This is one important respect in which local self-determination and cultural self-determination can be understood not as conflicting with but, rather, as requiring stronger global regulation.

A vision of global governance with local self-determination ought to make the inclusion of democratic values and institutions paramount. Those regimes and institutions existing today that coordinate and regulate global interaction beyond the jurisdiction of states are not very democratic. The growing global power of multinational corporations is explicitly undemocratic, for example. Existing tribunals of international law have few channels of democratic accountability. Especially because of the power and structure of the Security Council, the United Nations is not a democratic institution. Scholars and journalists bemoan the "democratic deficit" they observe in the operations of today's most complex and thoroughly developed transnational governance body, the European Union.[43] There are many complex issues involved in such democratization, of course; I will point to just a few.

First, one of the reasons to advocate localism, the devolution of sovereign authority onto more local units in nondiminutive institutional relationships, is to promote democracy. Participation and citizenship are best enacted at a local level. Democratic federated regimes of global regulation, however, do require institutions of representation and policy deliberation at levels far removed from the local. A global environmental regulatory decision-making body, for example, would not need to be any *more* removed from ordinary citizens than many national regulatory bodies currently are. Once we move beyond a local level, any polity is an "imagined community" whose interests and problems must be discursively constructed as affecting everyone because people do not experience most of the others in the polity. I believe that this problem is no bigger for transnational and global regulation than it is for large nation-states.

Activities of global governance ought to be public. Simple as this sounds, the deliberations of some of the most powerful global actors today, such as the International Monetary Fund or the World Trade Organization, are not public. Already the possibilities of transportation and communication in the world today see the formation of incipient public spheres composed of active citizens in global civil society.[44]

Institutions through which distinct peoples and locales can participate in formulating policies of global regulatory regimes would help render such global regulation compatible with a principle of self-determination. Self-determination does not mean sovereign independence, I have argued. It does entail, however, that to the extent that self-governing entities are obliged to follow more encompassing regulation, they have a real opportunity to participate with the others in formulating those regulations.

I have suggested above, for example, that there ought to be a stronger global regime to formulate global standards of individual human rights, and to monitor and enforce compliance with those standards. Having such a human rights regime does not impinge on local self-determination and local autonomy, I am arguing, as long as two conditions are met. (1) The peoples and communities obliged to observe these standards have had the opportunity to participate as a collective in their formulation. (2) They have significant discretion in how they apply these standards for their local context, and the means they use locally to implement them. As I hear their protests, those peoples in the world today who question the application of human rights covenants to their context do not reject general principles of human rights. They argue that the particular formulations of those rights applied today were developed largely by Western powers, and that in these changed times these formulations should be subject to review in a process that includes them.

This paper has criticized theories of liberal nationalism that continue to assume a conceptual distinction between a kind of group that is properly a nation, and thus deserves self-determination, and ethnic groups, which do not. I have argued that the distinction between nation and ethnic group is spurious, and that both ideas should be replaced by the idea of distinct peoples, relationally conceptualized. I have adopted cosmopolitan criticisms of nationalist arguments that claim that obligations of justice should extend only to conationals, even if there are some thinner human obligations to outsiders. Such an idea of the self-sufficiency of nations ignores the complex interdependency of the world's peoples today; obligations of justice are for this reason global in extent. Against the conclusion that affiliation with and loyalty to local and cultural groups is problematic, however, I have agreed with arguments for political recognition of multicultural difference. Distinct peoples should be recognized as self-determining. Self-determination should not mean sovereign independence, however, but relational autonomy in the context of global regulatory institutions that aim to minimize domination.

The purpose of accounts of global democracy to which I have briefly added is to jog the imagination into thinking about possibilities alternative to prevailing ideas and practices in the relations between societies and peoples. Accounts such as these are not and cannot be institutional designs, that is, specific proposals for practices with lawful legitimacy and practical force. The purpose of ideas such as those I and others have outlined is to inspire and motivate individuals and groups who aim to criticize existing international institutions, practices, and relationships, and who engage in actions intended to promote global democracy and justice. Visions such as these are contributions to a discussion of where we should collectively be going and why. Meaningful democratic change in global governance and its relation to local participation will come about only as a result of movements of public leaders and citizen activists pressuring for that change in concerted and thoughtful ways. The global organization of tens of thousands of people to bring positions and demands before several United Nations–sponsored conferences in the past decade is only one sign that such movements may be developing.

NOTES

I am grateful to the following people for helpful comments on an earlier version of this paper: Frank Cunningham, Omar Dahbur, Laurel Weldon, Alexander Wendt, Aaron Hoffman, Davis Bobrow, and Reiner Bauboeck.

1. Derrida, *The Other Heading*, trans. Pascale-Anne Brault and Michael B. Nass (Bloomington: Indiana University Press, 1991), 48.

2. Julia Kristeva reflects on this coincidence of French nationalism and cosmopolitanism in *Strangers to Ourselves* (New York: Columbia University Press, 1991), especially chapter 7.

3. Elizabeth Kiss attempts to cut a way between nationalism and cosmopolitanism in her essay "Five Theses on Nationalism," in John Chapman and Ian Shapiro, eds., *NOMOS XXXV: Democratic Community* (New York: New York University Press, 1993). Her essay shows how complicated a critique of nationalism must be but envisions little in the way of an alternative understanding of political community.

4. See, for example, Bhikhu Parekh, "The Politics of Nationhood," in K. Von Banda-Beckman and M. Verkuyten, eds., *Cultural Identity and Development in Europe* (London: University College of London Press, 1994).

5. For recent examples of a cosmopolitan position see Martha Nussbaum, "Patriotism and Cosmopolitanism," in Joshua Cohen, ed., *For Love of Country* (Boston: Beacon Press, 1996); Veit Bader, "Citizenship and Exclusion: Radical Democracy, Community and Justice, or, What Is Wrong with Communitarianism?" *Political Theory* 23:2 (May 1995): 211–46; In more recent work, however, Bader is less unambiguously cosmopolitan, giving more attention to ethnocultural commitments; see " The Cultural Conditions of Transnational Citizenship," in *Political Theory* 25:6 (December 1997); Jeremy Waldron, "Minority Cultures and the Cosmopolitan Alternative," in Will Kymlicka, ed., *The Rights of Minority Cultures* (Oxford: Oxford University Press, 1995).

6. See Will Kymlicka, *Liberalism, Community and Culture* (Oxford: Oxford University Press, 1989), especially chapters 4, 5, and 8; Charles Taylor, "Multiculturalism and the Politics of Recognition," in Amy Gutmann, ed., *Multiculturalism* (Princeton: Princeton University Press, 1992); Yael Tamir, *Liberal Nationalism* (Princeton: Princeton University Press, 1993), chapters 1 and 2.

7. David Miller, *On Nationality* (Oxford: Oxford University Press, 1995), especially chapter 4.

8. Will Kymlicka, *Multicultural Citizenship* (Oxford: Oxford University Press, 1995).

9. Miller, *On Nationality*, 18–21.

10. Ibid, 172–75.

11. Ibid, 68–70, 172–73.

12. Kymlicka, *Multicultural Citizenship*, 11.

13. See Margaret Canovan, *Nationhood and Political Theory* (Brookfield, Vt.: Edward Elgar, 1996); Mary Kaldor, "European Institutions, Nation-States and Nationalism," in Daniele Archibugi and David Held, eds.,

Cosmopolitan Democracy: An Agenda for a New World Order (Oxford: Polity Press, 1995).

14. Tamir, *Liberal Nationalism*, 121.

15. The "engine" metaphor is Margaret Canovan's. See *Nationhood and Political Theory*. In this book Canovan does not justify nationalism morally; indeed, she is worried about its potentially destructive consequences today. She argues, however, that nationalism is necessary to the functioning of states.

16. Compare Miller, *On Nationality*, chapter 3.

17. Miller, for one, explicitly distances his argument from the implication that dominant nationals do not have the same obligations of redistribution to members of ethnic or immigrant minorities. See *On Nationality*. As long as one links obligations of justice to national identification, however, the wedge is set to separate those culturally closer from those more culturally distant, and to prefer the former in redistributive policies.

18. See Michael Walzer, *Spheres of Justice* (New York: Basic Books, 1983).

19. Alan Wolfe and Jytte Klausen argue for greater immigration restrictions in the United States on the grounds that they are necessary to renew popular support for redistributive welfare policies. See "Identity Politics and the Welfare State," *Social Philosophy and Policy* 14:2 (Summer 1997): 231–55.

20. Thomas Pogge, "Cosmopolitanism and Sovereignty," *Ethics* 103 (October 1992): 48–75; Charles Beitz, *Political Theory and International Relations* (Princeton: Princeton University Press, 1979).

21. Onora O'Neill, *Toward Justice and Virtue* (Cambridge: Cambridge University Press, 1996), chapter 4; see also O'Neill, "Justice and Boundaries," in C. Brown, ed., *Political Restructuring in Europe: Ethical Perspectives* (London: Routledge, 1994).

22. I have proposed to replace the dichotomy Kymlicka makes between nation and ethnic group with a continuum of more or less distinct people; see "A Multicultural Continuum: A Critique of Will Kymlicka," in *Constellations* 4:1 (April 1997). Yael Tamir's suggestion that we think of the idea of a nation as a "cluster" concept rather than a concept defined by a necessary list of essential attributes moves in this direction.

23. Martha Minow proposes a relational understanding of group difference; see *Making All the Difference* (Ithaca: Cornell University Press, 1990), part II. I have introduced a relational analysis of group difference in *Justice and the Politics of Difference* (Princeton: Princeton University Press, 1990), especially chapter 2, and in "Together in Difference: Transforming the Logic of Group Political Conflict," in Will Kymlicka, ed., *The Rights of Minority Groups* (Oxford: Oxford University Press, 1995).

For relational understandings of group difference, see also William Connolly, *Identity/Difference* (Ithaca: Cornell University Press, 1993), and Chantal Mouffe, "Democracy, Power and the 'Political,'" in Seyla Benhabib, ed., *Democracy and Difference* (Princeton: Princeton University Press, 1996), 245–56. James Tully proposes a similar deconstruction of substantive understandings of group differences in his idea of cultural difference as "aspectival." See *Strange Multiplicities* (Cambridge: Cambridge University Press, 1995).

24. Compare Neil MacCormick, "Liberalism, Nationalism and the Post-Sovereign State," *Political Studies* XLIV (1996): 553–67.

25. See, for example, the articles collected in R. B. J Walker and Saul H. Mendovitz, eds., *Contending Sovereignties: Redefining Political Community* (Boulder: Lynne Reiner, 1990); see also Richard Falk, "Evasions of Sovereignty," in *Explorations at the Edge of Time* (Philadelphia: Temple University Press, 1992).

26. Definitions of sovereignty abound, but they vary only subtly. See, for example, Christopher Morris, "Sovereignty is the highest, final, and supreme political and legal authority (and power) within the territorially defined domain of a system of direct rule." *An Essay on the Modern State* (Cambridge: Cambridge University Press, 1998), ms., 166. Thomas Pogge distinguishes degrees of sovereignty. For him, sovereignty is simple when an agent has unsupervised and irrevocable power. Given this distinction, I am concerned with absolute sovereignty. I find it a bit puzzling that Pogge includes the condition that the decisions and laws of a sovereign power are *irrevocable.* This seems quite unreasonable, since in practice many states revoke or revise decisions previously made and no one considers this a challenge to their sovereignty. The condition should rather be put that a sovereign's decisions cannot be revoked or overridden by *another* authority. See Thomas Pogge, "Cosmopolitanism and Sovereignty," *Ethics* 103 (October 1992): 48–75.

27. See Daniel Philpott, "Sovereignty: An Introduction and Brief History," *Journal of International Affairs* 48: no. 2 (Winter 1995): 353–68.

28. See Morris, *An Essay on the Modern State.*

29. Beitz, *Political Theory and International Relations;* O'Neill, *Toward Justice and Virtue,* chapter 4; see also O'Neill, "Justice and Boundaries," in C. Brown, ed., *Political Restructuring in Europe: Ethical Perspectives* (London: Routledge, 1994); Pogge, "Cosmopolitanism and Sovereignty." Pogge distinguishes two approaches to social justice, an institutional and an interactional approach. Whereas the interactional approach focuses only on the actions of particular individuals as they affect identifiable persons, the institutional approach theorizes moral responsibility for the fact of others insofar as agents participate in institutions and practices

that may or do harm them. An institutional approach as distinct from an interactional approach, Pogge suggests, makes issues of international justice and moral responsibility with respect to distant strangers more visible. I make a similar distinction between a distributive approach to justice and an approach that focuses on the way institutions produce distributions; see Young, *Justice and the Politics of Difference*. Focusing on how structures and institutional relations produce distributive patterns, I suggest, makes a connected international society more visible and the relations of moral responsibilities of distant peoples within it.

30. Beitz, *Political Theory and International Relations*.

31. The work of Samir Amin is classic here; for a recent statement of this argument, see Fernando Henrique Cardoso, "North-South Relations in the Present Context: A New Dependency?" in Martin Carnoy, Manuel Castells, Cohen, and Fernando Henrique Cardoso, eds., *The New Global Economy in the Information Age* (University Park: Pennsylvania State University Press, 1993), 149–59.

32. Kymlicka, *Multicultural Citizenship*.

33. For one account of different internal challenges to uniformity or universality of the law of sovereign states, see Jacob Levy, "Classifying Cultural Rights," in Ian Shapiro and Will Kymlicka, eds., *NOMOS XXXIX: Ethnicity and Group Rights* (New York: New York University Press, 1997), 22–68.

34. Hector Diaz Polanco, *Indigenous Peoples in Latin America: The Quest for Self-Determination*, trans. Lucia Rayas (Boulder: Westview Press, 1997), especially part Two.

35. Franke Wilmer, *The Indigenous Voice in World Politics* (Newbury Park, Calif.: Sage Publications, 1993).

36. In the context of conceptualizing the meaning of indigenous people's claims for self-determination, Craig Scott proposes a more relational understanding of the claim. See "Indigenous Self-determination and Decolonization of the International Imagination: A Plea," *Human Rights Quarterly* 18 (1996): 814–20.

37. Anna Yeatman's critique of the idea of independence underlying a contractual view of citizenship is important here; see "Beyond Natural Right: The Conditions for Universal Citizenship," in Yeatman, *Postmodern Revisionings of the Political* (New York: Routledge, 1994), 57–79; "Feminism and Citizenship," in Nick Stevenson, ed., *Cultural Citizenship* (London: Sage, 1998), and "Relational Individualism," manuscript; see also Jennifer Nedelsky, "Relational Autonomy," in *Yale Journal of Law and Feminism* 1:1 (1989); "Law, Boundaries, and the Bounded Self," in Robert Post, ed., *Law and the Order of Culture;* for an application of this feminist revision of autonomy to international relations theory, see Karen Knop,

"Re/Statements: Feminism and State Sovereignty in International Law," *Transnational Law and Contemporary Problems* 3:2 (Fall 1993): 293–344; see also Jean Elshtain, "The Sovereign State," *Notre Dame Law Review* 66 (1991): 1355–84.

38. Philip Pettit, *Republicanism* (Oxford: Oxford University Press, 1997).

39. Ibid., 67.

40. David Held, *Democracy and the Global Order* (Cambridge: Polity Press, 1995), part IV; Held, "Democracy and Globalization," in Daniele Archibugi, David Held, and Martin Kohler, eds., *Re-imagining Political Community: Studies in Cosmopolitan Democracy* (Cambridge: Polity Press, 1998); Pogge, "Cosmopolitanism and Sovereignty" (Tamir, *Liberal Nationalism*, chapter 7; Tamir argues for federated relations among culturally distinct nations; I think it is a mistake to try to separate the political the cultural in this way, but Tamir's discussion of federalism is much in the spirit of the vision I am promoting here). For reflections directed more explicitly at global governance, see Tamir "Who's Afraid of a Global State?" manuscript; Alexander Wendt offers an account of global functional regulation from the point of view of how such regulatory regimes can promote collective identities for problem solving. See "Collective Identity Formation and the International State," *American Political Science Review* 88:2 (June 1994): 384–96; Jordi Borja and Manuel Castells propose institutions of greater local autonomy in the context of more global interaction; see Borja and Castells, *Local and Global: Management of Cities in the Information Age* (United Nations Center for Human Settlements, 1997).

41. See John Gerard Ruggie, "Territoriality and Beyond: Problematizing Modernity in International Relations," *International Organization* 47:1 (Winter 1993): 139–74.

42. A federated relationship between self-determining entities might be interpreted as a way of implementing the relationship between "thin" and "thick" principles that Michael Walzer advocates. See *Thick and Thin: Moral Argument at Home and Abroad* (Notre Dame: Notre Dame University Press, 1994), 63–84.

43. See Thomas Pogge, "Creating Super-National Institutions Democratically: Reflections on the European Union's 'Democratic Deficit,'" *Journal of Political Philosophy* 5:2 (June 1997): 163–82.

44. Richard Falk, "The Global Promise of Social Movements," in *Explorations at the Edge of Time* (Philadelphia: Temple University Press, 1992), 125–59; Ronnie D. Lipschuts, "Reconstructing World Politics: The Emergence of Global Civil Society," *Millennium* 21:3 (1992): 389–420.

6

FALLACIES OF NATIONALISM

RUSSELL HARDIN

To begin, I should note that Iris Young and I are in substantial agreement on the critical account of nationalisms, liberal and otherwise, that she gives.[1] If we have any disagreement on her dissection of liberal nationalism, it is merely one of degree of hostility to it. But our differences here might turn on little more than conceptual clarification. We might not so fully agree on the value of her prescriptions on how to give local communities more autonomy in their lives. I am not sure that doing so generally can even make sense to those who accept her criticisms of liberal nationalism, but if it does, her prescriptions seem to be far from practicable. I wish therefore to present what I think is her critical argument in a very different vocabulary in the hope of clarifying it and, I hope, adding to its forcefulness. I will then close with some limited criticisms of the latter part of her essay. Along the way, I will try to anchor the discussion in relevant facts of actual experiences of demands for group autonomy.

COMPOSING A GROUP

As the French historian Ernest Renan remarked in the nineteenth century, to make their claims seem compelling nationalists misrepresent history. That is bad enough. But they also butcher logic. The conceptual problem with nationalism is that the ideas in it are incoherent. (This is as true of so-called liberal nationalism as of ordinary nationalism.) Fallacies of composition corrupt virtually all discussions of nationalism. It is a fallacy of composition to suppose without argument that a group has the characteristics of an individual member of the group. Of course, a group might have characteristics of its members. For example, a group of blacks or whites could meaningfully be called a black or white group. But certain things we commonly attribute to individuals often cannot be attributed to groups of individuals. Chief among these things for present purposes are will, intention, and values. Furthermore, if we unpack the notions properly, some things we can attribute to individuals can also be attributed to groups of individuals, but the attributions have, in a sense, different content. Chief among such things are interests. There is commonly a meaningful sense in which we can say a group has an interest that is the interest of its members taken individually. Nevertheless, it need not be the interest of any of the members to do what is ostensibly in the group interest that they do. This is, of course, a variant of Mancur Olson's logic of collective action.[2]

We can look at putative groups as defined in one of two distinct ways. First, we can identify a group by legal, economic, social status, or other characteristics that give its members a common interest. For example, American blacks in the era of Jim Crow legal discrimination had a common interest in gaining equal protection and treatment from the law. Call this an *external* definition of the group. Such a definition is often, as in the case of American blacks, imposed, as when a group's members are "segregated and stereotyped by a dominant group."[3] Second, we might identify a group by the self-declarations of its members. Call this an *internal* definition of the group.

While there might often be some vagueness about the inclusive nature of a group defined externally, there must invariably be great vagueness and even conflict over the inclusive nature of a large group defined internally, so much so that we cannot generally expect to speak of a common purpose or will of such a group. Therefore, such claims as Young's that "most groups want recognition as nations" are incoherent.[4] This conclusion is, of course, especially true for any group large enough to be a potential nation. The members of such a group must have enormously varied interests and purposes. Indeed, if they did not, they would

make a very poor nation, because they would not have the complementary capacities that make a society prosper (I will return
to this point below).

Some groups might have both external and internal definitions. For example, a minority language group within a larger nation might well be defined as a group by external agencies on the
fairly clear objective criterion of the language its members speak
as their first and, perhaps for many of them, only language. That
language group's members might also identify themselves as a
group, at least with respect to language issues, which might be
quite pervasive in many aspects of their social and political life.
Much of the literature on nationalism blurs the distinction between external and internal definition of groups, often perhaps
merely because the groups at issue are defined in both ways.

When there is genuinely no conflict of interest even in the
sense of the logic of collective action and also no problem of
defining a group's interests in terms of or as equivalent to the
interests of its members, then the group faces a pure coordination problem. All its members need to do is to act the way they
would want to act anyway so long as others act in tandem with
them to achieve a harmonious outcome for all of them. While
there may have been cases of groups facing such a situation, at
least approximately, there is surely no group anywhere of such
size as to claim status as a nation that could plausibly be characterized so idyllically.

Even if we had no problems of collective action, what undermines the notion of self-determination as a conceptual matter is
the difficulty or impossibility of saying who the relevant self is. If
you and I disagree on the self-definition of our group, whose definition is determinate? Consider the contests for the legal right
to define who is a Jew in Israel, what counts as authentic black
culture in the United States, or who speaks for Islam. There is no
agreement there because there is no self there. To assert a "right"
or even a political claim to self-determination in these cases is
therefore meaningless. Hence, Young's recommendation that we
rethink the concept of self-determination "along lines of autonomy and participation, rather than exclusion" is beside the
point.[5] Careful rethinking is death to the concept (I will return
to this point).

REASONS FOR GROUP AUTONOMY

Language groups often have a special place in the ranks of culturally defined groups in that their distinctive problem is restricted capacity to use the language of daily politics on which very much of their political representation and success might turn.[6] Their issue is not merely another interest, such as an interest in lower tariffs or in welfare programs but, rather, the capacity even to raise other issues or to participate fully in, especially, democratic life and politics.

One might say that a group has interests in merely being autonomous in order to express itself, or to give its members validation in some sense, or to protect its racial or other purity. I will generally treat only those groups that seek national status or other forms of political recognition or autonomy for one of two kinds of reason: either (1) they wish to satisfy the interests that their members have in the ordinary kinds of government policies that more or less all people have interests in or (2), as in the case of some linguistic minorities, they seek the capacity to participate reasonably fully in politics. The desire some might have to impose their religious views on others or to purge their societies of various ethnic, racial, or religious groups is not at issue here.

Reasons for incapacity to participate fully in politics might include not only linguistic incapacity but also exclusion from participation because of racial prejudice, lack of franchise, or even economic distress. Former colonial peoples have often sought autonomy because of their lack of political rights to participate in their own governance. Racial minorities have sought autonomy in order to escape their status as second-class citizens or even noncitizens. Peoples in the second category typically have a grievance that they are also *therefore* in the first category. Because their participation is hampered, their interests are relatively slighted by their governments. Although I will not specifically defend this claim here, I think that the only morally compelling cases for national autonomy are in this second category, and a very large fraction of these have been former colonial outposts.

In this brief essay, I am primarily concerned with groups whose members define themselves as a group, that is, with groups that are internally defined. This is, of course, the way liberal nationalists conceive their national groups. Among such groups, I will give special moral attention to groups that are also externally defined to their detriment, as the Jim Crow laws and practices defined American blacks to their detriment. When some members of a group demand autonomy and even separate nationhood, the central question to ask is, Why these interests? Surprisingly little—almost none—of the debate over various ethnic movements provides answers to this seemingly central question. This question is central because groups defined by any criterion overlap manifold groups defined by other criteria. You and I may be in the same group as defined by language but in different groups as defined by economic interests, religion, cultural values, and on and on and on.

The concern is compounded by the fact that, for many members of any potential national group, other interests clearly do seem, in their own views, to trump national autonomy. This may be because they expect the autonomous nation to be led into policies hostile to certain of their interests. The recent referendum in Wales on partial autonomy—devolution of political authority to a separate Welsh assembly—carried by the whisper-thin margin of 50.3 percent to 49.7 percent in an election in which only 51.3 percent of the electorate bothered to vote at all. An earlier referendum in 1979 went four to one against autonomy from the United Kingdom. Naturally, the split in the voting has very much to do with interests. The counties of Wales that border on Great Britain, where most people are either English-born or work in England, voted very heavily against devolution. Three more rural counties in which Welsh is spoken voted strongly for devolution—Gwynedd, Cardiganshire, and Carmarthenshire all voted nearly or more than 60 percent for devolution. Most of the opposing counties voted by similar margins against. In areas hit by the permanent recession of coal mining, where Welsh is not spoken at home but where *Welsh identification* is common, the vote was also for devolution.[7]

The disparity between the overall figures and the county-level figures in Wales is virtually an arithmetic inference from a typical statistical distribution. In going from smaller to larger samples, we commonly expect to see regression to the mean. That is, as the sample grows, its average member approaches the size or characteristics of the average member of the overall population from which the sample is drawn. Hence, where there is division of opinion on group autonomy—which is essentially to say that there is division between those who see themselves as members of the group and those who do not or between those who want to be governed by the group and those who do not—the division will be more, even much more extreme at local levels. If some principle of self-determination based on individual self-definitions says that the larger population should have autonomy, it will commonly say that some local groups should have even greater claim to autonomy from that larger population.

Other recent referendums have been similarly close overall and not at all close in localities. In Quebec, the votes are also regional, with substantial majorities in areas bordering on Ontario and in Montreal hostile to autonomy and the more rural French-speaking areas strongly in favor. According to Prime Minister Jean Chrétien, "Those Quebeckers who are most fearful of anglophones tend to live in regions where they probably haven't ever met one."[8] The real butt of their hostility might simply be the grand urban center of Montreal, which is not merely in large part anglophone but is also urbane.[9] Aboriginal peoples in the north of Quebec also are hostile to separation. Canadian politics is currently torn over the issue of just what the boundaries of an autonomous Quebec should be, with separatists insisting on the current boundaries of the province and federalists insisting, either maliciously or ironically, on local self-determination.[10]

In the face of such results, any claim that there is a trumping interest in national autonomy in most contexts is farcical. There typically are overlaid interests that are in conflict on precisely the issue of group definition. No definition trumps because many will lose no matter what national arrangements are made. We could construct nations to map the self-definitions of their citizens, with overlapping geographic regions, as though Jerusalem should be the model for other societies. It is hard to believe that such a scheme would trump other interests for any but a tiny minority of people in any actual polity.

If, say, the Welsh devolution had been subjected to a more complicated voting procedure that took all of this into account, the result might have been dramatically different. For example, voters might decide whether their region gains autonomy *only if* other regions also want it or *even if* that means that other regions do not join them in an autonomous government. And, on the other side, they might vote whether not to join an autonomous Wales even if other regions do. If only about half of Welsh counties are to become autonomous, perhaps majorities in all counties would prefer not to become autonomous. One can imagine that the counties contiguous to England would opt out of an autonomous Wales and that, if this happened, the residents of the other counties would doubt the wisdom of carving off only their part of Wales as autonomous. The prior decision on how the voting is to be done may therefore determine the outcome. Any claim that the outcome is simply evidence of group identification and group will must therefore be suspect. If the choice for Quebecker separatists is to hive off northern Quebec and the western regions contiguous to Ontario and to make an island enclave of Canadian Montreal, would they still want autonomy?

Composing a Nation from a Group of Individuals

For contemporary separatist movements, especially in Europe, the urgent question for us to ask and answer is why some of our interests might justifiably trump all the others in our self-definition as a group. The answer to that question almost surely turns on peculiarities of psychology, especially of social and group psychology, rather than on the inherent rightness or justice of the claim for priority of one self-definition over the others. This issue underlies one of the two large branches of social choice theory, the branch that was started by Kenneth Arrow's demonstration of his impossibility theorem. It is telling for present discussion that Arrow came to his theorem when he was challenged to show that a nation could have the character of a person because it would somehow represent the interests of its citizens taken in the aggregate.[11]

What Arrow showed, of course, was the contrary. His demonstration has fed a large and expansive literature in political science but it has, oddly, been almost entirely ignored in the branch of political science, international relations, to which it was first addressed. In the face of Arrow's result, the continuing effort of realist theorists in international relations to impute an interest to the nation as such is a remarkable flimflam. Hans Morgenthau's peremptory claim is that nations have an interest in aggrandizing their power.[12] It evidently does not matter for this thesis that the citizens of a nation need share no such interest. But there is nevertheless some warrant for concluding in favor of power as a national interest on the ground that, if the people could agree on certain things, such as national defense, relevant power would help them to achieve that goal. There is no such minimally compelling warrant for concluding in favor of mere national autonomy as the self-evident interest of a group of people.

The problem of a group identity or, as we should prefer to say, a group identification is an analog of Arrow's problem. Arrow queried whether the aggregation of individual welfares could be represented, *in the same terms*, as a group welfare. He showed that the quick inference from a claim that we can impute welfare to individuals to a claim that we can impute the same kind of welfare to a group of individuals is commonly a fallacy of composition. It might be true of some conception of welfare that we could do this, but we must show this to be true. Arrow imposed certain constraints that seemed reasonable enough and found that, under those constraints, individual welfares do not compose into group welfare no matter how welfare is conceived. If we accept Arrow's conditions, then we must conclude that the idea of group welfare as a generalization of individual welfare is incoherent. This is, of course, a conceptual and not merely an empirical claim.

Against his general conclusion, Arrow's conditions themselves may be seen to rule out certain conceptions of welfare. This is most obviously true for the one conception that he was attempting to avoid: straight additive utility, additive across individuals. In keeping with the ordinal revolution that was remaking economics in his time, Arrow intentionally designed his theorem to deal with conceptions of welfare that do not allow for such interpersonal comparisons and trade-offs. This particular exclusion from our consideration, however, should not bother anyone concerned with visions of group identification, because those visions typically presume a coherently shared identification rather than a summing of interests. Indeed, the whole point of most claims for group autonomy and self-determination is that groups have values that cannot simply be subsumed in some larger system of summed or compromised values. Hence, Arrow's theorem is more devastating for those who push for group autonomy than for many ordinary democrats who think a polity must and can make trade-offs across groups and individuals.

In general, I wish here to speak of interests—conceived as resources or capacities rather than as ends—rather than of welfare. It is an analog of Arrow's theorem that individual interests do not compose group interests *if the individuals want resources for their own particular welfare reasons.* But in either case, whether our concern is with welfare directly or with interests and only indirectly with welfare, it should be noted that the concept is capable of encompassing concern with manifold values, so that the focus of the discussion is not exclusively on economic concerns.

Addressing interests rather than welfare has the advantage that it does not so readily occur to us to suppose people are mistaken about their interests in the way that we seem often to suppose people are mistaken about their welfare because we think, perhaps, that we understand their psychology better than they do. There is a German adage that, sometimes, people have to be forced to their happiness. They do not often have to be forced to give attention to their interests. Clearly, it is generally against anyone's interests to suffer ill health or starvation, to lack shelter, to be illiterate, to lose substantial sums of money, and so forth. It is, of course, against their interests because such losses impair their welfare. But we need not have a uniform or ready answer to the question what a particular person's welfare is to be reasonably confident about this judgment of anyone's interests.

When, however, we focus on interests, we immediately see that the problem in composing individual interests into group interests is partially like that of the logic of collective action. The group interest conflicts with individual interest in its provision. Let us simplify for a moment and suppose that all our resources are monetary, so that we could readily aggregate our individual resources into group resources. But now the group must decide how to allocate its resources for various consumptions. In general, there may be some central allocations for essentially collective goods that have great value to each of us and that could not as efficiently be provided by us individually, so that all of us will be better off if we have the collective allocations. Of course, although I might benefit from all of the collective allocations we make, I would benefit even more from making my own allocations while all others make the collective allocations. And the same is true for everyone else in the group. We might, however, be able to vote collectively in favor of making certain collective allocations on the condition that all contribute to their costs. *A very large part of the apparent argument for national autonomy seems to be an analog of this general claim: that the individuals of a group require collective allocations of some kind to make the lives of all of them better in some sense.*

But this is not the end of the story of our interests in having our own government. Once we get a government in place, it has causal effects that need not be related to the original impetus for group autonomy. This is one of the inescapable facts of politics, that there are external effects of empowering a government. Suppose we wish to empower our government to impose draconian measures that would be in our interest. For example, suppose we want much greater equality, successful prosecution of national defense, or dramatic economic development, and we put our government in charge of these programs. That government must have substantial powers. Unfortunately, those powers cannot generally be designed in such a way as to restrict their use to the single purpose for which we have given them to our government. In particular, they can be used to suppress many of us for various reasons. Many of the opponents of devolution in Wales and of separation in Quebec oppose what the new autonomous governments would do *beyond merely being autonomous.* After all, those governments are likely to be led by the most hardened and intransigent advocates of autonomy, the people who have built their political careers on the issue. Once in power, these separatists might reasonably be expected to neglect or actively oppose the interests of those not strongly in favor of the separatist goal. Their occasional public statements and the actions of their followers understandably give antiseparatists a chill.[13]

The argument for group autonomy is often framed as though it were merely an analog of the concern for individual autonomy. It is nothing of the sort. Even if we suppose that the self is quite divided and multiply directed, it is still typically coherent to speak of the interests of the self in a way that often makes no sense for a group. It is also supposed that individual autonomy depends on group autonomy. There may be causal links for the latter claim. But neither claim is conceptually correct. If I am personally autonomous, then I control the allocation of my own resources, including my own share of our joint resources. Now, as an individual member of our group, I am likely to come into conflict with others in deciding how to allocate our joint resources. Indeed, I may even conceive the distinction between my own private resources and what counts as our joint resources as meaningless, so that I have a substantial claim on a share of all of our resources.[14] My personal autonomy is restricted by the group's power if it has autonomous power. The claim that political autonomy is particularly moral or just in such cases is fatuous. It is merely political.

SELF-DETERMINATION: A BIT OF HISTORY

In its twentieth-century variant, the issue of so-called self-determination of peoples was raised by President Woodrow Wilson. It is noteworthy that he did so in a racist, elitist era and arguably in keeping with the racist values of his time.[15] Aspects of his concern might have been shared by leaders of many nations with respect to their domestic minorities, whom they might have wanted to exclude from their polities, as the United States partially excluded blacks. (Indeed, Wilson increased the exclusion on his own personal authority when he imposed Jim Crow on the Federal District of Columbia and on the armed forces. One might therefore suggest that his own values on race were more backward than those of most of his own fellow citizens.) But with respect to their colonial populations, whom they had no intention of including politically anyway, they were hostile to Wilson's vision. And of course, Wilson's own nation did not give political autonomy to Puerto Rico, Cuba, and the Philippines, which the United States had recently taken from Spain at the end of the Spanish-American War in 1898. And the U.S. Senate, under Republican Party hegemony, soon afterwards denied statehood to

Cuba on essentially racist or ethnic grounds, partly reinforced by anti-Catholic religious sentiments.

Hence, it is a perversity of the twentieth-century ideology of self-determination that it arguably arose from racist sentiments. That this is true does not rule out the possibility that the quest for group autonomy is moral. But it is at least a distasteful part of the past of such quests and, alas, all too often still of current quests—although now the racism is also often on the side of those who seek autonomy.

Earlier, I noted that there are two categories of grounds for a claim for group autonomy, even to the extent of separate nationhood. Of these, groups in the second category of those who lack capacities for political participation have strong moral claims for autonomy. It was generally true of Wilson's proposal for self-determination that it addressed "nations" in this category. Unfortunately, his proposal also went on to define the characteristics of a "nation" that should have autonomy. Those characteristics are what are commonly invoked today by subnational groups, such as Quebecker and Welsh nationalists and perhaps implicitly by proponents of so-called liberal nationalism. The argument of many is, in Young's words, "that a nation is a particular kind of cultural grouping with a unique claim to statehood."[16] What actually gave the colonies to which Wilson's proposal was directed their compelling moral claim was not such characteristics at all but, rather, their subjugation by their colonial masters and the denial of genuine participation in their political fates. Wilson's reframing of the justification of national autonomy has since polluted discussions of the issue.

By a trick of false association, the moral grounding those peoples had has been asserted for subnational groups that do not fit in the second category of grounds for autonomous national status. It was ironic in his own time that Wilson should have shifted the ground from the imposed incapacities of the colonial peoples to their self-defining characteristics because that shift essentially justified subnational groups among the Allied states—including in the United States—in making claims against their own governments. In general, simple characteristics such as common religion, language, ethnicity, and so forth are merely objective facts. As such, they have no moral implications. From an "is" we cannot derive an "ought." What gives a group a moral, and not merely a political claim, is that its treatment is unjust or its position is unfair in the larger context of politics over interests.

VARIANT NATIONALISMS

The discussion to this point is directed at nationalism without any differentiation into varieties of nationalism. In recent times there have been many advocates, including Will Kymlicka, David Miller, and Yael Tamir, of a vision of civic or liberal nationalism. They distinguish it as a good kind of nationalism in opposition to, for example, ethnic nationalism.[17] It is to the claims for such nationalism that Young addresses her chapter. The central objective claim of the liberal nationalists is that people just do identify with one another as a large, often national group. For example, Miller discusses "the potency of nationality as a source of personal identity."[18] Their normative claim is that people therefore suppose they have a special relationship with their fellow national citizens that in some respects gives a moral trump to their claims over the claims of anyone outside or not a citizen of their nation. The normative claim is oddly conventional: What is right for some group of people is what that group's members think is right.

The clear underpinning of both such liberal nationalism and the supposedly less appealing ethnic nationalism is self-identification with a group somehow defined. For the ethnic nationalisms of Nazi Germany, contemporary Serbia and Croatia, and many separatist movements, including those of Quebec and several nations in Europe, what the individual supposedly identifies with is a group in which membership is supposedly objectively defined by certain *individual* characteristics, such as race or ethnicity. In liberal nationalism the individual identifies with other citizens of their particular nation-state. In both cases, obligations are supposed to arise from and to be limited by the self-definition of the group members. The latter is not merely a pragmatic claim, such as a claim that a national government can practicably do more for its citizens than for others. Rather, it is supposed to be a compelling normative claim of prima facie rightness.

Because both liberalisms are founded in identification, both are subject to the standard possibility that they are undercut by the failure of many of the ostensible group members to share in the relevant identification. Hence, to speak of the group as defined by its members' identifications is likely to be a fallacy of composition. This is as true of the nice liberal form of nationalism as of the rude ethnic form of nationalism. Without the relevant identification, the normative claims of the nationalists do not follow—and this is for reasons that are at the core of the very definitions of the nationalist group. Hence, the normative claims do not even follow for the theorists of the variant nationalisms, neither for ethnic nor for liberal nationalism. All of the conceptual arguments against nationalism adduced above therefore apply to both variants of nationalism. All that is left of any claim for either nationalism is politics, not morality.

FUNCTIONAL DIVERSITY

If a modern society is to prosper, it must have extensive division of labor and therefore extensive variation in individual interests and, especially, capacities. This is true not only of the market society for which Adam Smith—and David Hume and others before Smith—argued the point. Socialist and other societies must also have extensive division of labor merely for the reason that specialization enhances productivity. Hence, the general claim is true of virtual necessity if production is to go much beyond subsistence agriculture and cottage production. While individuals have many interests, their interests in their roles in the economy loom especially large in modern societies. Ethnic, linguistic, religious, and other interests might sometimes be thought by at least some members of a particular group to trump such economic interests. Or, alternatively, some might suppose the economic interests could be handled well enough by a smaller, ethnically defined state, while only such a state could handle the ethnic interests of the group.

Strangely, in recent years ethnic divisions that were long dormant in western Europe have come back into political play. Part of the reason for the renewal of ethnic identification and conflict might simply be that the European economies are being reconstructed in some respects into a more or less single gigantic economy run by the European Union. Hence, the need for economic diversity and for the integration of many economic interests into a more productive whole is handled by the new suprastate. This both makes the states that are members of the union less important economically and also therefore politically weakens those states. On both counts, local groups are enabled to assert themselves at lessened cost and for much more trivial reasons than could have motivated localistic politics in the recent past.

Often one might suppose that it is localist political leaders who spark the new assertiveness and that they do so for career reasons rather than merely out of commitment to the ethnic values of their groups. But, of course, this is merely politics as usual. That it is possible to succeed with such politics is the interesting fact of the recent changes. This is an especially difficult issue if, as discussed so far, the interests of a potential national polity are diverse and are mostly not related to whether the polity has the status of an autonomous nation. Clearly, the urge for national autonomy cannot seriously be viewed as a spontaneous popular movement that somehow drowns out all other concerns of the time.

So what is the role of leaders in mobilizing such movements? Arguably, they essentially frame the issue and bring attention to it to the general exclusion of many other issues. For such framing, there need not be any actual event or change in status to justify initiation of a claim to autonomy. For example, one might suppose the sudden contemporary rise of the movement to get the U.S. government to sanction nations that sponsor so-called persecution of Christians is the result almost entirely of successful framing by a small number of professional framers in Washington rather than the result of any actual change in the extent of the supposed problem.[19] In many of the nationalist and ethnic and religious purification movements of our time, the issue gets framed at the level of the most scurrilous common denominator.

Although specific changes in the nature of the claim for autonomy need not be the cause of the sudden rise of a political movement, changes of relevant material matters might enable a leader successfully to reframe an issue to get it into central place on the political agenda. As noted, for example, this might be an important part of the reason for the newfound energy of the subnational movements in Europe after the successes of the European Union in taking governance of various economic matters away from the nations that compose the union. If nations do not govern the economy, which is one of the most important places for the requirement and exercise of functional diversity, they can more safely—that is, at lower cost—be put to other uses, such as narrowed nationalism.

Albert O. Hirschman has argued that the rise of market economic thinking from Bernard Mandeville to Adam Smith was partly a moral urge to preempt the use of government to enforce values of various kinds, including, disastrously, values of nepotism and cronyism in the awarding of monopolies over parts of the economy.[20] The beauty of the focus on self-interest was to wreck the focus on familial and party interests in the running of the economy. When the ayatollahs rail against godless capitalism and the values of American society, they are de facto agreeing with Hirschman's thesis. They actively wish to impose values other than individual prosperity and autonomy on their citizens, and they recognize that material concerns tend to soften or displace concern with such values. The less virulent nationalists of local groups in Europe are partially saved by the supranational reorganization of their economies from having to trade off individual prosperity and autonomy against subnational autonomy.

INTERGENERATIONAL AUTONOMY

Very briefly, I wish to note a corollary issue in the quest for group autonomy. If that quest were to affect only those who follow it, even if it were to affect only them and their compatriots from whom they wish to separate, it might have a kind of acceptable moral status. It would not be morally commendable or laudable. But it might at least be morally okay in something like the way John Stuart Mill supposed individuals should be allowed to harm themselves or to be frivolous with their lives if that is what they wish to do. In part it is okay because the alternative of coercing them to do otherwise is likely to be more odious than letting them choose for themselves. Of course, we do not hold this view with respect to children, and Mill himself did not hold it with respect to colonial peoples, such as the people of India, whom he evidently considered to be like children in their incapacity to judge for themselves.

But this is not the whole story of most drives for group autonomy. Suppose that, practicably, a contemporary subnational group's demands for autonomy could be addressed only by a separate state. Then there are likely to be very complex intergenerational issues that define, yet again, a fallacy of composition in speaking of the group as having an interest. Our generation may gain some kind of autonomy, but our children's and grandchildren's generations may actually lose personal autonomy thereby. For example, if the autonomy our generation seeks is the political use of its minor language, our group autonomy may depend in the short run on the education of our own children in that language as their first and, for practical purposes, perhaps only language. Lest this seem a trivial concern, it should be noted that there are thousands of separate languages spoken in the world, including very many that have at most a few hundred speakers and no serious literature of any kind in any field.[21]

Nationhood for all language groups would be a massive, dreadful tragedy in our world. It would give the English-, Chinese-, and Spanish-speaking communities huge advantages over virtually all others. If political empowerment in many of the extant language communities depends on using other languages, the current generation will be poorly empowered. Suppose we are the few thousand speakers of language X. If we gain empowerment by having a government and nation in our own language, our children and grandchildren will lose—arguably, they will lose more than our present generation gains. The choices of these future generations in the world our generation creates for them will be far more limited than they might otherwise have been. That is to say, *we constrict their autonomy*, and we do that in the name of autonomy. Therefore, when seen in its full range of implications, our claim for autonomy is itself a violation of the autonomy of our own progeny. For simple causal reasons, including intergenerational effects, the very notion of group autonomy in our world is often internally contradictory.

Rethinking Self-Determination

Young proposes that we rethink self-determination to fit it to a world in which sovereign states do not govern the relations of self-defined groups. In this proposal, there are two big points that seem to run counter to her arguments against liberal nationalism. First, she objects to the territorially based version of sovereignty that dominates our world and most of our theory. She says such a system *supposes* "a coincidence of one distinct people for each state."[22] This claim is not plausible. Theorists of the territorial version of sovereignty do not and cannot assume anything of the sort in our actual world, in which the number of states is radically smaller than the number of linguistic communities or ethnic communities. Some states, such as, notably, the United States and France, have attempted to meld diverse groups into a single national citizenry with a common language. But even more states have lived with great diversity—perhaps the most extreme instance is India. Young's resolution of this problem is to split up government functions across various levels, leaving some issues to be handled by group-level institutions.

She goes on to say that "a people has the prima facie right to set its own governance procedures and make its own decisions about its activities, without interference from others."[23] Unfortunately, this claim is vitiated by its implicit fallacy of composition. Indeed, the very idea of a particular right may be one that cannot be applied to *both a group and its members individually*. To assert the collective right of self-determination is radically too glib to be of help to us in redesigning the world, if we wish to be so bold. How is a people's assertion of its will to be ascertained? Did the people of Uganda will their nondomination by foreign powers in the days of Idi Amin? And if a people is to "define [its own] membership rules," why should we not expect many (most?) groups to be exclusive or exclusionary to an even worse degree than might be allowed by the liberal nationalists whom Young criticizes, partly on this ground?

Second, Young wishes to honor difference with public and *political* recognition. This cannot sensibly be unpacked in a way that fits most of Young's criticisms of liberal nationalism. For example, if, in my view, I am a member of some clearly defined group, how do I or my fellow group members need or even benefit from public and political recognition?—unless, of course, the political recognition is merely the recognition that every citizen should have. Do Catholics *as such* in, say, Italy, which is overwhelmingly Catholic, the United States, which is substantially Catholic, or Japan, which has very few Catholics, need some special recognition from government? If our groups are valuable to us, as Young and many communitarians keep saying they are—even to the point of being definitive of us—can they not make it on their own without state support? Should the state step in to enforce our group norms on us? Should our state be antipaternalist with respect to individuals but paternalist with respect to groups? For example, should the state penalize one of us for violating our religious norms or enforce our norms on our young in order to make sure our group has a membership in the next generation? Just what is it that groups should get from states? Surely they should get no more and no less than what the aggregation of their members as individuals should get, that is, all of the standard legal and political protections in various lists of political rights. Why should merely being a member of a group, somehow self-defined by value or cultural commitments, change a person's political rights or expectations?

I apologize for resorting to questions rather than to argument. But the problem here is that the claims of the liberal nationalists and of Young herself on behalf of groups are far too unspecific to argue against them. Group autonomy sounds okay, perhaps even lovely, when it is kept unspecific and glib. But it sours quickly when we try to imagine it on the ground. In supposing that the values of groups are worthy of political recognition, presumably these scholars mean something like legal "protection" of their values. If a group is to have some kind of protection from the state, either that is a protection of its members against impositions that any other individual should also be protected against or it is a protection against its own members' derelictions with respect to their group's demands—or, and this is symptomatic, as these scholars would prefer to say, the group's values.

In their actual working, protections of the group against its own members' derelictions are penalties against the individual members. Hence, group rights typically entail violation of individual rights. They are likely to be analogs of the notorious decision in the case of *Wisconsin v. Yoder et al.*, which allows parents to deny education to their children beyond age fourteen—this in a larger society in which education to age sixteen is required and in which a mere eighth grade education is virtually a disqualification from most employments and thus a form of entrapment in the Amish community.[24] If this is what groups should be getting from government, individuals should cry shame against their government. Again, as noted earlier, some groups might need special attention from the state if they have *liabilities that inhibit their political participation.* This might be true of minority language groups. But to go beyond this seems to violate Young's powerful arguments against liberal nationalism (she acknowledges that readers might think this[25]).

Young evidently would exclude some group values from even the kind of protection offered by *Yoder* on the ground that they are exclusionary. For example, many whites may have wanted to continue to have a society of their own in the South during the 1960s and thereafter. If the protection of the value of segregation had been left to the local levels that Young approves, they could have maintained this value, perhaps indefinitely. But the national government of the United States would not protect this value for them by allowing them to maintain segregation in schools and other places.[26]

The decision in *Brown v. Board of Education* that ended legal segregation in public schools did more or less the opposite of what *Yoder* did. It *ended* local control. *Yoder* devolved control to the local group. The Jim Crow values of the South are values that, of course, Young opposes in principle because they are exclusionary. The saving grace of *Yoder* is that it stopped a bit short of state enforcement. Is what the groups Kymlicka, Young, and others want for their members merely freedom from state impositions? Or do they want active intervention by government, whether national or local? (If the intervention is to be by local authorities, as in some of Kymlicka's societies, the relevant local societies will have to be empowered—in which case they will be empowered to do far more than Kymlicka intends. They will be empowered to do things that Kymlicka's arguments do not justify, that, indeed, would violate these arguments.) Or do they want at least the power locally to manage their own impositions on their members, some of whom might be recalcitrant?

This is the main irritant in the prescriptions of liberal nationalism and of local autonomy in defense of group values. *If a group needs help from a state to live its purported values, then its members evidently do not hold those values dearly enough to live them.* That is, the claim that those are the group's values either is, in fact, (1) a fallacy of composition, or is (2) not a moral claim at all but is a political assertion on the part of some members of the community to control or impose on other members of the community.

John Dewey thought we needed a new version of liberalism to combat the power of institutions over individuals.[27] He advocated social and institutional liberalism to liberate people from the domination of social norms and large private institutions, much as traditional political and economic liberalisms liberated people from the control of government. Of course, breaking the hold of a social norm may mean loosening the hold of a particular community on its members. For example, undercutting destructive religious norms is likely to undercut ties to a religious community and even to create conflict within such a community, in either case causing a decline in group cohesion.

Advocates of liberal nationalism and of local autonomy want, on the contrary, to grant institutions such powers specifically on behalf of supposed group values. Dewey surely had the better understanding of what such programs would mean. Since *Yoder* was about children, it did not require state coercion to entrap them in their culture while they were children. Rather, *Yoder* merely authorized the Amish community de facto to do this even beyond the age of childhood. Typically, the state cannot give such power to a local institution because groups have no available devices actually to enforce their values on their children once the children reach adulthood. Blocking education may not be the only way to entrap people past childhood, but it is probably a very effective way, and the Supreme Court's rationale for its decision actually acknowledged this purpose.[28]

Admittedly, there may be a problem in sustaining some values without legal enforcement. For example, lifetime monogamy in marriage and in sexual practice evidently cannot be sustained in our liberal world except by legal fiction and draconian imposition. But that sounds like one of the best of reasons for the state to keep its hands off the matter.

Concluding Remarks

The interests that all members of some putative group literally have in common and that are distinctive to the group will generally be quite limited except in conditions of severe crisis or grievous subjugation. It is commonly implausible that such limited interests could be of sufficient import as to require a separate state to address them. They might be poorly addressed by the state or states in which the group lives—but many of us have interests that are poorly addressed by our states. Why should the particular forum for addressing such interests be a separate state for that group alone? In the face of diverse interests and values in any substantial group, no matter how defined, the program of group autonomy threatens to be an analog of the economic mercantilism against which Smith railed in the Great Britain of his time. Under the system of mercantilism, the king gave monopoly patents to various entrepreneurs to produce various goods and services. The ideology of mercantilism was roughly the rationale of the modern patent system. Entrepreneurs supposedly had to be guaranteed monopoly rights in order to justify their investment in productive facilities and talents. The actual working of the system was to reward associates of the king and, unfortunately, to block the competition that would have enhanced the lives of most people by leading to lower prices and better goods and services. In the contemporary system of group autonomy, certain people who claim grouphood are given a local monopoly over the establishment of values. Their monopoly can be as destructive to the interests of particular individuals as any of the king's patents was. The ayatollahs have understood this inference better than have the liberal nationalists and communitarians of our academies.

Among the many fallacies of composition that litter analyses in political science, beginning from Aristotle at the latest, and that corrode our daily understanding in manifold ways, that of nationalism and ethnic group identity has surely been the most destructive of lives in our time, indeed, in our century. To assert national identity or to argue for group autonomy would be, if this claim were not itself a fallacy of composition, a case of group romanticism. People can strive all they want for the incoherent. They cannot achieve it on the ground. It can seem to exist only in their convoluted thoughts. This is actually a more devastating point for liberal than for ethnic nationalists. It seems likely that a rabidly illiberal, exclusionary group could come far closer to meeting the test of composition without fallacy than that a genuinely liberal society could.

The mere fact that a group's members define their group to value X does not make X valuable or good in any sense that the state should honor. Hence, there is no reason, at least no moral reason, that others or states should honor the convoluted visions of either kind of nationalist by helping in the forlorn attempt to put them into practice. We may be forced politically into stepping aside in the face of such attempts. But we owe groups that make such attempts nothing. And we may even owe others, including future generations, some duty to oppose the goals of such groups. Either way, nationalism is generally a corrupt and corrupting idea. Liberal nationalism is too good to be true, and ordinary nationalism is too true to be good.

NOTES

1. Iris Marion Young, "Self-Determination and Global Democracy: A Critique of Liberal Nationalism," this volume, chapter 5.

2. Mancur Olson, Jr., *The Logic of Collective Action* (Cambridge: Harvard University Press, 1965); see also Russell Hardin, *Collective Action* (Baltimore: Johns Hopkins University Press for Resources for the Future, 1982), chapters 1 and 2.

3. Young, "Self-Determination and Global Democracy," 147.

4. Ibid., 155.

5. Ibid., 172.

6. Russell Hardin, "Communities and Development: Autarkic Social Groups and the Economy," in Mancur Olson, Jr., ed., *A Not-so-Dismal Science* (Oxford: Oxford University Press, 2000), 206–227.

7. *Economist*, 27 September 1997, 62.

8. Mordecai Richler, "O Quebec," *New Yorker* (30 May 1994): 56.

9. The conflict in former Yugoslavia was also partly antiurban on the

part of mostly rural Serbs. See further, Russell Hardin, *One for All: The Logic of Group Conflict* (Princeton: Princeton University Press, 1995), chapter 6.

10. See the letter of Stéphane Dion, Canadian federal minister of intergovernmental affairs, to Quebec Premier Lucien Bouchard, *Toronto Globe and Mail*, 12 August 1997, A17. Dion, a francophone and former academic who has written in favor of francophone identity, wrote, "Neither you nor I nor anyone else can predict that the borders of an independent Quebec would be those now guaranteed by the Canadian Constitution." The tough line is part of the Canadian government's so-called Plan B.

11. For the lovely story, see Kenneth J. Arrow, *Collected Papers*, vol. 1: *Social Choice and Justice* (Cambridge: Harvard University Press, 1983), 1–4.

12. Hans Morgenthau, *Politics Among Nations: The Struggle for Power and Peace*, 5th ed. (New York: Knopf, 1978).

13. North American press coverage of harsh Quebecker sentiments has been extensive. See, for example, *New York Times*, 5 November 1995, 1.10 and 20 October 1996, 4.4.

14. Without much exaggeration, this could be said to be the central point of the theory of John Rawls, *A Theory of Justice* (Cambridge: Harvard University Press, 1971).

15. For a rich discussion, see Daniel Patrick Moynihan, *Pandaemonium: Ethnicity in International Politics* (Oxford: Oxford University Press, 1993), 63–106.

16. Young, "Self-Determination and Global Democracy," 147.

17. Will Kymlicka, *Multicultural Citizenship* (Oxford: Oxford University Press, 1995); David Miller, *On Nationality* (Oxford: Oxford University Press, 1995); Yael Tamir, *Liberal Nationalism* (Princeton: Princeton University Press, 1993). For discussion, see the "Special Issue: Nationalism," *Critical Review* 10 (Spring 1996).

18. Miller, *On Nationality*, 11.

19. Jeffrey Goldberg, "Washington Discovers Christian Persecution," *New York Times Magazine* (21 December 1997): 46ff.

20. Albert O. Hirschman, *The Passions and the Interests: Political Arguments for Capitalism before Its Triumph* (Princeton, NJ: Princeton University Press, 1977).

21. See further, Hardin, *One for All*, 67–68, 219.

22. Young, "Self-Determination and Global Democracy," 170.

23. Ibid., 172.

24. *Wisconsin v. Yoder et al.*, 406 U.S. 205–49. See further discussion in Hardin, *One for All*, chapter 7.

25. Young, "Self-Determination and Global Democracy," 147.

26. Among the other places, housing was a major arena of segregation, as in the covenanted cities and towns of the North. For example,
Levittown, on New York's Long Island, barred blacks and other non-Caucasians from living in its homes and required owners to include a
covenant barring sale to non-Caucasians. Such covenants were enforceable in courts until they were declared unconstitutional by the U.S.
Supreme Court in 1948, although the practice of refusing to sell to
blacks has evidently continued. To this day, Levittown's county, Nassau,
is by one measure the most segregated suburban county in the United
States. *New York Times*, 28 December 1997, 1.23 and 26.

27. John Dewey, *Liberalism and Social Action*, in *Later Works of Dewey,
1925–1953*, vol. 11 (Carbondale: Southern Illinois University Press, 1987
[1935]). For further discussion, see Russell Hardin, *Liberalism, Constitutionalism, and Democracy* (Oxford: Oxford University Press, 1999),
appendix.

28. *Wisconsin v. Yoder*, 222–34.

7

BETWEEN PHILOSOPHY AND LAW: SOVEREIGNTY AND THE DESIGN OF DEMOCRATIC INSTITUTIONS

ROBERT POST

A major thesis of Iris Marion Young's stimulating paper is that "a principle of state sovereignty lacks moral legitimacy,"[1] and that we ought therefore to aspire toward a "global governance system"[2] which supersedes independent nation-states and devolves powers to "self-determining peoples."[3] In these brief remarks I shall discuss this thesis, which I find deeply unconvincing. I shall argue, first, that Young's thesis rests upon an inadequate understanding of the nature of sovereignty, which is important to get right in order to comprehend the design of democratic institutions. I shall argue, second, that Young's thesis derives from a partial and misleading perspective on issues of institutional design, a perspective often associated with philosophical, as distinct from legal, treatments of such issues.

I.

Young's attack on "claims of state sovereignty"[4] advances on several distinct fronts. In this section of my remarks, I shall discuss Young's argument that state sovereignty necessarily implies the impossible notion that a sovereign state possesses a kind of "final authority," so that "no other state and no transnational body has the authority to interfere with its actions and policies."[5] In the next section of these remarks, I shall address two additional moral arguments against state sovereignty proposed by Young, which turn on the increasing entanglement of modern states in obligations of international and domestic justice.

Young's most fundamental objection to the concept of the "independent sovereign state"[6] is that it embodies a "principle of nonintervention," such that a sovereign state possesses "final authority" over its "territory and people, and no outside state or agent has legitimate claim to interfere with the decisions and actions of that authority."[7] Young apparently believes that sovereign rights must be broadly characterized in this fashion because the concept of sovereignty flows from the principle of "freedom as noninterference."[8] Young writes as though this principle uniquely justifies the right of sovereign states to prevent others from intruding upon their internal affairs. But it would strange indeed if as universal and as fundamental a concept as sovereignty should in the end turn on a particular and controversial account of freedom.

Although Young's characterization of the attributes of sovereignty certainly has respectable warrant,[9] it is inaccurate, as even Young herself appears to concede. No contemporary state has the kind of sovereignty that Young describes. This suggests that Young's theoretical explanation of sovereignty might also be deficient. In fact, any assessment of the concept of sovereignty, as it currently exists, requires us first to develop an alternative explanation of the concept that is more descriptively precise and theoretically convincing.

A more plausible account is that the concept of sovereignty derives from the fundamental question of how states assume the status of collective agents. This status is assumed whenever we speak of states as having the capacity to speak, act, promise, and so forth. The status is assumed whenever we claim that states should be accorded moral liberties characteristic of persons, like freedom. The very concept of the state, in short, presupposes that it is a special kind of agent, an agent composed of a collection of persons.

Young certainly does not disagree that groups of persons can acquire collective agency. In fact, she explicitly invites us to imagine an international order in which collectivities (like "states"[10] or "peoples"[11]) enjoy relationships of "relational autonomy"[12] that are characterized by the kind of freedom that signifies "non-domination."[13] This vision of the international order presupposes that groups of persons have established some form of collective agency, for Young understands relational autonomy as promoting "the capacity of agents to pursue their own ends in the context of relationships in which others may do the same,"[14] and she understands "freedom as nondomination" as safeguarding "an agent's choice situation" from improper constriction.[15]

The legal concept of sovereignty underwrites the capacity of groups of persons to forge this kind of collective agency. The concept is used to safeguard the processes by which collective agency is constructed. In the words of one commentator, "Sovereignty's value lies in the fact that it creates a legal space in which a community can negotiate, construct, and protect a collective identity. Sovereignty, simply speaking, permits the expression of collective difference."[16]

Framed in this way, sovereignty protects whatever processes a group uses to construct its collective agency. I have no theoretical explanation of how this happens in states generally, but I have written elsewhere at some length about how democratic states establish collective agency.[17] In brief, democratic states are organized to achieve collective self-governance, which means that the people in such states aspire to rule themselves. How this happens is quite complex, but suffice it to say that it entails a continuous negotiation between individual and collective self-determination within the medium of a shared public culture. A state's democratic legitimacy depends upon its fidelity to the process of collective will formation inherent in this negotiation, and this legitimacy in turn underwrites a democratic state's capacity to assume collective agency on behalf of its citizens.

Of course within democratic states the "will" of the people is always putative, never determinative or final. Domestic politics consist of a continuous competition for the mantle of speaking "in the name of" the people. From the external perspective of international affairs, however, where foreign peoples and states are excluded from this ongoing process of democratic will formation, the agency of a democratic state presents itself as fixed by whatever mechanisms of distributing power have been democratically and antecedently authorized.

This theoretical and moral account of the agency of democratic states explains why it is said that in democracies "the people are sovereign."[18] The collective agency of a democratic state is supposed to express the popular will of the people. We might thus say that sovereignty within a democratic state is located in the ultimate source of the state's collective agency, in, as Hobbes presciently put it in his definition of sovereignty, the locus of the "Artificial *Soul*" of the state.[19] The democratic sovereignty of the people represents a "final authority" in the sense that no appeal can lie to any other authority in determining the identity of the state.

On this account, sovereignty does not derive from any particular principle of freedom but, instead, from the necessity of attributing collective agency to states. We recognize sovereignty to the extent that we wish to safeguard the creation of a collective agent capable of managing the monopoly of force characteristic of government institutions. We recognize democratic sovereignty to the extent that we wish to safeguard the creation of a collective agent designed to manage the monopoly of force in a way that expresses the popular will of a particular collection of persons. For this reason, the sovereignty of democratic states reflects the value of self-determination. We can override democratic sovereignty only at the price of compromising that value.

It does not follow from this analysis, however, that democratic states cannot be "interfered with," for sovereignty is "final" only in respect to the constitution of collective agency. Thus sovereign democratic states can and are subject to a range of international obligations. These obligations, however, must be of a kind that can justifiably be applied to collective agents. Obligations that can justifiably be imposed on individual agents can often also properly be applied to collective agents. Just as a person can be obligated to keep her promises, so can a democratic state be obligated to keep its contracts and treaty engagements. Just as a person can be required to obey the constraints of domestic law, so can a democratic state be required to obey the constraints of international law. (But because the authority and sources of international law are so obscure, the vast majority of international constraints imposed upon democratic states are conceptualized in terms of a voluntary assumption of obligations.)

In an important passage, Young seeks to describe how she would envision a world without independent sovereign states:

> First, self-determination means a presumption of noninterference. A people has a prima facie right to set its own governance procedures and make its own decisions about its activities, without interference from others. Second, insofar as the activities of a group may adversely affect others or generate conflict, self-determination entails the right of those others to make claims on the group, negotiate the terms of their relationships, and mutually adjust the terms' effects. Third, a world of self-determining peoples thus requires recognized and settled institutions and procedures through which peoples negotiate, adjudicate conflicts, and enforce agreements. Self-determination does not imply independence but, rather, that peoples dwell together within political institutions that minimize domination among peoples.[20]

It is evident from this passage both that Young confounds sovereignty as noninterference with sovereignty as the construction of collective agency, and that she also fails to grasp the full implications of the latter. Contrary to Young's assertion in this passage, "self-determination" most certainly does "imply independence," at least with respect to the construction of the collective agency of a democratic state. That agency is designed to express the popular will of a particular group of persons, and not the popular will of others. Yet this independence is not necessarily inconsistent either with a democratic state's recognition of the rights of third parties or with its participation in international dispute-settlement mechanisms. Just as a person can submit to legal procedures and recognize the just claims of others without necessarily losing her own status as an agent, so also can a democratic state.

In fact, to the extent that Young invites us to imagine a world order that is characterized by relational autonomy and freedom as nondomination, she must *presuppose* the kind of sovereignty that preserves the integrity of the processes by which the collective agency of groups is established. Sovereignty is therefore actually a condition precedent to the kind of international order Young envisions. Her emphasis on international interdependence is best

understood as a way of specifying the moral and practical obligations that ought to bind collective agents, like states.

II.

Once sovereignty is understood in the way I have proposed, it is
clear that Young's two additional arguments against the independent sovereign state must also fail. The first of these arguments is that "globalization makes peoples interdependent and
thereby brings them together under the scope of justice."[21] The
second is that sovereign states "do not sufficiently recognize and
accommodate" the "prima facie rights of self-governance" of "national and cultural minorities."[22]

That the sovereignty of democratically legitimate states reflects the value of collective self-determination has important implications for Young's first argument. We do not generally regard
obligations of justice as inconsistent with the agency of persons;
in fact, we commonly interpret the requirements of justice so as
to make them compatible with that agency. For analogous reasons, we ought to interpret the demands of international justice
so as to render them compatible with the collective agency of
democratic states, and hence with the independent sovereignty
of such states. Even if the demands of international justice were
to prove incompatible with democratic sovereignty, however, we
would at most confront a conflict between the fundamental good
of self-governance and the value of justice, and nothing Young
says authorizes us unambiguously to choose the latter.

A proper understanding of democratic sovereignty also has
important implications for Young's second argument, which rests
on the claim that rights of "national and cultural minorities" to
self-determination tend to be inadequately recognized within
sovereign states. Young's argument may be taken to mean that
particular groups or peoples within specific democratic states are
so dominated that they feel excluded from processes of collective
will formation and hence do not regard the state within which
they happen to reside as democratically legitimate. On its face,
however, this is not an argument against the sovereignty of democratic states as such, but an argument against the democratic legitimacy of particular states. The implication of the argument is

either that democratic legitimacy in such states should be reconstructed or that sovereignty ought to be relocated to the "distinct peoples" who, on Young's account, "have prima facie claims to self-determination."[23] For the "self-determination" of such distinct peoples to have integrity, however, it must itself also be protected by the legal shield of sovereignty.

I should note in passing that Young's notion that distinct peoples have prima facie claims to self-determination seems facially inconsistent with Young's own account of what she calls a "relational rather than substantial social ontology."[24] Young convincingly argues that peoples and groups are matters of degree, that they become distinct "as a function of" their relations to others rather than because of the "essential nature" of their own members, and that therefore there are no "clear conceptual and practical borders that distinguish one group decisively from others and distinguish its members decisively."[25] This argument would seem radically to undermine the notion of "distinct" peoples, and hence to efface any reliable guide as to where "prima facie" rights of self-determination might actually lodge.

In fact, it is precisely because "peoples" and "groups" have such fuzzy boundaries, because individuals so often belong to various overlapping groups and peoples, that most democratic states choose to use essentially political criteria to distinguish those included in the process of constructing collective agency from those who are excluded. These criteria are defined not by reference to standards of group identity, but instead by reference to the shared *political* commitment to self-governance conveyed in the status of citizenship, a status often defined by criteria quite distinct from those of group identity.

Young sometimes seems critical of the very idea of such criteria. She complains that "[s]overeignty entails a clear distinction between inside and outside,"[26] and that any such distinction falsely flattens the complex interdependence of the world. Yet if ultimate decision-making authority in a democratic state lies in its people, some differentiation must be made between those who are included in the democratic polity and those who are excluded. Either a person does or does not have the right to participate in processes of democratic self-definition. Because the sovereign people in a democratic state is authorized to act in the name of the state, we must have criteria for ascertaining exactly who is included within the contours of that "people." To put the matter crudely, we must be able to distinguish those who may vote from those who may not.

The creation of such boundaries can theoretically be avoided in only one way. If self-determination were to be relocated to the global level, so that every person in the world were to participate in the construction of a universal democratic state, the sovereignty of individual democratic states would indeed be rendered theoretically superfluous. Young seems in her essay to advocate some such "a global governance system"[27] that would express "democratic values and institutions."[28]

The concept of world democracy, however, is not inconsistent with the concept of democratic sovereignty. It instead relocates such sovereignty to the people of a world community. The collective agency of that community would assume a final sovereign authority to define its own nature and identity. A world democracy might well choose, as Young seems to advocate, to devolve and decentralize power to more local units.[29] This is what now happens in federal countries like the United States, where the people of the nation have chosen to allocate their sovereignty between a centralized federal government and decentralized states. But this choice expresses, rather than compromises, democratic sovereignty. It designates how a sovereign democratic people have decided to distribute their power.

Although the ideal of world democracy is theoretically unobjectionable, I should note that it suffers from disabling practical objections. Self-governance requires the creation of a public culture within which the negotiation between individual and collective self-determination can occur.[30] It is through the medium of such a culture that citizens come to identify with their states in ways that are necessary to achieve democratic legitimacy.[31] It seems wildly implausible to postulate the existence of any such global public culture within the foreseeable future.

Young's claim that global regulatory bodies need not "be any *more* removed from ordinary citizens than many national regulatory bodies currently are"[32] is simply unresponsive to this point. In successful democratic states national regulatory bodies are responsive to a national democratic public culture that facilitates the formation of a national popular will. Democratic legitimacy is impossible without such a culture, which cannot simply be summoned out of thin air. Democratic public cultures emerge from a shared history, from good luck, from common norms and commitments. Even relatively homogeneous Europe is facing formidable difficulties in forging such a common public culture at the level of the European Union. There is currently no such global public democratic culture, nor is there any hope of establishing one for a very, very long time. We can expect, therefore, that for the foreseeable future institutions that possess democratic legitimacy will continue to assume the attributes of sovereignty at something like the geographical level of contemporary states.

III.

If the analysis I have so far offered is correct, Young's assault on the concept of sovereignty is unconvincing. The question I shall address in this section of my remarks is why Young might have been tempted to take the position that "self-determination does not mean sovereign independence."[33] To a lawyer, it is merely a solecism to apply this position to a state. My hypothesis, however, is that Young's position flows from a particular perspective on questions of institutional design, a perspective that tends to characterize a philosophical, as distinct from a legal, approach to these questions.

I should begin by noting that there is a way of understanding self-determination that renders manifestly true Young's claim that "self-determination does not mean sovereign independence." Self-determination is sometimes understood to be a good that exists in the world, a good that is in fact often distributed in ways that do not correspond to sovereignty. Modern institutions do not establish mechanisms of self-determination in an all-or-nothing way. The good of self-determination comes in degrees and kinds, and it is often disconnected from legal sovereignty. In the United States, for example, residents of cities exercise considerable self-determination, and yet cities are not sovereign. Shareholders of corporations exercise the kind of nonsovereign, nonterritorial self-determination that Young seems sometimes to envision.[34] Young properly celebrates these manifold forms of self-determination that appear to flourish without the seemingly artificial shield of sovereignty. Her project is to propose the fairest and most reasonable way of distributing the good of self-determination among the people of the world.

We must, however, distinguish between two different ways in which the good of self-determination can be exercised. That good can either reflect an originary power, or it can exist at the sufferance of higher power. Cities and corporations, for example, have charters that circumscribe the limits of their self-determination; the charters specify who can vote, in what ways, and to what ends. Cities and corporations lack the originary power of self-determination with respect to these charters, because the charters are imposed upon cities and corporations by states. When it comes to the content of their own charters, cities and corporations do not have the originary power ultimately to determine the structure of their own self-determination.

Whether we choose to characterize a particular exercise of self-determination as originary depends upon the context and purpose of the characterization. Within the confines of its charter, a city or a corporation can have the originary power to exercise its self-determination as it chooses. But it lacks this originary power with respect to the terms of the charter itself. We can think of originary power, therefore, as a kind of chain, with each democratic institution exercising originary self-determination with respect to some aspects of its power, but deferring to the originary power of some more authoritative institution with respect to other aspects. Cities defer to states, which in turn defer to the federal government, which in turn defers to the people of the United States.

When we speak of sovereignty in a democratic state, we refer to the ultimate originary power of self-determination with respect to institutions of government and of law. Sovereignty is located where deference to a higher originary power ceases. Democratic sovereignty designates the ultimate authority of a group of persons to become the author of their own forms of self-government; their authority is ultimate because the collective agency of their government will reflect their popular will, and not the will of others.[35] Within a democratic state, all other forms of political self-determination exist at the sufferance of sovereignty. In this sense, therefore, ultimate originary self-determination with regard to matters of government and law does indeed imply "sovereign independence."

At the root of Young's rejection of sovereignty lies her failure to theorize the aspects of self-determination that are originary. This failure stems from Young's general approach to the task of institutional design. Young writes as though the purpose of institutional design were to articulate the fairest way of distributing human institutional goods, like the good of self-determination. Institutional designs are better or worse depending upon how cogently their proposed distribution of goods can be justified. This perspective renders originary self-determination both irrelevant and suspect.

It is irrelevant because there is no need for sovereignty if Young has actually offered the best possible allocation of the good of self-determination. The distribution of that good is fixed by the reasons that justify her design; if these reasons are persuasive, they are presumed to be convincing to rational persons. Sovereign independence thus becomes superfluous because rational persons, even if vested with originary self-determination, would only recapitulate the features of Young's design. It is also rendered suspect because sovereignty would seem to serve no purpose except to hide the desire to authorize a (presumably unjustifiable) distribution of goods in ways that contradict the convincing reasons that underwrite Young's design.

Young's rejection of sovereignty thus comports with her more general approach to questions of institutional design. That approach focuses primarily on the reasons offered to justify the fair distribution of goods, like the good of self-determination. The force of these reasons tends to eclipse the independent agency of those to whom goods are to be distributed, because rational agents are assumed to accept persuasive reasons. It should be entirely unsurprising that this perspective on institutional design, which stresses reasons and fair shares, is frequently associated with the work of philosophers.

Lawyers, by contrast, tend to view issues of institutional design primarily from the perspective of implementation. They assume that disputes will arise about reasons and fair shares, and they therefore tend to focus on the question of who will be authorized to interpret and enforce the application of an institutional design. This is because lawyers are by profession acutely aware of what John Rawls has termed the "burdens of judgment," burdens that lead reasonable persons to disagree about important matters.[36] Lawyers tend to believe that no area of human affairs is exempt from the burdens of judgment, including even the interpretation and application of principles of justice.

For this reason, lawyers conceptualize decision making as reflecting not only the impersonal force of abstract reason, but also the authorship of particular decision makers. Lawyers therefore deem the allocation of decision-making authority to be central to questions of institutional design. Because it matters very much *whose* interpretation of an institutional design carries final authority, the question of originary self-determination assumes fundamental importance within legal thought.

Viewed from this perspective, Young's proposals do not transcend the necessity for sovereignty. They merely refuse to face the question. We need to parse Young's vision of international relationships by asking *who* would have the ultimate power to define and enforce the complicated details of the dispersed and decentralized forms of self-determination she proposes. If Young were to respond to this query, she would have to identify the collective agent with final authority to determine the shape of its own nature in matters of government and law. She would in this way locate sovereignty.

IV.

It would of course be merely tendentious to argue that there is a necessary distinction between philosophical and legal perspectives on issues of institutional design. It is John Rawls, after all, who has offered the most compelling account of the burdens of judgment. Yet when all is said and done, there do seem to be important differences between approaches to institutional design that stress reasons and fair shares, and those that stress implementation. These differences do seem to track the distinct foci of the two professions.

My objective in these short remarks has not been to defend one approach or the other. It is clear to me that any reasonable account of institutional design must be responsive to the professional concerns of both philosophers and lawyers. An acceptable institutional design must justify its allocation of goods, and it must also pay attention to the distribution of ultimate decision-making authority in the implementation of that allocation.

That having been said, it is also necessary to acknowledge that there is some tension between these two distinct approaches. Although institutional designs sometimes involve only matters of process and implementation, they often also turn on the substantive values expressed by their justifications and by the fair outcomes they are created to achieve. Final decision-making authority to interpret and apply these justifications and outcomes must lodge somewhere. Final decision-making authority will necessarily encompass the capacity to act in ways that the author of an institutional design might well regard as inconsistent with her understanding of its justifications and of its expected fair outcomes.

This tension is at its zenith when dealing with designs for the distribution of the good of self-determination, a subject that is surely at the heart of the organization of democratic institutions. The reasons justifying any institutional design for the allocation of this good necessarily will strain against the need of those exercising the originary capacity of self-government to both interpret and implement those reasons.

We are thus moved into the territory of paradox and compromise. Young's article illustrates the impossibility of any clean solution. Even if the reasons offered by Young to justify her preferred distribution of the good of self-determination were completely convincing, a subject I have not explored in these remarks, her proposed institutional design would fail because of its refusal to acknowledge the need for self-determination as an originary act. The sign of this refusal is Young's full-scale attack on the concept of legal sovereignty.

In the design of democratic institutions, however, it is perilous to ignore the necessity of sovereignty. We can be sure that in any actual democratic social structure the originary power of self-determination will lie somewhere, and its location ought to be accounted for within our institutional designs. If sovereignty does not lie in a single, all-encompassing, world democratic government, sovereignty will continue to lodge in the potentially divisive hands of independent states. But, if I am correct in my suggestion that a world government is unlikely within the foreseeable future to carry democratic legitimacy, this may not be such a bad state of affairs.

Young is certainly correct to anticipate that as international interdependence expands, we can expect sovereign states to become bound in increasingly close terms of cooperation with other sovereign states. Eventually this may lead to the development of a public culture of global proportions, which may indeed propel us toward the visionary terminus imagined by Young. The appearance of a legitimate world democracy would certainly be a happy day, in no small part for the reasons so eloquently advanced by Young.

NOTES

1. Iris Young, chapter five, this volume, 164.
2. Ibid. at 174.
3. Ibid. at 172.
4. Ibid. at 163.
5. Ibid.
6. Ibid. at 169.
7. Ibid.
8. Ibid. at 170.
9. See, e.g., Lassa Oppenheim, *International Law*, vol. 1 (New York: Longmans, Green, 1905), 101. For a discussion of traditional concepts of sovereignty, see Neil MacCormick, "Beyond the Sovereign State," 56 *Modern Law Review* 1 (1993).
10. Young, at 172.
11. Ibid.
12. Ibid.
13. Ibid. at 171.
14. Ibid. at 170–171.
15. Ibid.
16. Patrick Macklem, "Distributing Sovereignty: Indian Nations and Equality of Peoples," *Stanford Law Review* 45 (1993): 1311, 1348.
17. For a full statement of the argument sketched in this paragraph, see Robert Post, *Constitutional Domains:* Democracy, Community, Management (Cambridge: Harvard University Press, 1995), 6–10, 179–96, 268–89.
18. *McIntyre v. Ohio Elections Commission,* 514 U.S. 334, 346 (1995); see *U.S. Term Limits, Inc. v. Thornton,* 514 U.S. 779 (1995). Neil MacCormick,

while recognizing the principle of "the sovereignty of the people," oddly concludes that "the principle belongs to the theory of democracy as ideal moral theory, rather than to a descriptive or analytical legal or political theory." Neil MacCormick, "Sovereignty, Democracy, Subsidiarity," 25 *Rechtstheorie* 281, 285 (1994). At least from the American perspective, this conclusion seems demonstrably incorrect.

19. Thomas Hobbes, *Leviathan*, ed. C. B. MacPherson (Harmondsworth: Penguin, 1968), 81.

20. Young, at 172–173.

21. Ibid. at 164–165.

22. Ibid. at 167.

23. Ibid. at 162.

24. Ibid. at 161.

25. Ibid.

26. Ibid. at 147.

27. Ibid. at 174.

28. Ibid. at 176.

29. See ibid.

30. For a discussion of the nature of that culture, and for an argument that it will be more likely to be successful if it transcends the limitations of any single community or "people," see Post, *Constitutional Domains*, 134–50.

31. See ibid., 1–96, 286–88; Robert Post, "Community and the First Amendment," *Arizona State Law Journal* 29 (1997): 473.

32. Young, at 176.

33. Ibid. at 178.

34. Ibid. at 163.

35. There is of course room for ambiguity, since we do ordinarily view as incompatible with democratic sovereignty that it must be exercised in a way that is subject to certain constraints. It is not usually regarded as self-contradictory, for example, to say that the originary power of self-determination cannot be exercised in such a way as to violate human rights. To observe this, however, is to mark the difference between the originary power of self-determination, exercised pursuant to particular constraints, and the transfer of the power of self-determination itself. The line between these two conditions can sometimes grow blurry, and this creates a kind of dynamic ambiguity. One can see this ambiguity at work in the gradual and imperceptible evolution from, for example, separate European sovereign states to a single sovereign European Union.

36. John Rawls, *Political Liberalism* (New York: Columbia University Press, 1993), 55.

8

DESIGNING A DEMOCRACY FOR THE EURO-POLITY AND REVISING DEMOCRATIC THEORY IN THE PROCESS

PHILIPPE C. SCHMITTER

From the perspective of democratic theory, the European Union (EU) is a puzzling entity. On the one hand, the requirement that all of its member states be democratic has provided a powerful stimulus for the transformation of autocratic regimes—first, in southern Europe and, more recently, in eastern Europe. Without stable democratic institutions, no country in Europe can aspire to attaining full access to the EU's integrated market and decision-making process. Moreover, membership in the EU is widely regarded as one of the best insurance policies that a nascent democracy can take out to prevent its eventual regression to autocracy.[1]

On the other hand, the EU itself is not a democracy and shows only very limited signs of becoming one. Neither its "executive power" (the Council of Ministers) nor its "administrative power" (the Commission) is directly accountable to its continent-wide citizenry. Despite some recent increases in the powers of the European Parliament, the actual governance of the EU lies in the hands of a duopoly of national governments and supranational bureaucrats. It has all the trappings of a normal Western democracy, including such "bells and whistles" as an independent quasi-constitutional court, an impressive array of organized interests, an extraordinary variety of consultative bodies, and even an ombudsman, but it does not function as one—and this is an evaluation that is increasingly shared by the individuals and groups that are subject to its authority.

In this essay, I shall first examine the nature of the EU's democracy deficit. Then, I shall consider some of the generic difficulties that are posed by the prospect of democratizing such an unusual polity. In the third section, I shall briefly outline some specific institutional suggestions as to how this might be accomplished. And, finally, I shall address the issue of "why bother?"—that is, why should the EU deal with its democratization now when it is simultaneously facing so many more immediate and pressing issues, such as monetary unification and Eastern enlargement?

I. Why Is the EU Not a Democracy?

In principle, an eventual Euro-democracy would have to satisfy the generic qualities of any modern political democracy, which Terry Karl and I have defined elsewhere as follows:

> "Modern Political Democracy" is a regime or system of governance in which rulers are held accountable for their actions in the public realm by citizens, acting indirectly through the competition and cooperation of their representatives.[2]

Note that, according to this definition, democracy does not consist of any particular configuration of institutions/rules. It is a property that emerges from the relationship among three distinctive sets of actors, regardless of their size, scale, or scope: rulers, citizens, and representatives. And, it is a relationship that may (or may not) characterize very different types of polity, that is, it is not restricted to so-called nation-states.

Simplifying considerably, an eventual Euro-democracy would have to become a regime with a public realm of its own in which *citizens* from the polity as a whole would have to be capable of ensuring the accountability—by means of the competition and cooperation of their political *representatives*—of those *rulers* entitled to make and implement those decisions that are binding on all members of that polity. This presents us with three continent-wide sets of actors whose behavior has to be institutionalized in such a way that accountability is ensured, at the same time that binding decisions are taken and implemented for the polity as a whole.[3]

Let us examine briefly each of the concepts in the above definition in terms of the present practices of the European Union (EU).[4]

1. A *regime* (or *system of governance*) is an ensemble of patterns that determines (1) the forms and channels of access to principal governmental positions; (2) the characteristics of the actors who are admitted to or excluded from such access; (3) the resources or strategies that these actors can use to gain access; and (4) the rules that are followed in the making of publicly binding decisions. To produce its effect, the ensemble must be institutionalized, that is, the various patterns must be habitually known, practiced, and accepted by most, if not all, of the actors. Increasingly, this has involved their explicit legalization or constitutionalization, but many very stable regime norms can have an implicit, informal, or prudential basis.

By these criteria, the EU is definitely a regime, although not a democratic one. The characteristics of the actors (that is, citizens) who are permitted direct access to its institution are not fully defined (or are contingent upon specifications established by its national member states) and the absence of anything like an explicitly constitutional bill of rights means that which resources or strategies are legitimate are also largely defined at the national level or left to the vagaries of practice at the supranational level. Finally, the modifications embedded in the Single European Act (SEA) and the Maastricht Treaty on European Union (TEU) concerning qualified majority voting do not constitute a definitive statement of the decision rules that actors expect to live with for the indefinite future.

2. The *rulers* are those who occupy dominant positions in the formal structure of governance. Democracies are not anarchies. They are not voluntarily or spontaneously coordinated but depend upon the presence of persons who occupy specialized roles and can give legitimate

commands to others. What distinguishes democratic rulers from nondemocratic ones are the norms that determine how they become rulers and the practices that hold them accountable for what they do once they have become rulers.

Here, the key issue is whether the supranational authorities of the EU have sufficient capacity for giving direct commands legitimately and effectively. Not only are there relatively few Eurocrats and not only do they dispose of vastly less resources than the rulers of their member states but also they devote most of their effort to giving commands to these national rulers who remain directly responsible for the actual acts of governance. As the mounting complaints testify, the compliance of these more numerous and more resourceful authorities at the national and subnational levels cannot be taken for granted.

Moreover, the EU's rulers are accountable only en bloc to the directly elected representatives of citizens. They cannot be refused or dismissed as individuals responsible for specific tasks. Although the data are not clearly apposite, the public opinion surveys of Eurobaromètre do suggest that most of the EU's subjects/citizens do not feel directly obligated by or identified with its commands and they have increasingly raised serious doubts about the legitimacy of some of its highly secretive and technically obscure decision-making practices. Finally, the opt-out, opt-in provisions of several EU policy arenas (for example, the European Monetary System and the Schengen Agreement on cooperation in police and internal security affairs) and the subsequent sanctification of this sort of variable geometry in several clauses of the TEU would seem to indicate that countries (and, hence, their citizens) that do not agree with certain measures will not necessarily be bound by the decision of the majority—whether qualified or not.

3. The *public realm* involves that part of the collective choice process in which norms binding on the society as a whole and backed by the coercive force of the state are made. This realm can vary a great deal across democracies depending upon how previous decisions have drawn distinctions between the public and the private, between state and society, between legitimate coercion and voluntary

exchange, between collective needs and individual preferences. Differences of opinion over the optimal mix of the
two provide much of the substantive content of political
conflict within established democracies.

There is no question that these issues involved in delimiting the
public realm have been debated extensively in the EU—but they
have not been definitively resolved. The notion that the Single
European Act of 1985–86 had definitively opted for a narrowly
"liberal" conception has been denied by subsequent developments. While its nature has changed substantially, regulation of
economic exchanges has increased, not decreased, with the implementation of the SEA. *Pace* the provision of regional funds,
however, the arrangement has yet to engage in any substantial
and deliberate redistribution of funds within its class and territorial borders—other than the sectorial welfare state it has created
for agriculture.

4. *Citizens* provide the most distinctive element in democratic
   regimes. All types of regime have rulers of some sort and a
   public realm of some dimension; only democracies have
   citizens.

The EU has only just recently begun to specify the distinctive rights
and obligations of its individual citizens and, so far, they are far in-
ferior in quality and quantity to those defined and protected by its
national member states. Nevertheless, the Treaty of European
Union signed at Maastricht in 1992 formally specifies in its Arts. 8,
8a, 8b, 8c, 8d, and 8e a set of rights, involving such items as (1) the
enfranchisement of residents of other EU member states to vote
and run as candidates in local elections, which could be the first
step in extending the right to all Euro-citizens to vote in all elections in the constituencies where they permanently reside regardless of their national citizenship; (2) the reaffirmation of the rights
of all individuals, nationals, and resident foreigners to petition the
European Parliament; (3) the creation of an ombudsman office at
the EU level; and (4) a pledge to make the proceedings of EU institutions more "transparent" in the future. The last of these articles
(8e) even invites the Council of Ministers "acting unanimously"
and only on a proposal from the Commission and after consulta-

tion with the European Parliament to strengthen or to add to this list in the future. When one combines these newly founded aspects of *political* citizenship with the "four freedoms" of economic citizenship already promised by the Single European Act of 1986, that is, free movement of trade, capital, services and persons, one has the potential basis for the development of a varied and consequential "Euro-citizenship" above and beyond existing national citizenships guaranteed by its member states.

It should be noted, however, that Euro-citizenship differs in one fundamental aspect from national citizenship. While it conveys equal rights and opportunities upon individuals (and firms), their collective *political* weight in EU decision making is highly unequal, given the complex formulae that systematically overcompensate the smaller countries. Moreover, its exercise is relatively marginal, given the weakness of the European Parliament (EP) in the process as a whole. Granted that overrepresentation of rural districts and other peculiarities of malapportionment and gerrymandering are never completely absent from national democracies, the EU's weightings across member states is of a qualitatively different magnitude. It could also be argued that national parliaments have lost influence relative to other decision-making bodies within national polities, but the EP has never had much influence to lose.

5. *Competition* has not always been considered an essential defining condition of democracy, although at least since the *Federalist Papers* it has become widely accepted that competition among more or less permanent factions— also known as political parties—is a "necessary evil" of all democracies that operate on a more than local scale.

The most widely diffused conception of this competition makes it virtually synonymous with the presence of regular, fairly conducted, and honestly counted elections of uncertain outcome. Without denying their centrality for democracy, these contests between candidates are held sporadically and only allow citizens to choose between the highly aggregated alternatives offered by political parties. In between, however, individuals can compete to influence public policy through a wide variety of other intermediaries: interest associations, social movements, locality groupings, clientelistic arrangements, and so forth.

Modern democracy, in other words, offers a variety of competitive processes and channels for the expression of interests—associational as well as partisan, functional as well as territorial, collective as well as individual. All are integral to its practice.

Nor is there agreement on the appropriate rules of competition. There is certainly a commonly accepted image of democracy that identifies it exclusively with the principle of rule by the majority. The problem, however, arises when *sheer numbers* meet special *intensities,* when a perfectly properly assembled majority (especially a stable majority) produces decisions that negatively affect some minority (especially a threatened cultural or ethnic minority). Another way of putting this intrinsic tension between numbers and intensities would be to say that "in modern democracies, votes may be counted, but influences are also weighted "carefully."

On these grounds, the democratic status of the EU is highly ambiguous. Partisan competition is recognized and enshrined in the elections to the EP and in its internal legislative operations—even if the lines of cleavage and aggregation are often inconsistent from country to country and change frequently at the European level.[5] Voters in Euro-elections are simply not offered an opportunity to choose between rival partisan elites presenting alternative programs at that level of aggregation. In any event, this principle of party-structured competition does not govern the formation of the Commission or its policy deliberations. Nomination by national governments according to fixed quotas prevails and those who are subsequently appointed are explicitly not supposed to represent the interests of their respective governments. Most important, there is virtually no way that individual citizens voting in free, equal, fair, and competitive Euro-elections could influence the composition of Euro-authorities, much less bring about a rotation of those in office.

Votes are taken by simple majority in the EP, but they are not generally binding or determinant—even if they have been increased in importance through the codecision procedures of

Maastricht. It remains impossible to translate a majority produced by the European electorate at large into an effective and predictable change in government or policy. The best one can expect is an indirect expression through a qualified majority of the member states, which themselves all have majoritarian governments—at least on the range of issues that is subject to this decision rule. The closest analogy might be German democracy with only the Bundesrat and no Bundestag.

Otherwise, the EU is a rather extreme case of a type of emerging democracy that stresses the weighting of intensities, especially those intensities that are aggregated and expressed as "national interests." Not only are small countries overweighted in the voting formula of the Council of Ministers but on a wide range of important issues unanimity is still required. The new codecision procedures between the Council and the European Parliament prefigure a system of concurrent majorities. However, the absence of statutory guarantees for the powers of national, provincial, and/or local governments—*pace* the recent references to subsidiarity—means that a federalist consensus on the distribution of powers has not yet been established. One could describe the process of forming the Commission as a sort of consociational arrangement in that all member states are included in a Grand Coalition and, by tradition, those with more than one commissioner have tended to nominate their commissioners from opposing domestic parties. Repeated efforts by the Eurocracy (and, most recently, by the former president of the European Commission) to create a viable "social dialogue" between capital, labor, and themselves have yet to produce any regularized channeling of class-based interest intensities. The advisory Economic and Social Council has never made a serious contribution since its founding in the late 1950s.

Supplementing the institutionalized expression of national—and, hence, allegedly majoritarian—interests through the Council of Ministers, is the less visible but nonetheless pervasive expression of minority interests through interest associations. From its founding, the Eurocracy has attracted (and, occasionally, sponsored) organizations representing specialized class, sectorial, and professional interests. Especially since the SEA, Bruxelles has been literally invaded by an increasing variety of "Euro-lobbies"—not just formal interest associations but also social movements, individual enterprises, and law firms. While all this is entirely appropriate for a modern democracy, the normative issue is whether these channels are freely and fairly available to all minorities with intensive preferences. So far, the evidence suggests a mobilization of bias in favor of business and systemic problems in adjusting to the expanded scale of genuinely European interaction.

6. *Cooperation* has always been a central feature of democracies. Actors must combine with one another by some voluntary process to make collective decisions binding on the polity as a whole. Most obviously, they must cooperate in order to compete. They must be capable of engaging in collective action through parties, associations, and movements that can select candidates, articulate preferences, petition authorities, and influence policies.

But beyond this unavoidably "adversarial" aspect to democracy, its freedoms should encourage citizens to deliberate among themselves, to discover their common needs and to resolve their possible conflicts without relying on centralized political authority. The "classical" conception of democracy stressed these qualities and they are by no means extinct—despite repeated efforts by contemporary theorists to stress the analogy with behavior in the economic marketplace and to reduce all its operations to competitive interest maximization.[6]

As mentioned above, no viable party system has yet emerged at the level of the European Union as a whole. To a limited extent, members of national parties do cooperate under supranational labels within the legislative process of the EP, but candidates for Euro-deputy are neither nominated nor funded through supranational parties. On the contrary, their selection by national party oligarchies and election by proportional representation, usually within a single national constituency (except for Great Britain with its traditional first-past-the-post individual constituencies), more or less ensure that the winning candidates will be unknown to the citizens who have elected them. In any case, none of this effort at partisan cooperation has been translated into cooperation in the formation of governing coalitions or cabinets.

Moreover, the sheer scale of the Euro-polity—not to mention its potpourri of languages and political traditions—seems to have inhibited the sort of deliberation among individual citizens that Tocqueville regarded as so crucial. With the exception of academic cooperation and the proliferation of policy centers and think tanks, there are very few sites at which Europe's practices and purposes can be discussed. During the difficulties that surrounded the ratification of the TEU, this sense of alienation from Bruxelles became manifest. Individuals proved willing to accept almost any rumor presented to them about arbitrary behavior on the part of Eurocrats—in large part because they were ill-informed and unable to discuss these issues reasonably with their peers.

7. The principal agents of modern political democracy are *representatives*. Citizens may elect them or choose to support the parties, associations, or movements they lead, but representatives do the real business of governing. Moreover, most of these persons are not amateurs but professionals. Without individuals who invest in democracy to the extent that they orient their life's career around the aspiration to fill its key roles, it is doubtful that any democracy could survive. The central question is not whether or not there will be a "political elite" or even a "political class" but how that group of representatives will be composed and subsequently held accountable for its actions.

The EU is indeed surrounded by representatives, but these are hardly representative of the citizenry as a whole. At the functional level, they are overwhelmingly skewed to favor business interests. With the increased importance of the EP, there is some evidence of a shift of attention and greater access for social movements, consumer groups, and environmental constituencies—but they have a long way to go before they have redressed the imbalance. At the territorial level, representatives owe their allegiance almost exclusively to national constituencies. Recently, the TEU officially opened up an opportunity for the representation of subnational polities with the creation of the advisory Committee of Regions, but this may have no more effect than the preceding establishment of the Economic and Social Council.

What is missing are the *professionals* who represent transnational interests and passions. With the exception of the relatively unknown Eurocrats who labor away in its core bureaucracy, there are few persons who identify exclusively with the Euro-polity. The careers of the politicians-cum-technicians who are momentarily active in its Commission or who are elected to its Parliament continue to be much more affected by what is happening in their countries of origin. Very few lose an election or fail to gain a promotion for something they have done in Bruxelles or Strasbourg—and many are sent there after their real careers are over. The composition of Europe's emerging "political class" may be more varied and less predictable than that of its component parts, but it is much less coherent and capable of defending its distinctive practices and purposes.

This exploration of the EU's status as a "generic democracy" may have helped us to identify its practices and rules, but it has not told us much about how the EU should operate as a democracy. The simplistic answer to be found ad nauseam in the literature on democratic theory is that it should be governed "by the consent of the people." The more complex but accurate answer is that the EU should be governed "by the contingent consent of politicians acting under conditions of bounded uncertainty."

1. *Contingent consent*: In a democracy, representatives agree to compete in such a way that (1) those who win greater electoral support or those who gain greater influence will not use their (temporary) political superiority to impede those who have lost from taking office or exerting influence in the future; and (2) those who have lost in the present will respect the right of the winners to make binding decisions, in exchange for being allowed to take office or influence decisions in the future. In their turn, citizens are expected to obey the decisions ensuing from such a process of competition, provided its outcome remains contingent upon their collective preferences as expressed through fair and regular elections or open and repeated negotiations in the future.

   The challenge is to find a set of rules that embody contingent consent, not a set of goals that command widespread consensus. This "democratic bargain," to use Robert Dahl's expression, varies a good deal from society to society depending on cleavage patterns and such subjective factors as the degree of mutual trust, the standard of fairness, and the willingness to compromise. It may even be compatible with a great deal of dissensus on specific policy issues.

2. *Bounded uncertainty*: All democracies involve some degree of uncertainty—about who will be elected and what policies they will pursue. Even in those polities where one party persists in winning elections or one policy is consistently implemented, the possibility that they could be reversed by independent collective action still exists, vide the Scandinavian social democracies. If not, the system is not democratic, vide Mexico (until recently) or Indonesia.

But the uncertainty embedded in the core of all democracies is bounded. Not just any actor can get into the competition and raise any issue he or she pleases— there are previously established rules that must be respected. Not just any policy can be decided and implemented—there are contingencies that must be respected. What the emergent practice of democracy does is to institutionalize "normal" uncertainty with regard to actors and policies. These boundaries vary from country to country. Constitutional guarantees of property, privacy, decent treatment, self-expression, personal movement, and "the pursuit of happiness" are part of the effort. But the most effective boundaries are generated by the processes of competition between interests and cooperation within civil society. Whatever the rhetoric— and some polities appear to offer their citizenries more dramatic alternatives than others—once the rules of contingent consent have been agreed upon, the actual variation is likely to stay within a predictable and mutually acceptable range.

The strongest reasons for denying the EU its bona fides as a political democracy lie in these underlying operative principles.

Regardless of its formal trappings, it simply does not "function" like a democracy. Without even the remotest prospect of a rotation in power, there is no reason to worry about contingent consent. Except for the highly unlikely defection of a member state (not even contemplated by the Treaty of Rome), the invulnerability of its rulers is virtually assured. Discontent with particular measures, grumbling over technocratic decision making, selective implementation of unpopular policies, difficulties with transposition and ratification, and even occasional threats to opt out of specific obligations—yes, but nothing like the prospect of being disgraced or ejected from office as in a normal democracy.

Nor is the EU's uncertainty bounded in the same way. The absence of a formal constitution, combined with the European Court of Justice's conversion of the existing treaties into a "quasi constitution," makes the functional boundaries of its attention and authority ambiguous—and potentially unlimited. There is not even a clear delimitation of its territorial boundaries. Granted that the Council of Ministers can be counted on to impose restrictions on initiatives that encroach too far on national prerogatives, but even its rules for doing so are not yet definitively fixed.

In most modern settings, the regularity and reliability of these relationships requires that they be (at least, in part) protected by formal legal norms. Given both the nature of the contracting parties and the process whereby their bargaining over these norms takes place, it is highly likely that this would eventually have to involve the negotiating, drafting, and ratifying of an explicit European Constitution.[7] Which is not to say that progress toward democratizing the EU has to await this sort of "big-bang" founding event. As we shall see in the third section, there are many things that could be done less auspiciously and less controversially to improve its accountability to the Euro-citizenry.

II. WHY IS IT SO DIFFICULT TO DEMOCRATIZE THE EU?

At first glance, it is the sheer scale and complexity of the enterprise that seems so daunting. Even with the present fifteen members, the total population of the EU (371 million) is already greater than that of the United States (249 million)—moreover, that involves ten official languages expressing very resilient political and social traditions that are rooted in polities whose claims to sovereignty go back hundreds of years. The disparities in size and level of development between its smaller or poorer and its larger or richer units are much greater than was the case of the United States at its founding or is the case of the United States today. Moreover, many of its member states have histories of fierce rivalry and armed conflict with one another that are still fresh in the minds of their older citizens.

And if that were not enough, the EU is slated to expand its membership in the proximate future. According to "guesstimates," it could eventually have between twenty-seven and thirty-five member states or a total population from 478 million to 572 million (and this without either Russia or Ukraine!), speaking twenty to thirty "national/official" languages and who knows how many "subnational/unofficial" ones! The disparity in development levels would shoot up with such an enlargement—not to mention the differential burden imposed upon the late-entering former-Communist countries by their need to adopt and adapt capitalist practices in such a short time frame. Also, the fact that so many of these newcomers have much smaller populations than the previous average EU member means that the existing disparities in voting power will be exaggerated beyond recognition and it will very quickly become possible for a small minority of Europe's citizens to veto decisions or to impose disproportionate burdens on the much larger majority.

My hunch, however, is that the principal difficulty lies not with scale or complexity—although both obviously would have to be taken into account in any effort to democratize the EU. After all, India has a population of 815 million, even more languages, much less of a gross national product, vast territorial and class disparities, all the stresses of playing "catch-up"—and it still manages to be democratic.[8] I am convinced that what makes it so hard to even imagine a Euro-democracy is the *type of polity* that the EU has become, associated with the fact that democratic theory is of little or no help since it presumes exactly what the EU is not—namely, the (prior) existence of a state or, even, a nation-state.

Any prospective democratizer of the emerging Euro-polity would have to take into consideration a set of unique conditions and adjust his/her expectations-cum-recommendations accordingly. He or she must first be aware of what the EU is *not*, and then concentrate on what it is becoming—rather than to presume either that it is already a state and likely to become a nation.

1. The emerging Euro-polity has *not* yet acquired its definitive institutional configuration, in terms of its territorial scale, its functional scope, or its level of political authority.[9]

2. The Euro-polity in its present, provisional, configuration is *not* a democracy and will not become one unless and until its member states decide explicitly to endow it with new rules and rights.[10]

3. The conjunctural forces affecting its configuration are *not* currently pushing the Euro-polity in a uniform direction but toward diverse outcomes with no stable equilibrium likely to emerge in the near future.[11]

4. Nevertheless, its most likely outcome within the medium-term (say, twenty years) is a form of nonstate, nonnational polity or stable political order that is novel, that is, will *not* resemble either an intergovernmental organization or a supranational state or any of the possible points along this institutional continuum.[12]

5. If, eventually, its member states decide to transform this novel polity into a democracy, they will have to experiment with new forms of citizenship, representation, and decision making in order to be successful. Merely copying the institutions of existing national democracies, even federal ones, will *not* suffice—and could even have counterproductive effects.[13]

6. No matter how reluctant they may be and how ill-informed about what to do, the member states of the Euro-polity will eventually have to democratize it, or risk the loss of what they have already attained (that is, a high level of economic interdependence and a reliable degree of security community) through declining legitimacy with mass publics.[14]

The core of the emerging Euro-polity's novelty lies in *the growing dissociation between territorial constituencies and functional compétences.* In the classic model of the state (if not invariably in its praxis), the exercise of public authority in different functional domains is coincident or congruent with a specific and unique territory.[15] When one arrives at its physical borders, the legitimate exercise of coercion in all these domains ends. The polity on the other side has, in principle, no right to command obedience in any domain on one's own side—and there presumably exists no superordinate entity exercising authority over both sides.

In the emergent Euro-polity, the functional and the territorial domains of authority have become less rather than more congruent over time. What seems to be asserting, and even consolidating, itself is a plurality of polities at different levels of aggregation—national, subnational, and supranational—that overlap in a multitude of domains. Moreover, the EU authorities have few exclusive *compétences,* and have yet to assert their hierarchical control over member states—except by means of the limited jurisprudence of the European Court of Justice and in such specified functional domains as competition policy. Instead, these multiple levels negotiate with one another in a continuous way in order to perform common tasks and resolve common problems across an expanding range of issues. Without sovereignty—without a definitive center for the resolution of conflicts or for the allocation of public goods—there is only a process and, hence, no definite person or body that can be held accountable for its actions in the public realm. Moreover, the participants in this process are not just a fixed number of national states but an enormous variety of subnational units and networks, supranational associations, and transnational firms.

Elsewhere, I have argued that the EU is likely to become something qualitatively different, *neither* an intergovernmental *confederatio* nor a supranational *stato federatio* but one of two novel forms of political domination I have called a *consortio* or a *condominio.*[16] As an ideal type, the *consortio* assumes a fixed and irreversible set of member states within defined territorial boundaries but with varying policy responsibilities (*"L'Europe à géométrie variable"* seems to capture this property well). Subsets of members would pool their capacity to act autonomously in domains

that they could no longer govern at their own level of aggregation but would be free to determine—either at the moment of
joining or when subsequent revisions were made—which specific
common obligations they were willing to accept. Presumably,
they would form a singular and relatively contiguous spatial bloc,
but they would arrange their common affairs within a multitude
of distinctive functional authorities, only some of which would be
coordinated from a single center or secretariat.

The emergence of something resembling an ideal-type *condominio* would be an even more unprecedented outcome, that is,
the one that least resembles the preexisting Euro-state system. In
it, both territorial as well as functional constituencies would vary.
Not only would each member country be able to select from a
menu of potential common tasks but each European institution
would be composed of a different (although presumably overlapping) set of members. Instead of a single Europe with recognized
and contiguous boundaries, there would be many Europes: a
trading Europe, an energy Europe, an environmental Europe, a
welfare Europe, a defense Europe—*et ainsi de suite*. Instead of
one "Eurocracy" that coordinated all the distinct tasks involved in
the integration process, there would be multiple regional institutions acting autonomously to solve common problems and produce different public goods. Given its formidable coordination
problems—not to mention its unprecedented nature—one can
hardly imagine the deliberate establishment of such a cumber-
some arrangement. It could emerge only in an improvised and
incremental fashion from successive compromises among members with divergent interests and institutional legacies.

If either of these models better describes the medium-term
outcome than those that lie on the more orthodox continuum
connecting the intergovernmental organization with the supranational state—something that admittedly is a matter of conjec-
ture—and if democratization cannot be indefinitely postponed,
then it seems reasonable to me to presume that *the Euro-Polity will
have to invent and implement new forms of ruler accountability, new
rights and obligations for citizens, and new channels for territorial and
functional representation.* For all existing conceptions of democracy—with the limited exception of those involving small-scale,
highly localized forms of direct democracy—presume the exis-

tence of a political unit with the minimal properties of a state. Only if there is a ruling person or body with a legitimate command of legitimate violence can it be made accountable to citizens through the appropriate channels of representation. Without such a prior coincidence between external and internal sovereignty, the most that one can expect is a confederation or intergovernmental arrangement that does not have to legitimate itself as democratic to remain a persistent political institutions..

III. WHAT CAN BE DONE TO MAKE THE EU MORE DEMOCRATIC?

Elsewhere I have explored a set of specific reforms in three institutional domains: (1) *citizenship*; (2) *representation*; and (3) *decision rules* that I believe could make a substantial contribution to democratizing the EU, although even if enacted together they would not complete the job. I also believe that these reforms are feasible, in the sense that they do not require radical transformations and are compatible with existing national practices—although I confess that I have yet to find a solution to the "agency problem" that might bring them about. Below, given the limitations of space (and time), I will list only these "modest reform proposals,"[17] but I can supply greater details upon demand.

  I. Citizenship
    1. Referenda with Euro-elections
    2. Status for denizens
    3. Dual voting (for deputies and their terms)
    4. Electronic or mail-in voting
  II. Representation
    1. Universal membership in EP—coupled with
    2. Deliberation-amendment by functional committee
    3. EP control over Euro-election funds
    4. Secondary citizenship by means of vouchers
  III. Decision Rules
    1. Proportional proportionality
    2. Three Colegii (or Groupings) by size of country
    3. Concurrent majorities
    4. Tripartite Commission (by Colegii)

Since none of these "arrangements" currently exists at the national or subnational level, it is important to recognize the "root dilemma" that this creates: *If the EU as a nonstate will have to come up with novel institutions if it is to democratize itself, then it will run the risk that both politicians and citizens may find it difficult initially to recognize these novel rules and practices as "democratic."* Eventually, they may come to agree that these arrangements do offer the best possible means for rendering rulers accountable, but it may take some time before they can be cured of their "national habits" that are so different.

IV. Why Bother to Begin Democratizing the EU Now?

The preceding discussion should have convinced the reader that it is neither feasible nor desirable to democratize the Euro-polity *tutto è súbito*—completely and immediately. Not only would we not know how to do it, there is no compelling evidence that Europeans want it. Nothing could be more dangerous for the future of Euro-democracy than to have it thrust upon a citizenry that is not prepared to exercise it and that continues to believe its interests and passions are best defended by *national* not *supranational* democracy.

However, I hope that the arguments have convinced the reader that it is possible and may even be timely to begin to improve the quality of Euro-democracy through some reforms in the way citizenship, representation, and decision making are practiced within the institutions of the European Union. We may not yet have a comprehensive vision of what the end product will look like, but there are specific and incremental steps that could be taken to supplement (and not supplant) the mechanisms of accountability that now exist within its member states. If my initial hunch was correct, that is, that the rules and practices of an eventual Euro-democracy will be quite different from those existing already at the national level, then it is all the more imperative that Europeans act cautiously when experimenting with political arrangements whose configuration will be unprecedented and whose consequences may prove to be unfortunate.

There are, in my opinion, two reasons that it may be timely to begin this experiment with supranational democracy sooner rather than later:

1. There is considerable evidence that rules and practices of democracy at the national level have become increasingly contested by citizens. This has not (yet) taken the form of rebellious or "unconventional "behavior but of what Gramsci called "symptoms of morbidity," such as greater electoral abstention, decline in party identification, more frequent turnover in office and rejection of the party in power, lower prestige of politicians and higher unpopularity of chief executives, increased tax evasion and higher rates of litigation against authorities, skyrocketing accusations of official corruption, and, most generally, a widespread impression that contemporary European democracies are simply not working well to protect their citizens. It would be overly dramatic to label this "a general crisis of legitimacy," but something isn't going well—and most national politicians know it.

2. There is even more compelling evidence that individuals and groups within the European Union have become aware of how much its regulations and directives are affecting their daily lives, and that they consider these decisions to have been taken in a remote, secretive, unintelligible, and unaccountable fashion. Whatever comfort it may have given them in the past that "unwarranted interference" by the Eurocrats in Bruxelles could have been vetoed by their sovereign national government, this has been dissipated by the advent of qualified majority voting. Europeans feel themselves, rightly or wrongly, at the mercy of a process of integration that they do not understand and certainly do not control—however much they may enjoy its material benefits. Again, it would be overdramatizing the issue to call this "a crisis of legitimacy," but the "permissive consensus" of the past is much less reliable—and supranational officials know it.

Combining these two trends expedientially—and they may even be causally related—opens up a rather unusual political opportunity space: a potentiality for acting preemptively before the situation reaches a crisis stage and before the compulsion to do something becomes so strong that politicians may overreact.

Moreover, if my second hunch is correct, that is, that the so-called "Monnet Method" of exploiting the spillovers between functionally related issue arenas to advance the level and scope of integrative institutions has exhausted its potential—precisely because of increased citizen awareness and politicization—then switching to an overtly political strategy of democratization might be sufficient to renew the momentum that has clearly been lost since the difficult ratification of the Maastricht treaty. If only one could rekindle within the process of Euro-democratization that same logic of indirection and gradualism based on an underlying structure of functional interdependence and an emerging system of collective problem solving, then the process of European integration might be given the *relancement* that it has so frequently sought and so badly needs. Except that this time, the result may not be so foreseeable or controllable. Democratization, especially in such unprecedented circumstances and for such a large-scale polity, is bound to activate unexpected linkages, to involve less predictable publics, and to generate less limited expectations.

We have good reasons, thanks to various theories of democracy, for believing that specific forms of citizenship, representation, and decision making are closely interrelated in a self-reinforcing fashion in stable democratic regimes. But, thanks to the absence of much theorizing about democratization, we are a lot less well informed about how these elements came together historically and even less well informed about how they might combine under contemporary circumstances. The pseudosubdisciplines of "transitology" and "consolidology" have only just begun to draw attention to these dynamic relations within the neodemocracies of the post-1974 wave of democratization—and it is far from evident that their (tentative) conclusions would have any relevance for democratizing an interstate organization composed not of relatively recent democracies but of relatively ancient ones.[18] About all that we can assert with confidence is that there have been and still are many different sequences involved in the relation between citizenship, representation, and decision making—and that these sequences have produced rather substantial differences in both the rapidity with which democracy was consolidated and the type of democracy that subsequently emerged.

But why bother? And, especially, why bother to act now? After all, there is monetary unification in Europe's near future. Will it not generate lots of spillover effects and, thereby, provide the process of economic integration with a renewed momentum? Why not wait until things get worse and then—as the prointegration forces have done several times in the past—exploit the contradictions to push the process further? Preemption is hardly the most compelling of motives in politics—and certainly, one of the least noble. And how do we know, anyway, that the EU is bound for such a crisis? Maybe, it is time to call a halt to all this business of further integration. Why not leave well enough alone and simply consolidate the present gains of regional free trade and factor mobility? Why not leave what remains of market regulation, welfare provision, and security protection to national polities that have (presumably) been strengthened by the process and that (demonstrably) still have a predominant claim on the loyalty of their citizens? And, even if there are some areas of positive policy making that must remain Europeanized, why not just strengthen national democratic processes to monitor and control them?

So, why bother with this much riskier process of European political integration through democratization? Might it not produce a contrary effect, that is, even greater resistance to cooperative policy making and the further "pooling" of national sovereignties? Worse yet, might it not just trigger an increase in expectations on the part of newly empowered Euro-citizens, a proliferation of channels for Euro-representation that will just confuse those who attempt to use them, and the establishment of new decision-making agencies that are even more bureaucratic, remote, and alienating than the national ones they are displacing?

These are all serious queries. Any eventual serious effort at Euro-democratization would have to cope with them and provide convincing counterarguments. I, alas, do not have answers for all of them, and the answers I do have are more in the nature of impressionistically compiled hunches than scientifically confirmed observations:

1. Monetary unification, if and when it occurs, will be so contained institutionally and so confined functionally that it will not have the same potentiality for generating spillover as did policy expansions in the past.

2. Even so, the politicization of mass publics at the national level will make it increasingly difficult for technocrats and organized interests to exploit its side effects without resistance.

3. The process of economic integration cannot be stopped at will; least of all, it cannot be confined to the status of a mere free trade area without jeopardizing the *acquis communautaire* that is essential for sustaining the political consensus and economic rules that reproduce that market.

4. Moreover, if that *acquis* of consensus on rules and substantive distributions is significantly threatened, so will be the very institutions of the EU, and that will eventually force the member states to revise their general policy in Europe, which could jeopardize its status as a security community.

5. The mere prospect of endangering Europe's security community, that is, the shared faith that force will not be used, under any circumstances, to resolve disputes between states, would so risk undermining the interests of all EU member states that they will do (almost) anything to prevent it.

6. National states and their political processes—*pace* the protestations of such scholars as Donald Puchala, Alan Milward, and Andrew Moravscik—have not been strengthened by the process of European integration (whatever their intentions) and, hence, they have irretrievably lost the capacity to act autonomously and effectively in many policy areas—even if the EU should disappear altogether.

7. National citizens are sufficiently aware of this and the costs involved in returning to the status quo ante so that only a minority would be willing to pay the price for such a retrenchment. Most would support a further enlargement of EU *comp*tences* rather than risk the collapse of the *acquis* and even more, the security community behind it.

8. Regardless of how national citizens might divide on this issue—and even more if they are seriously divided on it—it is not conceivable that their collective efforts at that level alone would be sufficient to ensure the accountability of supranational authorities—without significant changes in the formal rules of EU citizenship, representation, and decision making—and that would require unanimous intergovernmental agreement, that is, a treaty, if not a Euro-constitution.

9. Finally, it will be virtually impossible for national or supranational actors to do nothing about EU decision-making rules since the admission of, at least, some of the eastern European countries cannot be avoided in the near future, and this is bound to put an unbearable strain on these rules—not to mention, on existing distributions of benefits.

I began this essay with some general assumptions about the current status of the EU that I thought were plausible. I have concluded it with some specific assertions about where the EU may be headed that I admit are more speculative. It is my hope that between these two extremes, the reader will have gleaned something useful or, at least, thought provoking.

NOTES

1. And, once the Amsterdam Treaty is ratified, the premium will go up since this agreement stipulates that member states that are judged to have violated norms of human rights or democratic procedure will be suspended or expelled. These provisions were obviously inserted in anticipation of eastern enlargement, when the newcomers are expected to have less consolidated democratic regimes.

2. "What Democracy Is . . . and Is Not," *Journal of Democracy* 2:3 (Summer 1991): 75–88.

3. It would be more accurate to say that "accountability appears to be ensured in a way that satisfies the legitimate expectations of the citizenry," since this can vary rather considerably from one political culture to another. Needless to say, in the context of contemporary Europe, national differences over such things as "parliamentary sovereignty," "party

government," "transparency in the actions of public officials," and so on will make it all the more difficult to arrive at a consensual perception of what is involved in accountability.

4. For better or worse, the future of Euro-democracy rests with the set of institutions called—following the Treaty of Maastricht (1992)— the European Union (EU). Formerly, it was given the name of the European Economic Community and, then, the European Community when the secretariats of the European Coal and Steel Community, Euratom, and the EEC were merged in 1972. There are many other, independent European-level institutions, not the least of which is the Council of Europe, which contribute to the orderly and, sometimes, democratic governance of this part of the world, but no one seems to doubt that the EEC/EC/EU is destined to be preeminent among them.

5. In fact, it is at least arguable that, since the TEU in its Article 138a specifically mentions the role that European political parties should play in the integration process, this particular channel of representation gets more of a formal recognition at the European level than in the constitutions of most, if not all, of its member states.

6. See Jane Mansbridge, *Beyond Adversarial Democracy* (New York: Basic Books, 1980).

7. Hence, it is very unlikely to emerge from the interpretive procedures that the European Court of Justice has resorted to in order to convert the Treaty of Rome into a quasi constitution. Indeed, it is resistance to the further expansion of these norms that may provide one of the strongest incentives for explicit constitutionalization.

8. Although I wonder whether, under contemporary circumstances, a democracy on the scale and complexity of India could ever be created *ex novo*.

9. I have substantiated this in "Examining the Present Euro-Polity with the Help of Past Theories," to be published in Gary Marks, Fritz Scharpf, Philippe C. Schmitter, and Wolfgang Streeck, *Governance in the European Union* (London: Sage Publications, 1997), chapter 1.

10. The literature on the so-called Democracy Deficit of the EU is enormous—and, by and large, substantiates the observation that its existing institutional configuration falls considerably short of being democratic. As one wag put it, "[S]ince the EC requires that its members be democratic, if the EC were ever to apply to join itself, it would have to turn itself down." What is also (if less overtly) presumed is that there is no "indirect" or "functionalist" strategy that can fill this deficit. Hence, its members will have to agree "formally and intergovernmentally"—if and when it becomes imperative to address the issue.

11. Elsewhere, I have explored the four factors that seem (to me) to be

pushing the EU in such contrary directions: (1) the problem of enlarge-ment—especially to the east, (2) the increase in the politicization of inte-gration issues, (3) the growing implementation deficit, and (4) the rising need to deal with issues of European security after the Cold War. NB the tacit implication that the democratization deficit alone has (so far and for the foreseeable future) *not* been of sufficient magnitude to compel the member states to make a serious good-faith effort to eliminate it—even though some of the impetus behind the rising controversiality and wider public attention to EU affairs (politicization) probably has something to do with a general increase in questioning the democratic legitimacy of EU procedures and policies. Cf. my "The Future Euro-Polity and Its Impact upon Private Interest Governance within Member States," *Droit et Société* 28 (1994): 659–76, for further elaboration of this point.

12. The issue of how to label this emerging nonstate order poses a se-ries of difficulties. I have rejected "confederal" or "quasi-federal" be-cause these would limit the possible options to the existing continuum that runs between an intergovernmental organization and a suprana-tional state when it is precisely my contention that the Euro-polity is more likely to evolve toward (and, to a certain extent, already is) some-thing quite different. Elsewhere, I have proposed neo-Latin terms, *con-sortio* and *condominio*, to capture two of the alternatives in which either the functional or the territorial and the functional components of politi-cal order would vary from one member to another over an extended pe-riod of time. "Imagining the Future of the Euro-Polity with the Help of New Concepts," in Gary Marks, Fritz Scharpf, Philippe C. Schmitter, and Wolfgang Streeck, eds., *Governance in the European Union* (London: Sage Publications, 1977), last chapter.

I might have used EURO-OPNI ("European *objet politique non-identi-fié*") in honor of Jacques Delors, who once used this expression to (sort of) define what the EC/EU was and would remain for the foreseeable fu-ture, but I decided to forgo that opportunity. So, I have decided to stick with the innocuous label *Euro-polity.*

13. For a first effort at addressing this issue, see my "Alternatives for the Future European Polity: Is Federalism the Only Answer?" in Mario Telò, ed., *Démocratie et construction européenne* (Bruxelles: Éditions de l'U-niversité de Bruxelles, 1995), 349–61.

14. It should be observed that if the EU had not already expanded beyond the limits of intergovernmental cooperation, the issue of its de-mocratization would be moot. There is no compelling reason that citi-zens would expect such an arrangement to be accountable—provided that their own democratically accountable rulers could either veto its ac-tions or withdraw from its jurisdiction with little or no effort.

15. And, in the *nation*-state model, these domains are supposed to be coterminous with a distinctive and unique national identity based on a common language, culture, descent group, or "community of fate" (*Schicksalsgemeinschaft*).

16. I have subsequently discovered that I am not alone in concluding that the EU may be heading for novelty. Ben Rosamund, for example, has suggested that "integration may be coaxing (or perhaps even is) the evolution of new state forms which are not *nation*-states." "Mapping the European Condition: Theory of Integration and the Integration of Theory," *European Journal of International Relations* 1:3 (September 1995): 403.

17. Philippe Schmitter, *Come Democratizzare l'Union Europea e Perche* (Bologna: Il Mulino, 2000).

18. Guillermo O'Donnell and Philippe C. Schmitter, *Transitions from Authoritarian Rule: Prospects for Democracy: Tentative Conclusions about Uncertain Democracies* (Baltimore/London: Johns Hopkins University Press, 1986). Also, Philippe C. Schmitter, "Transitology: The Science or the Art of Democratization?" in Joseph Tulchin, ed., *The Consolidation of Democracy in Latin America* (Boulder: Lynne Rienner, 1995), 11–44.

PART III

LIMITS TO INSTITUTIONAL DESIGN?

9

CONSTITUTIONAL DESIGN: AN OXYMORON?

DONALD L. HOROWITZ

Now that the latest wave of worldwide democratization has apparently ended, debates have begun about institutions appropriate to the consolidation of new democracies. Lively controversies have raged about the respective merits of presidential and parliamentary systems, proportional and plurality electoral systems, unitary and federal governments.[1] No sooner have these debates captured the imagination of academicians and policymakers than it has become clear that a peculiar set of problems surrounds the maintenance of democracy in societies severely divided along ethnic lines. For these societies, special sets of institutions seem to be required to insure that minorities who might be excluded by majoritarian systems be included in the decision-making process and that interethnic compromise and accommodation be fostered rather than impeded.

These issues are of pressing importance in conflict-prone societies all around the world, from Northern Ireland in Western Europe to Bosnia, Slovakia, Romania, Bulgaria, Macedonia, and Cyprus in Eastern Europe, to Tatarstan, Georgia, Kazakhstan, and Moldova in the former Soviet Union, to Sri Lanka, Pakistan, and Fiji in Asia and the Pacific, to South Africa, Nigeria, Kenya, and Sudan in Africa. Perhaps surprisingly, there is no agreement on the political and constitutional arrangements most likely to be conducive to peace and accommodation in a democratic context. Some scholars advocate one set of electoral and governmental arrangements; others favor an alternative set. Practitioners often have different views altogether. More often than not, for reasons I shall elaborate below, inapt institutions or peculiar mixes of institutions are adopted, with little discernible effect on the conflicts they are intended to ameliorate and sometimes with clearly dysfunctional effects on those conflicts and on the future of democracy in the affected countries.

The present paper seeks to move beyond debates over the configuration of appropriate institutions and to focus on the reasons that democratic institutions appropriate to the predicament of severely divided societies are unlikely to be adopted by them. The debates thus far have had a curiously abstract air about them, in the sense that the participants lay down prescriptions for the affected societies, rather as a physician prescribes for a patient, operating on the assumption that the patient can simply choose to take the medicine. The trouble with this unspoken assumption is that there is no single patient involved at all; instead, there are collectivities. To put the point directly, it is very difficult for divided societies to adopt coherent institutional packages or to follow even the very best advice, whatever that might be. The reasons for this difficulty need careful specification, which they have not yet received (the issue has hardly even been noticed), for in this difficulty lie the seeds of a great many failures of democracy and of interethnic accommodation, even in otherwise favorable circumstances. Those who prescribe institutions may be quite right to think that they would have important consequences, were they adopted, but they have been remiss in failing to give equal attention to the process that determines whether they will be adopted.

Following a brief description of the substance of the debates in this field, the essay turns to the issues surrounding constitutional and political innovation in severely divided societies. After enumerating the obstacles to innovation, the essay then considers whether and how the obstacles can be overcome. In its present form, this effort is very much a provisional report on research that is still far from completed. The preliminary finding—really, still a hypothesis—is that, even in circumstances apparently most conducive to the adoption of coherent institutions, their adoption is unlikely.

THE CONTENDING PRESCRIPTIONS

A great many students of ethnically divided societies have done inventories of measures undertaken to promote interethnic accommodation, either within a democratic or an authoritarian framework.[2] Without attempting to be comprehensive, others have occasionally advocated particular measures or policies that seemed promising. Still others, particularly recently, have assumed or argued that no such measures are likely to be sufficient and have suggested that, for groups that are not territorially intermixed, secession should be looked upon with much greater favor than it has habitually received.[3] The growing receptivity to secession is really a counsel of despair that suggests the urgency of the issues dealt with here. In fact, secession is usually a very bad alternative to attempts of ethnic groups to live together in peace, if not in harmony. For one thing, secession places an international boundary between former domestic antagonists, thereby transforming their domestic conflicts into international conflicts, as partition did for India and Pakistan and as multiple secessions did for the former Yugoslavia. For another, secession cannot provide a clean break, since virtually all secessionist regions are themselves heterogeneous. Rather, secession simplifies intergroup confrontations by breaking up ethnically complex states into smaller compartments in which the struggles of a few groups tend to take a bipolar (or at most tripolar) form and in which one group usually emerges dominant and able to take possession of the new, smaller state for its own ends. In practice, to endorse secession is not so much to fulfill aspirations to self-determination as to allow some groups to determine the future of others.[4]

Although receptivity to secession is growing, it is certainly not the main academic approach to the problems of severely divided societies, as it is not the main approach in practice. Two other approaches have gained a measure of scholarly acceptance, but neither has much to show for itself in the actual practice of severely divided societies.

The first, and better known, approach to the problems of severely divided societies is consociation, a prescription for treating the multiethnic state for some purposes as if it were more than one polity and for according to each of the subpolities—the main ethnic groups—a considerable degree of veto power and autonomy.[5] Consociational democracy is not majoritarian democracy but a form of consensual democracy, in which all major groups are represented in governing grand coalitions in proportion to their numbers, in which elections are conducted by proportional representation in order to insure ethnic proportionality, in which major decisions are made by consensus (and so groups are accorded vetoes over them), and in which matters of concern to only one group are delegated for decision to that group. This is an approach to government that takes ethnic group divisions very seriously and is prepared to prevent majorities from ruling minorities by altering the rules of the game away from majority rule. Ethnic groups and ethnically based political parties are taken to be the building-blocks of the system, and conflict is to be contained by keeping each out of the affairs of the others and allowing each to prevent governmental action impinging on its distinctive interests.

Consociationalism is, then, a plan by which the ill effects of adversary democracy in divided societies are to be kept at bay, for electoral minorities need not risk total exclusion. Everyone is to be included in a grand coalition—that is, a coalition of parties representing all the groups, rather than representing any collection of parties with more than half the seats. Elites form a cartel to produce this result. As Arend Lijphart says, "The primary characteristic of the consociational democracy is that the political leaders of all significant segments of the plural society cooperate in a grand coalition to govern the country."[6]

I shall make no effort in this paper to conceal my view that consociational methods are inapt to mitigate conflict in severely divided societies, that they are more likely the product of resolved struggles or of relatively moderate cleavages than they are measures to resolve struggles and to moderate cleavages. Nor shall I do more than mention the powerful objection that, if indeed consociationalism really works as specified, it creates an altogether too cozy relationship among parties included in government and provides no room for a feature vital to democracy: opposition.[7] Instead, I shall recapitulate some objections to consociational theory that I have voiced in various other places,[8] but from then on ask not whether consociationalism is effective when adopted but whether it can be adopted intact. For there is no doubt, as we shall see, that various features of consociational democracy have attractions to some political leaders, usually minority leaders. And whatever its deficiencies as a means of reducing conflict, consociational democracy, in its original formulation at least, constitutes a coherent program: its parts are meant to fit together. As I shall suggest, the adoption of certain pieces of the program without others can produce results at odds with the goal of conflict reduction. The question I want to focus on here is whether consociational democracy or any other coherent plan can be adopted. But first the critique.

To some extent, lack of adoption of consociational schemes may be a function of the insights of decision-makers that those schemes will not help them out of the predicament they face as leaders in divided societies. It is certainly true that few severely divided societies have gone in this direction, some that are asserted to have adopted consociational methods have not actually done so, and some that have been coerced toward a consociational course (such as Cyprus and, recently, South Africa) have rapidly turned away from that course.

Insofar as consociationalism requires leaders to parcel out sovereign power to ethnic groups in divided societies, it seems plain enough that those who have all of state power within their reach have no incentive to take a large fraction of it and give it away. The most likely motive advanced, the awareness by leaders of the risk of mutual destruction, is based on a time horizon not generally employed in the calculations of political leaders: *après moi le déluge.* In any case, it certainly is not clear to them in advance that disintegrative conflict is not best deterred by a system that keeps power in their own hands. Furthermore, the sentiments of leaders and followers in divided societies are hardly conducive to what are regarded as concessions to the other side. If statesmanship is required, then it needs to be pointed out that the assumption that elites are invariably less ethnocentric than their supporters is without foundation. Most studies do not show leaders to be less ethnocentric than their followers, and some studies show that ethnocentrism actually increases with education.[9] Whatever the dispositions of leaders may be, when leaders have tried to compromise, it has been shown repeatedly that leadership leeway is very narrow on issues of ethnic power in severely divided societies. Compromisers can readily be replaced by extremists on their flanks, once the latter are able to make the case that a sellout of group interests is in progress. In short, no mechanism can be adduced for the adoption or retention of consociational institutions, particularly no reason grounded in electoral politics.

In conditions of free elections, the very creation of an interethnic coalition, whether intended to be a grand coalition or not, gives rise to ethnic opposition parties and so precludes such a coalition, even if it endures, from becoming a grand coalition. It is no accident that not one of the four developing countries asserted by Lijphart to be consociational in the 1970s—Lebanon, Malaysia, Surinam, and the Netherlands Antilles—had a grand coalition. Each had a coalition of parties, opposed by others, not a "coalition of the segments,"[10] and some violated other consociational criteria as well. Malaysia followed rules of disproportion, rather than proportion, had no mutual vetoes, and allowed only limited cultural autonomy. Lebanon had a presidential system, which Lijphart argues is inimical to power-sharing. India, asserted by Lijphart to have followed the consociational course,[11] has never had a grand coalition in the independence period and is a leading example of adversary, rather than consensual, democracy in Asia.

The electoral system favored by consociationalists, list-system proportional representation, insures the representation of ethnically based parties in proportion to their underlying votes, but this hardly can guarantee conciliatory results. If it fragments the electorate, list PR may give rise to coalitions, but there is nothing inherent in that electoral system that provides incentives to create an inclusive or grand coalition, as opposed to the usual sort of majority coalition. In many countries using list PR, adversary, majoritarian democracy has flourished. Where parties are ethnically based, as they are in severely divided societies, list PR is perfectly compatible with the domination of some groups by others.

The combination of list PR and ethnically based parties is inimical to incentives to make electoral appeals across group lines that might reduce the exclusive character of ethnic outcomes. With ethnic parties and list PR, the zero-sum relations of party lists to each other translates into a zero-sum competition between ethnic groups as well.[12] Absent PR, various distortions of electoral outcome—for example from accidents of electoral demography that produce wasted majority votes—might accidentally give minorities more than a proportionate share of seats and thus mitigate the severity of minority exclusion. PR eliminates distortions, benign as well as malign.

A rather different approach also takes ethnic group politics as the starting point and aims at multiethnic government, but without reversing majoritarian practices. Instead, it aims at majoritarian decisions made by a moderate, interethnic center. The underlying mechanism is based on incentives. The objective is to make multiethnic participation and compromise rewarding to all the participants who practice it. The approach differs in yet another way from consociationalism, because it does not require that leaders act on conciliatory feelings that do not exist; it assumes only that they will follow their interests.[13] Unlike consociationalism, this approach does not rest on a specified set of structures to be adopted invariably from country to country but upon certain mechanisms that the structures are to be designed to bring into play.

Since such an approach is based on political incentives, it requires some institutions that are specially tailored to majority rule in divided societies. The underlying mechanisms lie in inducements to politicians and their followers to engage in interethnic cooperation. Sometimes these inducements are supplemented by structures that simultaneously heighten intraethnic divisions, for fractions of groups may have greater incentives to cooperate across group lines than do entirely cohesive groups. The institutions that have such effects are largely territorial or electoral.

Depending on how boundaries are drawn, federalism can fragment groups and induce intergroup accommodation. When Hausa-Fulani dominance of all of Northern Nigeria was broken by new federal arrangements that divided the former Northern Region into states, new parties arose in minority areas of the

North, for now they had a chance to control a state rather than engage in a futile competition with a majority party within the undivided region. The weakened grip of the Hausa-Fulani provided a strong inducement for Hausa-Fulani politicians to seek allies from among other groups, something that a feature of the electoral system introduced in 1978 also induced them to do. I shall return to this example shortly.

Electoral systems are crucially important institutions in pushing political leaders toward ethnically conciliatory or ethnically exclusive strategies. If, for example, an electoral system rewards parties and politicians who take account of the interests of voters from groups other than their own, those parties and politicians will learn how to behave in an accommodative fashion. If the goal is to produce a moderate, interethnic center, it is necessary to provide ethnically based parties with electoral incentives to take moderate positions on issues of interethnic relations and to form electoral alliances and governing coalitions with moderate parties of other ethnic groups. Absent such electoral incentives, where parties break along ethnic lines, as they habitually do in divided societies, democratic business-as-usual results in the bifurcation of the included and the excluded. Group A, whose party holds 60 percent of the parliamentary seats, simply excludes Group B, with 40 percent.

Some multiethnic states have stumbled across apt institutions to mitigate polarization of this kind, often using electoral incentives to encourage moderation, and a few have begun to explore more deliberate constitutional measures to achieve these objectives. To be sure, ethnic demography often makes the task difficult. Heterogeneous constituencies, usually essential to the creation of conciliatory electoral systems, are not always easy to construct. Group settlement patterns may result in territorial separation. And it will require coherent packages of institutions, not partial adoptions, to make such incentives to intergroup accommodation effective.

Because this approach is designed to reward political leaders for interethnic moderation, sustaining the system, once it is adopted, will be much easier than sustaining consociational arrangements that are based merely on exhortations and constitutional constraints, devoid of political incentives. The politician who has benefited from appealing to voters across group lines will obviously see this behavior as being in his or her interest. Still, the threshold problem of adoption remains. Rather than innovate with an explicit view to conciliation, most states, most of the time, have adhered to institutions associated with their former colonial power or to institutions that were otherwise familiar to them. Very few states have learned from the actual experience with ethnic conflict of any other state.

THE COHERENT PACKAGE PROBLEM

This, then, is the depressing state of the available wisdom on one of the most important problems of the contemporary world: how to achieve democratic inclusion in severely divided societies. Two main approaches compete for acceptance, neither yet verifiable by the actual experience of divided societies, due to a threshold problem: precisely because the societies are divided, their divisions prevent them from taking action to breach their divisions, and so one cannot say whether the action would be effective if taken.

Both approaches need coherent packages of institutions to reduce conflict. Consociational theory demands (1) grand governing coalitions of all the main groups; (2) proportional representation elections; (3) proportional representation by ethnic groups in cabinet membership, public offices, and distribution of resources; (4) consensual rather than majority decision-making—that is, mutual group vetoes; and (5) a large measure of group autonomy. This is an elaborate set of interlocking structures, a fixed basket of institutions.

If consociational measures work to reduce conflict, they work together. If some parts of the package were adopted but others were not, the results could be worse than doing nothing at all. For example, with list-system proportional representation in a system of ethnic parties (the usual situation), the number of seats won by the various parties will tend to reflect the ethnic proportions of the voting-age population. If, as a concession to obtain adoption of proportional representation, the group that wanted PR agreed in return to abandon the equally consociational demand for consensual decision-making (that is, group vetoes), the result would be the worst of both worlds: majority exclusion of the minority, abetted by an electoral system that, by assuring the minority could gain only minority support, perfected the exclusion and made it more predictable. A good case can be made that just such an incoherent compromise is the fate of many consociational proposals once they are negotiated. The more general point is that the way in which the features of a constitutional design combine or break apart has much to do with outcomes that are intended or perverse. Proportional representation may look functional in a divided society if group vetoes guarantee consensual outcomes, but it looks dysfunctional without those vetoes. Again, the total package is decisive.

The incentives approach does not require specific structures. It is, for example, at home with any of several different electoral systems, depending on the context—and I shall soon mention a couple of these systems—provided that the system is strongly conducive to interethnic moderation in the appeal for votes and provided that the system is adopted across the board, so that moderation in one governmental body is not undone by countervailing incentives to extremism in another. But coherent, consistent packages of this kind are most unlikely to be produced by the political process that typically surrounds the adoption of innovations to reduce conflict in severely divided societies. This is for reasons I shall specify in a moment.

The disjunction of process and substance forms the core of my argument. So many forces favor the pursuit and exacerbation of conflict—and even deadly violence—in severely divided societies that anything less than a coherent package is unlikely to provide a sufficient counterweight to those forces, and yet only partial measures that are doomed to fall short of the coherent package stand a real chance of adoption most of the time.

To see why this is so, it will be necessary to delve into some actual examples of ameliorative measures that were adopted but proved inadequate, but first I want to make explicit a point I only hinted at earlier. Those polities that most need institutions to reduce interethnic conflict are those that are most unlikely to adopt them. The very conflicts that make compromise essential preclude agreements to facilitate compromise. Politicians benefitting from hostile sentiment toward other groups are unlikely to transform the conflict-prone environment that supports their political careers. That does not mean that conflict-reduction measures can never be adopted—the subject of this paper would be completely uninteresting if this were the case—but that they can be adopted, if at all, only at limited times and under certain conditions. Usually, political leaders will conclude, as Archbishop Makarios did with respect to the consociational measures that gave Turkish Cypriots weight in government far out of proportion to their numbers, that there is no reason to make such concessions.[14] Timing and leadership motivation are crucial variables here.

Now to examples of ameliorative measures that were adopted but proved inadequate—Nigeria, Sri Lanka, and Malaysia—and one ongoing example—Fiji—that, while still in the formative stage, also promises to be inadequate. In each case, policymakers hit upon an appropriate conciliatory device but found it insufficient to bear the full weight of ethnic conflict by itself.

In Nigeria (1978), the device adopted was the separately elected president, combined with an electoral system designed to guarantee that the winning candidate was moderate on matters of interethnic relations. The electoral formula involved two sets of requirements: plurality plus geographic distribution. The winning candidate had to receive the largest number of votes plus at least 25 percent of the vote in at least two-thirds of the then-19 states. Since territory was a proxy for ethnicity, the intention was to preclude even two of the three main groups (Hausa, Yoruba, and Ibo) from combining to win the election without minority support. The system worked exactly as intended. The victor in the first presidential election, Shehu Shagari, proved to be a panethnic figure. The problem was that no similar electoral system was adopted for the Nigerian legislature, whose members were elected from largely homogeneous constituencies on a formula requiring only a plurality. Those members acted simply as representatives of their own ethnic groups; they were not inclined to interethnic conciliation; and their pursuit of conflict helped cancel out Shagari's pursuit of accommodation. So here is a case in which the benign effects of one institution—even when combined with another, the federalism that reduced Shagari's party's core support and so made it even more inclined to accommodation—were outweighed by the negative effects of still others. This is a paradigm of the inadequacy of anything less than a coherent package.

In the same year (1978), Sri Lanka also moved to a presidential system, partly to enable strong leadership to take the measures required to achieve a compromise with the Tamils. There, too, an accommodative electoral formula was adopted. The president was to be elected by a system of alternative voting, a method of election that had enormous potential for minority votes to tip the balance between two Sinhalese candidates and so to provide incentives for one of them to be moderate on issues of concern to Tamils. As in Nigeria, the legislature was elected under a different system likely to produce less conciliatory results. Unfortunately, moreover, by the time of the first presidential election under the new system, ethnic conflict had become so acute that Tamils essentially did not participate, thus effectively forfeiting the potential influence of Tamil voters in the presidential election. By the time of the next election (1988), a civil war was being fought in the Tamil areas, and an electoral boycott was conducted there. In short, the very promising alternative vote system never had a chance because it had been adopted so late in the development of the conflict. This, too, is a recurrent feature of ameliorative innovations: when there is time to act, the matter is not urgent; when the matter is urgent, there is no longer enough time.

The third example is Malaysia, where, at independence, Malaysians had stumbled upon an accommodative political arrangement for their very deeply divided society. For a variety of idiosyncratic reasons, a Malay party, a Chinese party, and an Indian party had formed a coalition to pool each others' votes. To do so, the coalition partners had to compromise on interethnic issues. For some years, those compromises saved Malaysia from becoming a deadly society of the sort Sri Lanka has become. But two problems continued to erode the Malaysian arrangements and the compromises that sustained them. Both are characteristic of the forces that work against durable democratic institutions in divided societies.

The first derived from the process of interethnic bargaining by which the Malaysians came to their constitutional agreement in the first place. The Malays and Chinese had traded some incommensurables, among them citizenship to the Chinese in return for unspecified measures to advance the Malays economically. The former (citizenship) was conferred at a stroke; the latter, a matter of economic development, could not be handled in the same way. When, years later, Malays regretted the little they had achieved economically, that realization greatly unsettled the basis of the constitutional bargain, jeopardized any further interethnic compromise, and in the end reduced the extent to which the Chinese were included in the political process.

The second, more powerful force for erosion derived from the Malaysian electoral system, which made the exchange of Chinese and Malay votes for coalition candidates a significant phenomenon in only some parliamentary constituencies, rather than all. Whether the moderate interethnic center could prevail over the respective Malay and Chinese extreme parties by pooling moderate Malay and Chinese votes depended on the particular demography and pattern of party support in a given constituency. Consequently, the need to pool votes across ethnic lines—which, according to the incentives view of conciliation, is the very foundation for interethnic compromise—could easily be weakened by changing the territorial boundaries of parliamentary constituencies. By 1974, electoral boundaries had been thoroughly gerrymandered so as to produce more Malay-majority constituencies and to pack Chinese voters into fewer constituencies, but with much greater Chinese majorities in the latter. In such constituencies, Chinese would essentially waste their votes by electing fewer legislators but with overwhelming support.[15]

On the one hand, then, accommodative institutions were undermined by other features of the founding compromise that encouraged the groups to measure the benefits and declare any shortfalls a breach of the agreement, casting the legitimacy of the constitutional settlement in question. And, on the other hand, precautions had not been taken against alteration of the electoral situation that had provided the foundation for compromise.

Finally, a quick look at what is emerging in Fiji, a dangerously divided society with a chance to restore a democratic and inclusive system. In 1996, the Fiji Constitution Review Commission rendered a long and thoughtful report, informed by the desire to make Fiji a democratic society that can manage its ethnic problems between Fijians and Indians.[16] In 1987, a military coup by Fijian forces had rejected an elected but disproportionately Indian government. Three years later, the military regime had promulgated a strongly pro-Fijian constitution that triggered considerable international criticism. As a result, the regime had been forced to promise a serious review. Among other things, the Constitution Review Commission proposed an electoral system, based on alternative voting, intended to foster political cooperation between moderate Fijian and Indian parties. Were it possible for this system to be adopted for a large number of ethnically heterogeneous constituencies, there is little doubt that it would produce a moderate, multiethnic, coalition government. Each of the two major groups has habitually divided its support between two parties of unequal electoral strength. These subethnic divisions, reflected in party politics, would provide conditions conducive to the formation of an interethnic coalition, flanked by ethnic parties opposing its compromises. Even after considerable enlargement of constituencies, however, the fraction of significantly heterogeneous seats was less than half of the total. Fiji, moreover, has a long history of reserving large numbers of seats for members of particular groups who are elected on the votes of members of their group alone (that is, reserved seats and communal rolls). Much as it might have liked to do so, the Commission felt itself unable to abolish all reserved seats, for that would have been an unsettling break with tradition and a step into the unknown that would surely have made the Commission's recommendations unacceptable. Instead, the Commission recommended that 25 reserved seats (12 Fijian, 10 Indian, 3 other minorities) be retained, and that the remaining 45 open seats (about 30 of them heterogeneous in composition) be elected by alternative voting.

Necessary though this course may have been, what it did at the outset was to dilute the conciliatory effects of alternative voting and to permit the members elected from reserved seats to constitute a built-in drag on compromise, for the electoral dynamics of their homogeneous constituencies will propel them to take extreme positions. As in Nigeria, one set of institutions would work against the other, producing an inconsistent set of incentives.

Following receipt of the Commission's report, the balance between reserved and open seats was altered further by a Joint Parliamentary Select Committee on the Constitution, which recommended 46 reserved seats and only 25 open ones (23 Fijian, 19 Indian, 4 other).[17] At the same time, it recommended constitutional provisions for a compulsory "multi-party Cabinet which would, as far as possible, be a fair representation of all parties represented in Parliament."[18] Both of these proposals were incorporated in the new constitution, which provided for much smaller, and therefore less heterogeneous, constituencies and for a requirement that all parties with at least 10 percent of the seats in the lower house be invited to be represented proportionately in the cabinet.[19] However, this requirement of party inclusion in government was not accompanied by any constitutional requirement for consensual government. Rather, government needs only the confidence of the majority of the house.[20] Minorities are not to have a veto.

What seems to have happened is that the desire of minority politicians to find their way into government conjoined with the desire of Fijian politicians to restore the international legitimacy Fiji had lost after the events of 1987.[21] The desire for certainty of inclusion in government pushed Indian politicians toward consociational impulses, while a desire for certainty of representation had frightened Fijian politicians into retention of a majority of reserved seats. Meanwhile, British parliamentary conventions had produced the usual provision about the confidence of the house. The result is a little consociationalism (if a minority option to join the cabinet can be considered consociational), even less in the way of electoral incentives to accommodation, and a large, residual dose of majoritarian institutions. Within a matter of months, the smaller of the two Fijian parties had joined, and some months later already left, the cabinet, so that the inclusive character of the coalition had already been ruptured. The leader of the larger Indian party declared the long constitutional crisis resolved, and Fiji was readmitted to the Commonwealth from which it had been expelled ten years earlier.

This was a hybrid constitution, if ever there were one. (Whether any constitution is other than a hybrid is a question to which I shall return.) From the standpoint of consociationalism, a proportional electoral system, cultural autonomy, and mutual vetoes are absent. From the standpoint of electoral incentives, unreserved seats are too scarce, the unreserved seats are insufficiently heterogeneous in composition, and, because post-electoral coalitions are not based on compromise necessary to lure votes across group boundaries, they are inadequate to foster conciliation. From the standpoint of majority rule, proportional inclusion of all parties in the cabinet means the end of opposition. (If some parties leave the cabinet, on the other hand, the consociational impulse is defeated.) Containing many professions of the need for interethnic accommodation, the new constitution is assuredly more liberal than its predecessor, but it points toward no clear path to conciliation.

The Common Sources of Difficulty

In these diverse examples—and in many others—there are a number of common sources of difficulty. (There are also a number of hopeful possibilities, even in these examples, but these I leave for the concluding section.) It is necessary to identify the common impediments to coherent institutional packages that are necessary to reverse the conflict dynamics of severely divided societies, both to see how recurrent—and even built-in—they are and to think about how they might be overcome.

First, there is the problem of knowledge. Decision-makers, including constitutional engineers, in most countries are utterly unaware of the techniques that have been utilized and the measures that have been adopted in other divided societies to promote interethnic accommodation. In many countries, there has been until recently only a most imperfect awareness of even the commonality of problems from one country to another: most have tended to think their problems were unique. When they seek to innovate, most decision-makers borrow (or sometimes avoid) institutions from countries with which they are most familiar, whether or not the institutions are apt for their predicament. Ex-colonial countries typically opt for the institutions associated with the mother country, often with unfortunate results. Benin, for example, adopted the French presidential runoff system, thereby turning its tripolar ethnic cleavages into more intractable bipolar ones. Negative learning also takes place. Although both Serbia and Macedonia might have benefited from federal institutions that accorded a measure of autonomy to their unhappy Albanian minorities, both "learned" from the dissolution of Yugoslavia that federalism promotes disintegration, rather than integration. There is a very large failure of knowledge at both ends: (1) failure of states to analyze their own problems accurately and to cast a net widely and in the right direction and (2) failure of external agencies to help in the dissemination of usable knowledge.

Second, related to failures of knowledge at the site of innovation, there is a failure of expertise more generally. Many specialists, called in to help design systems in lands far from home, simply bring along their usual tool kits, which were developed for more or less homogeneous societies. One might well call these visitors provision merchants. In the electoral field, reflecting debates that have little pertinence to the problems of divided societies, they typically advocate (depending on their own preferences) systems that will produce proportionality of seats to underlying votes, or strong and cohesive parties, or a limited number of parties and stable governments, or representatives in close touch with those who elected them. These, after all, constitute the usual evaluative criteria for electoral systems in societies that are not severely divided. More narrowly, they are the ingredients in the enduring but for present purposes inapposite debate between advocates of plurality and of proportional systems. The only purpose of electoral innovation that is of life-or-death relevance to the problems of divided societies—producing inducements to compromise and accommodation—finds no place in this debate, no place in the traditional literature on electoral systems, and generally no place in the on-site advice of experts.

A splendid example is the electoral system adopted in Papua New Guinea at independence. There, an even narrower set of issues dominated debate over the electoral system. The system, borrowed from the colonial power, Australia, was alternative voting, a preferential system with, as I have suggested, considerable power to foster intergroup accommodation, by requiring candidates who wish to reach the majority required for election to gain second-preference support from voters of groups other than their own. This system, imposed as if by accident, had exactly the conciliatory results one might anticipate.[22] Soon after independence, however, the alternative vote was scuttled, in favor of first-past-the-post, on grounds a simpler system was more desirable. The results were immediately apparent in the next elections, in which candidates were returned on small pluralities and with no support outside their own group.[23] Expertise had failed Papua New Guinea miserably by focusing only on the mechanics of balloting. Ironically, this was a case in which a more apt ex-colonial institution was rejected in favor of a less apt one in greater currency elsewhere.

Third, beyond any problems of knowledge, there are enormous disjunctions between what severely divided societies require and the methods that are used to decide on the institutions that will govern those societies. Typically, although the setting varies widely, negotiation is the method by which proposals are hammered out. Negotiation has its own exigencies; it entails bargaining, trading, and splitting differences. If obstacles arise because the participants have divergent preferences, they may exchange incommensurables to overcome the obstacles, thereby producing a mélange of institutions or even enshrining inconsistent solutions to problems within the same document. With negotiation, one may contrast planning, a process intended to produce internally consistent solutions to problems. Even from a process of planning, of course, perfectly coherent outcomes are unlikely, but in any case, in democratic constitutional design, bargaining and negotiation are the main modalities. Bargaining has much to commend it, but coherence is not among its virtues.

Of course, it is not bargaining alone, but the specific preferences likely to be entertained by ethnic party leaders in constitutional negotiations. They seek to reduce uncertainty in different ways. Majorities attempt to retain majoritarian institutions insofar as possible, while minorities search for guarantees. Consociational schemes seem to provide guarantees, however illusory they may prove to be in operation, and minorities find them attractive. Majorities are not keen on guarantees for minorities, needless to say, and they are certainly not inclined to the panoply of guarantees provided by consociational theory. If need be, they will agree to some fraction of guarantees, such as proportional cabinet representation or perhaps a PR electoral system, but they will find minority vetoes especially unattractive. Neither the leaders of majority ethnic parties nor of minority ethnic parties will be tempted to embark on electoral innovations that encourage candidates to seek marginal votes from voters of groups other than their own. Although such innovations are conducive to interethnic compromise, they risk electoral poaching on what would otherwise be the secure clienteles of ethnic parties, and they also pose the more general risk of uncertain electoral outcomes. When ethnic parties produce more or less predictable electoral results, a modicum of risk aversion will impel party leaders to reject systems that create greater uncertainty. Ironically, the very virtue of such systems for divided societies lies precisely in the uncertainty they generate by virtue of greater fluidity of party choice by the electorate. But interethnic virtue here constitutes intraethnic vice.

The result of this pattern of preferences is a distinctly suboptimal outcome. A few guarantees of minority participation, particularly in the cabinet, can be conceded by the majority. Especially if a majority-dominated regime is under international pressure to become less transparently ethnocratic, there are benefits for the regime in such a concession, which the minority will welcome. Incentive-based proposals will be less attractive to both sides. Unless there is external imposition of the constitution, as there was in Cyprus in 1960, or a minority regime is in an unusually strong position to dictate transitional institutions, as in South Africa in 1994, no strongly consociational scheme will be adopted. Even in these cases, the arrangements were not durable, just as the Nigerian and Malaysian incentive-based electoral institutions, both of them partial, were subject to erosion.

The pattern of preferences I have depicted explains the outcome in Fiji and implies that it is not idiosyncratic but is likely to be typical—not the only outcome, no doubt, but probably the most common. Those who plan constitutions may be persuaded that consociational or incentive-based arrangements are preferable, but their influence in the negotiations that lead to adoption is likely to be marginal.

I hasten to add, of course, that planning is a problematic category to begin with. Has anyone, after all, ever succeeded in planning any large institutional change? If we look to the United States Constitution, it may seem coherent in retrospect, but it was very much the product of *ad hoc* behavior at every step of its framing. Some of its institutions most celebrated as embodying its distinctive genius, especially those that support the separation of powers, were the product of compromise or usurpation. The bicameral solution to the big state–small state problem, with each state to have an equal number of votes in the Senate, was the result of the "great compromise" that saved the Philadelphia Convention; and the presidency was designed in committee by a small clique that wanted a vigorous executive and presented the office as a *fait accompli* to a convention deeply divided on the issue and certainly not disposed toward the proffered solution by anything like a majority.[24] By the same token, to say that bargaining determines outcomes is not to indicate anything about the identity, position, power, or preferences of the bargainers. Clearly, it matters whether some of them are in power and others out, whether some can thwart the constitutional change, whether the players are bargaining in the shadow of some larger forces, and so on.[25] I do not contrast coherence as an end with bargaining as a means in order to argue that either of these categories is truly homogeneous but only to suggest that the two deserve juxtaposition in this context.

I particularly want to insist on coherence as a virtue of constitutional design for severely divided societies, because their centrifugal forces are so strong that without equally strong, consistent, centripetal institutions their divisions tend to become acute. In a word, strong ethnic affiliations and ordinary democracy combine to produce political exclusion of minorities. The fact that coherence is rare and bargaining is common does not make me naive so much as it makes me skeptical. My central proposition embodies the paradox that substantial compromise on a plan to facilitate interethnic compromise decreases the likelihood of interethnic compromise in the operation of the plan once adopted.

Fourth, severely divided societies have not always been well served by well-intentioned third parties that have tried to assist in mediating solutions. Those third parties whose specialty is negotiation are most unlikely to know very much about severely divided societies. Third-party mediators tend to be interested, above all, in having the parties reach agreement. Mediators and negotiators receive their rewards (sometimes even Nobel Prizes) for reaching agreement: they receive an advance against performance that will not need to be repaid if performance later falls short. By then, they will be working on another problem. Third-party mediators have even stronger interests than negotiators do in reaching agreement, for they, unlike the participants, do not have to live with the results. They are often called "facilitators," a term that aptly describes their role, which is to "get people to the table," "maximize areas of agreement," or "get to 'yes.'" They measure success by the achievement of agreement, and their method is wholly processual, which is to say that it is content-neutral.[26] If anything is clear in the field of ethnic conflict, it is that the content of ameliorative institutions is not something about which the participants can afford to be neutral. It follows that not any agreement is preferable to none.

In some ways, the most dangerous people in a negotiation are third parties, those with only detachment to offer. Anything a third-party facilitator can point to in order to induce moderation is probably already discounted in the conflict. Does it stand to reason that those with less interest in the conflict are likely to see a reason for moderating the conflict that the parties, who are more intensely interested in it, have failed to discern? It may be that the incentive to join the European Union will soften the intransigent behavior of ethnic antagonists in Eastern Europe, although the willingness of Lebanese, Cypriots, and Sri Lankans to destroy their *entrepôt* and tourist trades suggests that the lure of prosperity is hardly infallible in inducing moderation. In any case, it is not merely a matter of altering the willingness to make concessions that is crucial—although this is what third parties focus on—but of altering the incentives and behavior of the antagonists once they have made concessions at the threshold, and this depends on what arrangements they agree to. Here third parties are generally not helpful, for at best they are process experts without substantive expertise in the institutions that would reduce conflict,[27] and they are likely to see the issue in terms of the antagonists' reluctance or inability to summon up the requisite "political will."

Fifth, the assumption is frequently made about severe conflicts that if the parties could not agree before and can agree on something now, this is a good first step, even if that something is not quite apt to ease their relations. If it is wrong at the outset, it can be fixed later. This assumption is usually incorrect. Interests quickly crystallize around whatever arrangements are adopted, even if they are dysfunctional, so that even if the institutions fail in their public objectives, there are actors whose private success comes to depend on the maintenance of the arrangements. This is most visible in the case of Fiji, where it proved impossible to dislodge the reserved seats even when a fresh start was to be made. Two of the most prominent techniques used by structural engineers (those who build bridges and buildings) to avert failure are redundancy—that is, extra capacity—and midcourse correction, using feedback. For constitutional engineers, midcourse correction is not readily available, since players quickly get attached to the initial institutions that facilitated their success. All that is left, therefore, is redundancy. As I have suggested, some features of the intractable ethnic conflicts dealt with here positively require redundancy, because the whole point of the arrangements is to create institutions that will counter, and counter strongly, again and again, the preexisting incentives of the parties that produced and sustain the conflict at high levels.

In a divided society, it is fortunate if consensus can be reached on any institutions, much less truly apt institutions. Yet it is wrong to think that whatever the parties agree to will be durable. All an agreement means is that it was acceptable to the parties at the moment it was consummated. Other agreements, including much better agreements, might also have been acceptable. It is a mistake to elevate the existence of agreement over the content of agreement when it comes to societies prone to violent conflict. Yet that is what is done, over and over again.

New Departures

Up to this point, it might be appropriate to read this paper as a lament. For the most part, after all, severely divided societies have not had the conflict-reducing institutions they need. In many cases—among them Lebanon, Northern Ireland, Bosnia,

Rwanda, and Sri Lanka—the results have been truly catastrophic. Further catastrophes are waiting in the wings. In the post-Communist world, Romania, Bulgaria, Macedonia, Kazakhstan, Kirghizia, Tatarstan, Bashkortostan, and Crimea, among others, have so far been very lucky. Much of the pessimism, as I have emphasized, derives from the difficulty of finding procedures that are likely to yield the institutional packages divided societies need. And so there is a certain *prima facie* reason for pessimism.

One could paint an even bleaker picture. I have not touched on the whole question of timing. A careful examination of the occasions for constitutional rethinking in severely divided societies reveals that those occasions are few. They tend to occur in the wake of disasters (thirteen years of civil war and military rule in Nigeria) or at those rare moments when momentous general changes are in place (the collapse of Communism or the end of colonialism). These are not everyday occurrences, and so, in addition to all the other impediments to arriving at apt arrangements, there is the prior condition: the existence of an occasion for rethinking the matter at all. Moreover, not all of these moments are conducive to apt innovation. If we ask what it takes to induce ethnic majorities or ethnic groups otherwise politically advantaged to agree to accommodative institutions that do not reinforce their advantages, we have limited the occasions for apt innovation considerably. The end of Communism or of colonialism alone was surely not sufficient.

The exceptional character of the occasions for innovation is suggested by one case in which the requisite inducements were present: Nigeria 1978. Nigerian leaders knew they did not wish to return to the institutions they (rightly) believed were conducive to conflict. More than that, they were unsure who would be victimized in the next conflict and so were eager to design institutions that would make ethnic domination difficult. That they did not fully succeed is attributable more to deficiencies of constitutional technology than of attitude. The Nigerians quite clearly wore John Rawls' "veil of ignorance." Most groups, most of the time, will come to the table unveiled.

Do the many failures of institutional innovation and the maladroit efforts of outsiders, then, necessarily consign the unlucky inhabitants of conflict-prone countries to lives that are precarious, uncomfortable, and possibly quite short? There are a few promising openings that remain to be explored at all and on which I intend to focus.

The first is that there is a small but discernible tendency toward the development of a more encouraging species of constitutional engineering. The worldwide growth of democracy has made it uncomfortable for regimes that observe democratic forms but exclude minorities from effective political participation to continue to do business this way. Moreover, when occasions do arise for constitutional innovation, it has become increasingly clear that the making or remaking of a constitution is an international and comparative venture in a way that it was not generally seen to be a couple of decades ago. This is an important change that has not received the notice it deserves. The Nigerians began to think in these terms in 1978, when their Constituent Assembly took at a closer look at unfamiliar American institutions that they believed might help them escape their predicament. Much more recently, the South Africans, in the making of their interim constitution and now in the making of their permanent constitution, have cast a very wide net in the search for ideas. Tatarstan gave some attention to practice elsewhere (Puerto Rico, in fact!) when it negotiated its asymmetrical federalism with Russia. The Fiji Constitution Review Commission traveled and consulted around the world, in a careful quest for institutions apt for the divisions it confronted. In general, the cascading democratizations of the early 1990s led those charged with constitutional innovation to begin to think their problems were not *sui generis.*

Yet a strong case can be made that more information has generally not translated into more usable knowledge, that it has meant either more blind copying or very crude adaptation of institutions in use (or in vogue) elsewhere, to produce yet more peculiar hybrids. There seems to be an emerging tendency, for example, toward the adoption of mixed electoral systems, with a newly imported system used for some seats or offices and the preexisting system used for the remainder. Constitutional borrowing in general is a subject for another day, but the more limited point can be made now that the comparative analysis that would need to be done by decision-makers to make borrowing effective in their home conditions has so far been done very superficially. This calls to mind the impulses of leaders in many divided societies a decade or two earlier to examine what would be required to make their countries just like Switzerland—cantonization and all.[28]

A second potentially promising development suggests a way out of the problem of inducing participants who benefit from the pursuit of ethnic conflict to embark on a quest for accommodative arrangements. In some of the most dangerous cases, it turns out that precisely those leaders who have interests in pursuing conflict are sometimes obliged to put constitutional decision-making in other hands. When that happens, there is an opening for breaking out of conflict-enhancing incentives. That was the case in Nigeria in 1978, when the military regime yielded to pressure to create a Constituent Assembly. It has been the case in Northern Ireland, where the British and Irish governments have been the sources of innovation; and it was also the case in Fiji, where, as in Nigeria, a military regime was obliged to create an independent constitutional commission. The contending parties on Cyprus have so far been conducting their prenegotiations under the aegis of the United Nations. (One could say that the Dayton Accords that produced the Bosnia-Croatia federation derive from a similar lifting of decision-making from familiar to unfamiliar hands, but the Dayton results are hardly of the sort that can be commended.) Finally, the need of governments to conform to Western standards of human rights or to quell the anxieties of investors may yet produce a comparable (and perhaps benign) involvement of outsiders in the process of constitutional innovation, although, as I have argued, the involvement of third parties who specialize merely in negotiation will surely be insufficient.

If this is so, then the prospects may not be quite as bleak as I have suggested they are. There will still be enormous problems of producing coherent and apt institutions, but at least the process will not always be foreclosed at the outset by the interests of political leaders. The focus of my ongoing research, therefore, is on discerning whether the involvement of outsiders (commissions of inquiry and the like) and the growing practice of turning constitution-making into a comparative exercise show signs of producing the sort of internally consistent, coherent plan that I have argued severely divided societies need. For if, as I have hypothesized, coherent constitutional plans for conflict reduction are unlikely to be adopted, then this hypothesis ought to be able to withstand a test in the circumstances most favorable to its falsification. If, for example, even in conditions most hospitable to elaborate constitutional innovation, what recurrently gets adopted is a mélange of inconsistent provisions, then it may be concluded that the hypothesis is true.[29]

There are several circumstances that may create such favorable conditions. There may be an element of constitutional imposition from outside, as in Northern Ireland. Alternatively, as I mentioned earlier, the existing regime may find its position sufficiently precarious or illegitimate that it is obliged to delegate the formulation of proposals to outsiders, as the Nigerian military regime did in the late 1970s and the Fijian military regime did in the 1990s. Similarly, a regime may find constitution-making power essentially usurped, as African regimes did in the early 1990s, when unofficial but powerful "national conferences" appeared on the scene in Benin, Togo, and elsewhere in Francophone Africa. In such cases, the weakened state of the regime renders it liable to accept plans it might otherwise dismiss, and the forces for bargaining that produce inconsistent outcomes may be temporarily disabled. In still other cases, new regimes may come to power as a result of civil war or the fall of Communism; and, committed to a fresh start on ethnic issues, they may be especially eager to receive expert advice. Eritrea had elaborate constitutional processes and proposals as a result of such a regime change. Regimes that are unusually dependent on the good will of outsiders, particularly the confidence of foreign investors that ethnic conflict will be kept under control, may go out of their way to propitiate external forces by constitutional designs. There are, then, many roads that lead to conditions hospitable to coherent constitutional plans for severely divided societies.[30]

I cannot say for sure what will result from this research, but perhaps I can introduce what may prove to be an important intervening variable: the ambition of the constitutional plan. That this is an important issue is suggested by the Northern Ireland Agreement of 1998.[31] The agreement is generally, but not perfectly, consociational,[32] largely because of the power of the external British and Irish authorities to dictate the overall shape of the arrangements (although not the particulars). The agreement contains numerous interesting features, but the one I wish to highlight here is its maximal ambition.

The agreement provides for a very large measure of ethnic proportionality in a variety of institutions, and it makes an advance promise of ethnic equality and—in a fascinating phrase—"parity of esteem" for the two main groups. The phrase is significant, because it goes right to the heart of what divided societies struggle over: whose country this is, who will dominate whom, what the terms of political incorporation will be. Certainly, groups in Northern Ireland have struggled over these issues, particularly the question of whose symbols were entitled to priority of esteem. At a stroke, the agreement promises to bring these struggles to an end, to preempt them, and implicitly to measure future political performance by its conformity to the objective of parity of esteem. Given the (at best) spotty record of political systems in divided societies in providing for the fair treatment of all major groups within them, the agreement sets Northern Ireland up for a possible shortfall. The aptness of the institutions established for Northern Ireland will be sorely tested by the need to meet such maximal standards, rather than merely to muddle along in a more or less peaceful state—which is what ordinarily passes for success when groups are inclined to severe conflict.

The proposed arrangements might just prove durable, were they intended to produce only incremental change in interethnic relations. Indeed, it is a frequent criticism of consociationalism that its arrangements, especially mutual vetoes, are conducive to minimal government in general. One would think that this extraordinarily ambitious agenda would require considerable political support for the emergence of a moderate middle to accomplish it. Institutions that include no likely electoral support for intergroup compromise, that in fact are premised on the electoral status quo,[33] form a particularly unpromising basis for such a political transformation. To put the point provocatively, how can the ambitions of the proposals be realized in the face of something approaching vetoes accorded to the unreconstructed ethnic parties?

If Northern Ireland promises to be a state freighted with burdens too great for its institutions, the Cyprus discussions may be going in an opposite direction, almost to the point of abandoning the interethnic state. A host of outside bodies is involved: the United Nations, Britain, the United States, the European Union, among them. The impulses of at least some of these outsiders seem to embody two main ideas: an extremely decentralized federation, with only those matters requiring central coordination to be handled by the central government, and a central government designed somehow to prevent majority domination.[34] Whereas government in Northern Ireland would be required to shoulder heavy burdens in contentious areas, the central government on Cyprus might be divested of all such burdens (and most others as well). So far as ethnic relations go, a new regime on Cyprus would have a light agenda indeed.

This leads me to speculate that there may be four likely outcomes of constitutional processes for divided societies. The outcomes are scaled by the ambition of their designers and the character of the institutions to be introduced. The first, suggested by Serbia and Slovakia, among many others, is ethnically exclusivist, either because the constitution identifies the state with a single group or because straightforward majority rule produces such a result *de facto*. This is, of course, an exceedingly common outcome. The second, exemplified by Fiji (1997) and Nigeria (1978), is a hybrid of institutions combined in such a way as to be inadequate to generate the requisite compromise. The third, illustrated by Northern Ireland, is largely consociational, but probably inadequate to sustain the heavy burden of change laid upon it by external forces eager to transform the conflict dramatically from the start. The fourth, possibly typified by Cyprus, is a minimalist regime, entrusted with doing nothing to change the status quo, because everyone is incredulous of any prospect of doing so. The ambitions range from roughly zero in the first case, to mere peacekeeping in the fourth, to modest accommodation in the second, to serious transformative efforts in the third. If this is the range of likely outcomes, the one combination it excludes is a coherent set of institutions, committed to compromise and capable of effecting at least modest conflict reduction.

It may be "that there is no constitutional solution to be found to the case of really radical social diversity."[35] That is, no institutions may be adequate to cabin the conflict. This conclusion is not yet warranted by the evidence, because particular structures do seem to produce particular benign results when they invoke appropriate mechanisms, even where the ensemble of institutions does not produce benign results overall. Still, it may be that no process is adequate to produce an ensemble of institutions that are adequate; and on that the proper view at this point, it seems to me, is pessimistic agnosticism.

NOTES

I am grateful to the United States Institute of Peace and the Harry Frank Guggenheim Foundation for the support that has facilitated the research on which this paper is based. I am also appreciative of the support of the Eugene Bost Foundation at Duke Law School and the hospitality of the STICERD Distinguished Visitor Program at the London School of Economics and of the Government Department at the LSE, where this paper was revised for publication.

1. See, e.g., Giovanni Sartori, *Comparative Constitutional Engineering*, 2d ed. (New York: New York University Press, 1997); Juan Linz and Arturo Valenzuela, eds., *The Failure of Parliamentary Democracy* (Baltimore: Johns Hopkins University Press, 1994); Mathew Shugart and J. M. Carey, *Presidents and Assemblies: Constitutional Design and Electoral Dynamics* (New York: Cambridge University Press, 1993); Donald L. Horowitz, "Presidents vs. Parliaments: Comparing Democratic Systems," *Journal of Democracy* 1:4 (Fall 1990): 73–79; Seymour Martin Lipset, "The Centrality of Political Culture," *Journal of Democracy* 1:4 (Fall 1990): 80–83; Juan T. Linz, "The Virtues of Parliamentarianism," *Journal of Democracy* 1:4 (Fall 1990): 84–91.

2. For some early inventories, see Claire Palley, *Constitutional Law and Minorities* (London: Minority Rights Group Report no. 36, 1978); Milton Esman, "The Management of Communal Conflict," *Public Policy* 21 (Winter 1973): 49–78; Eric A. Nordlinger, *Conflict Regulation in Divided Societies* (Cambridge: Harvard University Center for International Affairs, Occasional Paper no. 29, 1972).

3. See Chaim Kaufmann, "Possible and Impossible Solutions to Ethnic Civil Wars," *International Security* 20 (1996): 136–75.

4. There is a voluminous recent literature on secession, most of it hospitable, which I have reviewed in "Self-Determination: Politics, Philosophy, and Law," *Nomos XXXIX: Ethnicity and Group Rights* (New York: New York University Press, 1997), 421–63.

5. See Arend Lijphart, *Democracy in Plural Societies* (New Haven: Yale University Press, 1977).

6. Ibid., 25.

7. See Courtney Jung and Ian Shapiro, "South Africa's Negotiated Transition: Democracy, Opposition, and the New Constitutional Order," *Politics and Society* 23:3 (September 1995): 269–308.

8. Horowitz, "Self-Determination," 439–40; Horowitz, *A Democratic South Africa? Constitutional Engineering in a Divided Society* (Berkeley: University of California Press, 1991), 137–45, 167–71; Horowitz, *Ethnic Groups in Conflict* (Berkeley: University of California Press, 1985), 568–76.

9. The studies are collected in Horowitz, "Self-Determination," 457 n. 31, and Horowitz, *A Democratic South Africa*, 140–41, nn. 44–50.

10. Lijphart, *Democracy in Plural Societies*, 201, 205.

11. Arendt Lijphart, "The Puzzle of Indian Democracy: A Consociational Interpretation," *American Political Science Review* 90 (June 1996): 258–68.

12. I deal with list PR and its anticonciliatory tendencies in Horowitz, *A Democratic South Africa?* 167–76.

13. For general statements of the approach, see Horowitz, *A Democratic South Africa?*; Horowitz, "Ethnic Conflict Management for Policymakers," and "Making Moderation Pay: The Comparative Politics of Ethnic Conflict Management," in Joseph V. Montville, ed., *Conflict and Peacemaking in Multiethnic Societies* (Lexington, Mass.: Lexington Books, 1989), 115–30, 451–76.

14. See David Wippman, "International Law and Ethnic Conflict on Cyprus," *Texas International Law Journal* 31 (Spring 1996): 141–80, at 144–46.

15. This process actually began soon after independence. See Lim Hong Hai, "The Malayan Electoral System: Its Formulation and Change," Ph.D. dissertation, Faculty of Economics and Administration, University of Malaya, 1997, 225–337.

16. *Towards a United Future: Report of the Fiji Constitution Review Commission* (Suva: Parliament of Fiji Parliamentary Paper no. 34 of 1996). I was a consultant to the Commission but had no role in its deliberations or in the drafting of its report. The Commission consulted with proponents of several approaches to conflict reduction. Its report canvassed consociational and incentive-based approaches and opted for the latter

after a quite careful review that constitutes the most incisive analysis of issues of conflict reduction I have seen in a report by policymakers.

17. *Report of the Joint Parliamentary Select Committee on the Constitution* (Suva: Parliament of Fiji Parliamentary Paper no. 17 of 1997), 20.

18. Ibid., 17.

19. Constitution (Amendment) Act 1997 of the Republic of the Fiji Islands, 25 July, 1997, Arts. 50, 51, 54, 99(5). The alternative vote was retained, but the 25 open seats were to be elected in single-member constituencies, whereas the 45 proposed by the Commission were to be elected in 15 larger three-member constituencies, with each member to be elected separately.

20. Ibid., Art. 6(g).

21. For a summary of the Indian parties' submissions to the Constitution Review Commission that urge constitutionally mandated participation in the cabinet of any party that obtained more than 20 percent of the seats, see Yash Ghai, "The Recommendations on the Electoral System: The Contribution of the Fiji Constitution Review," in Brij V. Lal and Peter Larmour, eds., *Electoral Systems in Divided Societies: The Fiji Constitution Review* (Canberra: National Centre for Development Studies, Research School of Pacific and Asian Studies, Australian National University, 1997), 147–59.

22. Cf. Horowitz, *A Democratic South Africa?*, 188–95.

23. See Ben Reilly, "The Effects of the Electoral System in Papua New Guinea," in Y. Saffu, ed., *The 1992 PNG Election: Change and Continuity in Electoral Politics* (Canberra: Department of Political and Social Change, Australian National University, 1996), 43–76.

24. On the Senate, see Max Farrand, *The Framing of the Constitution of the United States* (New Haven: Yale University Press, 1913), 91–112. On the presidency, see Donald L. Horowitz, "Is the Presidency Failing?" *The Public Interest* 88 (Summer 1987): 3–27, at 7–11.

25. Samuel P. Huntington, *The Third Wave: Democratization in the Late Twentieth Century* (Norman: University of Oklahoma Press, 1991), describes a variety of modes of democratization that suggest multiple bargaining situations.

26. I have served on a number of occasions as a mediator, and I can testify to the powerful pull, inherent in the role, to help the parties end their dispute on any terms they find agreeable, no matter how lopsided the merits of the dispute may be.

27. Obviously, I am not referring here to outsiders whose expertise is not in negotiation alone but in measures to reduce ethnic conflict.

28. Sri Lankan Tamil leaders were particularly keen on the Swiss example in the 1950s and 1960s.

29. For the underlying logic, see Gary King, Robert O. Keohane, and Sidney Verba, *Designing Social Inquiry: Scientific Inference in Qualitative Research* (Princeton: Princeton University Press, 1994), 209–12. Cf. Harry Eckstein, "Case Study and Theory in Political Science," in Fred I. Greenstein and Nelson W. Polsby, eds., *Handbook of Political Science*, vol. 7 (Reading, Mass.: Addison Wesley Publishing Co., 1975), 79–137.

30. For some of the pertinent literature, see John R. Heilbrunn, "Social Origins of National Conferences in Benin and Togo," *Journal of Modern African Studies* 31:2 (June 1993): 277–99; Chris Allen, "Reconstructing an Authoritarian State: 'Democratic' Renewal in Benin," *Review of African Political Economy* 54 (July 1992): 43–58; Jean-Jacques Reynal, "Le renouveau démocratique béninois: modèle ou mirage?" *Afrique Contemporaire* 160 (4e trimestre 1991), 3–25; Jon Elster, "Constitutionalism in Eastern Europe: An Introduction," *University of Chicago Law Review* 58:2 (Spring 1991): 447–82; Allison K. Stanger, "Czechoslovakia's Dissolution as an Unintended Consequence of the Velvet Constitutional Revolution," *East European Constitutional Review* 5:4 (Fall 1996): 40–46; Edward W. Walker, "The New Russian Constitution and the Future of the Russian Federation," *Harriman Institute Forum* 5:10 (June 1992): 1–16; A. E. Dick Howard, "The Indeterminacy of Constitutions," *Wake Forest Law Review* 31:2 (Summer 1996): 383–410; Eric Stein, "Post-Communist Constitution-Making," *New Europe Law Review* 1:2 (Spring 1993): 421–75.

31. Agreement Reached in the Multi-Party Negotiations, April 10, 1998.

32. See Brendan O'Leary, "The British-Irish Agreement: Consociation Plus," unpublished paper, London School of Economics, May 13, 1998.

33. The Northern Ireland proposals take party alignments and support as given and make no pretense of trying to alter them.

34. See "Set of Ideas on an Overall Framework Agreement on Cyprus," negotiated by leaders of the Greek Cypriot and Turkish Cypriot Communities, January 20, 1997, available at http://www.access.ch/tuerkei/GRUPF/f616.htm

35. Robert E. Goodin, "Designing Constitutions: The Political Constitution of a Mixed Commonwealth," *Political Studies* 44:3 (Special Issue, 1996): 635–46, at 643.

10

DESIGNING DEMOCRATIC INSTITUTIONS: POLITICAL OR ECONOMIC?

BROOKE A. ACKERLY

Although Donald Horowitz argues that ethnic cleavages create political obstacles to coherent constitutional reform, the importance that ethnic cleavages take on may itself be a function of the socioeconomic opportunities associated with political power. Horowitz argues that coherent constitutional design is unlikely under conditions of ethnic cleavages due to the centripetal forces of political processes. He sets out to prove his hypothesis by examining the political processes of failed constitutional design in four ethnically divided societies where constitutional reform and democratization fail or stall. The evidence that Horowitz presents from Nigeria, Sri Lanka, Malaysia, and Fiji suggests that in these ethnically divided societies political forces prevented constitutional reformers from designing the coherent package of institutions that is necessary for inclusive democratization. However, evidence from these same societies suggests that explaining the political processes of constitutional design requires analysis of other factors—particularly socioeconomic conditions.

The literature on democratic transitions and constitutional design has paid attention to ethnic cleavages as a potentially significant factor in the failure of constitutional reforms. Other factors

285

include poor economic performance; inefficacious, weak, militant, and uncompromising political leadership; a political culture without tolerance, freedom, and competition; socioeconomic inequality; lack of associational life; a powerful centralized state; state control over the economy; party systems that do not cut across cleavages; constitutional structures that do not cut across cleavages; an autonomous military; and international factors including colonial and postcolonial factors.[1] One way to test Horowitz's hypothesis against the alternative hypotheses that any other of these factors could be decisive in the political failure to design a coherent constitution and supporting legal institutions would be to broaden the data set beyond his subset of countries with ethnic cleavages and political failure such that it include countries that were able to design appropriate constitutions despite ethnic cleavages and countries whose constitutional designs failed despite their *not* having ethnic cleavages.[2] With enough variability in each variable, the model could control for factors other than ethic cleavages and thus measure the latter's impact on the failure to design coherent constitutional reforms. Examining the political processes associated with the other obstacles to coherent constitutional design would improve the descriptive accuracy and predictive implications of Horowitz's project. Such a model could test competing hypotheses.

Drawing on one of Horowitz's examples, the case of Nigeria, I propose an alternative hypothesis about the failure of democratic institutions. I propose that where there are socioeconomic inequalities (particularly if they are worsening) and where high economic rewards accrue to those in political power, in competition for power political elites may resort to exploiting ethnic differences. Thus, socioeconomic cleavages and not ethnic cleavages underlie the centripetal political processes that prevent coherent constitutional design. If my alternative hypothesis is correct, we can be more optimistic about the possibility for coherent constitutional design in ethnically divided societies than Horowitz's "Constitutional Design" would indicate.

HOROWITZ'S METHODOLOGY

Horowitz's interest in studying the political processes affecting constitutional design is consistent with the broader democratiza-

tion literature that has turned away from the question of precon-
ditions of democracy to look more closely at processes.[3] The
problem with Horowitz's method, however, is that by selecting
only cases with the explanatory variable that his hypothesis pre-
dicts is most powerful—ethnic cleavages—and the outcome that
he wishes to explain—incoherent and thus failed constitutional
design—he risks overestimating the effect of ethnic cleavages on
failure of democratization due to incoherent constitutional design.[4] Further, his discussion of the cases is limited to analysis of
the ethnic cleavages and their impact on the political processes.
However, other factors—the economic premium of centralized
political power and socioeconomic conditions—may also have
important influences on political processes. The case of Nigeria
suggests that even in an ethnically divided society, ethnic divisions may not be or need not be decisive in political processes,
even the most important political processes of constitutional design and political institutional change.[5]

Horowitz's argument about the failure of constitutional design
in Nigeria is based on the 1978 electoral system, which required
that the president be elected by majority but that the winning
candidate must also get at least 25 percent of the vote in at least
two-thirds of the nineteen states. In response to regional and ethnic cleavages and party politics that emerged as politically decisive in the First Republic (1963–1966), constitutional reform
under General Murtala Muhammed included expanding the
number of states by creating seven new ethnic minority states,
and dividing the major Yoruba state into three and the major
Igbo state into two such that the federal structure worked against
rather than to encourage regional, ethnic, and party cleavages. It
banned political parties until just prior to the elections and it required political parties to have a panethnic appeal if they were to
be approved by the federal election commission. Horowitz argues that while the constitutional design of the Second Republic
(1979–1983) was conducive to electing a president with panethnic appeal and a political strategy of ethic accommodation, the
legislators were still elected by generally homogeneous constituencies such that they had no incentives to seek conciliation
across ethnic groups and thus worked in opposition to the efforts
of accommodation by the president.

Nigeria: Ethnic Cleavages, Economic Control, and Socioeconomic Inequality

Larry Diamond suggests a more complex explanation for the failure of the Second Republic that is borne out in subsequent events.[6] While many factors played a role in the failure of the Second Republic, conflicts that manifested themselves as regional-ethnic cleavages are better understood as competition among political elites over the economic resources of the state. Such an interpretation is more consistent with the events preceding and following the Second Republic than Horowitz's explanation that political processes related to ethnic conflict prevented Nigeria from designing coherent constitutional reforms.

Diamond attributes the failure of the First Republic to the economic premium associated with political power. The state controlled cash crop agriculture and mineral mining. State monopolies existed in other sectors, and private enterprise was discouraged while the state-owned economy grew. "By 1964, 54 percent of all wage earners were employed by some level of government, and most of the rest (38 percent) were employed by foreign capital."[7] For political elites and their clients, there were few opportunities for economic gain available without the power of the state. For communities, the resources of development and cultural integrity were at stake in political contests. "For communities, both rural and urban, [the state] was the source of schools, roads, clinics, pipe-borne water, electricity, factories, markets, and almost every other dimension of material progress. For cultural groups, it could be the primary threat to or the primary guarantor of their cultural integrity."[8] In this context of zero-sum competition for economic resources, accommodation was an ineffective political strategy. Political elites turned instead to tribalism to mask their own class interests and to mobilize their ethnic bases for political support. Thus party politics became ethnic and regional politics. Political elites used corruption and patronage to promote their economic interests and used election fraud to sustain their political power. The press's, the students', and the military's disgust with the abuse of power led the students to support the military coup against the corruption of the First Republic.

The political reforms leading up to the Second Republic were based on the recognition of the use of party and ethnic politics to divide the country and to advance the interests of political elites. The reforms prior to the Second Republic were designed to increase panethnic accommodation and to weaken party politics. As Horowitz notes, the increase in the number of states made the federalism structure more conducive to ethnic cooperation and regional cross-cleavages, but the election laws governing the selection of legislators did not create incentives to cooperate across ethnicities and regions in the same way that the presidential electoral reform did. The failure to construct incentives for legislators to cooperate across ethnic groups was not clearly a failure due to ethnically motivated political processes. Neither Diamond nor Horowitz suggests that political behavior prevented the reformers from implementing such a plan. It may simply have been an oversight. The real failure of the reformers was in failing to reduce the economic reward for political success.

According to Horowitz, although President Shagari was an accommodating political figure, he could not prevent his cabinet or the legislature from reverting to ethnic politics and infighting for political control. However, according to Diamond, when the military dictatorship ended the Second Republic, the splits in parties and between the parties in power and the opposition followed the economic cleavages created by the oil boom not ethnic cleavages. Legislators behaved opportunistically. The public became disillusioned with the corruption by political elites. Scandals "included the mishandling of $2.5 billion in import licenses by the minister of commerce, the alleged acceptance by legislators of large bribes from a Swiss firm, the rumored apprehension in London of a Nigerian governor trying to smuggle millions of naira into Britain, and the revelation by a federal minister that the country was losing close to a billion dollars a year in payroll fraud."[9] In every region, evidence of government mismanagement littered the landscape in the form of abandoned or incomplete schools, public health facilities, and public works projects. Election fraud was the decisive invitation to a military coup.

Although ostensibly to end corruption and reestablish democracy like the previous military coup, this military dictatorship ushered in a new era. The dictatorship of General Buhari became increasingly repressive. In a growing climate of fear, the people welcomed the subsequent coup led by Major General Ibrahim Babangida. Initially he freed the press (many journalists had been imprisoned) and promoted public dialogue about the negotiations with the IMF. However, Babangida's regime became increasingly authoritarian. The military became factionalized as officers competed for the economic spoils of political authority. Civilian political elites collaborated with the military and continued to exploit economic opportunities where possible. Ordinary citizens were increasingly alienated from the state. As resources and standards of living declined for most people, regional and ethnic competitions revived. When world oil prices surged in the 1990s because of the Gulf War and correspondingly the economic benefit of government control surged, Babangida twice postponed the scheduled transition to democratic rule and political elites increased their competition over the economic spoils of political power.

Eventually, on June 12, 1993, elections were held and Chief Moshood K. O. Abiola, a Muslim businessman, won 59 percent of the vote and carried constituencies in the North, middle, East, and Southwest (his own region). General Babangida nullified the elections. Overturning the 1993 election results on accusations of fraud that were not independently verified reminded the people of the fraud in the 1965 and 1983 elections. After a decade of political power and enjoying the economic spoils of political power, the military was uninterested in ceding control. However, under public, foreign, and internal military pressure, Babangida resigned as scheduled in August in favor of a civilian-led Interim National Government (ING). However, the ING did not maintain authority through the end of the year. In November, General Abacha persuaded the ING leadership to step down. Abacha's regime repressed political opposition, broke the oil union's strike, suppressed the media through detention or threat of detention, and staged trials of alleged traitors. Ogoni activists who were protesting the government and the Royal Dutch Shell company for causing environmental degradation and neglecting economic development in their region were tried for murder and executed following a trial that brought international attention and eventually U.S. sanctions.

Abacha's regime was succeeded at his death in June 1998 by that of General Abubakar. His regime shows signs of moderation in the use of force against civilians and of political opening, authorizing the new Independent Electoral Commission to oversee the registration of political parties in preparation for elections. The new electoral rules seek to promote the parties' panethnic appeal, but they may not be enough to counter the anger of the Yorubas, Ijaw, Ogoni, and other minority groups over their marginalization during the previous regime.

Moreover, it seems unclear that electoral reform and accommodating leadership are adequate antidotes to the economic premium of political power that is a function of the state and class structure of Nigeria's state-run economy. A process of liberalization and privatization will not solve the problem of incentives to exploit political power for economic gain. Those in political power will be able to influence privatization to their advantage and to the advantage of their cronies in a way that does not promise to undermine the system of patronage and corruption that has become the established economic and political norm. Further, with GDP per capita having declined from $1,000 in 1980 to $250 in 1996, with oil prices low, with Nigeria on the periphery of the global economy, and with little private industry or a domestic business class, the possibility of devolving political control over economic resources seems remote.

DESIGNING DEMOCRATIC INSTITUTIONS: POLITICAL OR ECONOMIC

The history and the present of the economics and politics of Nigeria suggest that political reform will not be successful—no matter how coherently designed, no matter how accommodating the political strategies of certain elected officials—if political power continues to be the most sure source of economic gain. In order to remove the temptation to corruption and election fraud, the link between political success and economic reward needs to be broken. The legitimacy of the nation's economic development plan will be as important as the legitimacy of its constitutional reform and its election practices.

Malaysia, another country that Horowitz uses to make his case for the impossibility of coherent constitutional design in a context of ethnic cleavages, provides an example of coordinated economic and political reform that was initially successful and then failed. This failure was due not to ethnic cleavages but to a failure to institutionalize changes in the economic and political landscapes.[10] Following riots in 1969, the Malaysian government sought to address political and economic inequality among ethnic groups. The Malays had political power but were not benefiting from Malaysia's economic growth. The Chinese were economically successful but lacked political influence. The Indians were regionally isolated on tin plantations. The groups agreed to promote Malay economic growth and to grant the Chinese political power. Horowitz argues that the political-economic pact failed because the incentives were not in place for the Chinese to share economic growth with the Malays in the same way that the Malays immediately shared political power with the Chinese.

However, failure to institutionalize change led to failure in both the economic and political plans. Five-Year Economic Plans beginning in 1970 were successively designed to incorporate Malays (and less so Indians) into Malaysian economic life. Chinese were given incentives to partner with Malays in order that the latter could develop their business and professional skills. Through the 1970s it appeared that there were shifts in the economy resulting in the greater participation of Malays. However, growth due to the oil boom of the decade gave the appearance of economic shifts that during the worldwide recession of the early 1980s were revealed to be less structural. Thus, while all groups benefited from the economic growth of the 1970s, the benefits were not structurally permanent. Similarly, the political agreement was also not structurally permanent. Over the course of the 1970s, Malays used redistricting to create more Malay majority constituencies. Thus, party politics conformed to ethnic groups, with the Malay party, the United Malays National Organization (UMNO), maintaining political dominance. By the time the economic failure was revealed, the districting changes had undermined the political component of the pact as well. The economic-political pact failed because the changes were not institutionalized.

The cases of Nigeria and Malaysia demonstrate that economic conditions, socioeconomic inequity, and perceived rates of change in those conditions have important implications for the success of constitutional reform. The difficulty in designing coherent constitutional institutions may be a function of competition for control over economic resources and not a function of ethnic cleavages. Economic benefits to political power may be a more decisive cause of divisive political competition than ethnic cleavages.[11] Thus attention to political control of economic resources, to the resulting socioeconomic inequality, and to the ways in which ethnic cleavages may be exploited to the benefit of political elites may prove more important and challenging to constitutional designers than merely accommodating and ameliorating ethnic cleavages. In order to better assess the impact of economic control, socioeconomic inequality, ethnic cleavages, and other factors on coherent constitutional design, we need to broaden the model of constitutional reform to include these other factors and to broaden our data set beyond severely divided societies whose constitutional reforms fail to include those whose constitutional reforms succeed.

Horowitz importantly draws our attention to the need to pay attention to the processes of constitutional design and not just to the features of a good constitutional design.[12] The example of Nigeria demonstrates that understanding the political control over economic rewards will help our analysis of the political processes of constitutional design and electoral reform in divided societies. Whether based on small or large sample sizes, qualitative or quantitative data, our analyses of political processes associated with constitutional design and electoral reform need to consider socioeconomic conditions and the incentives they create for political actors. Where ethnic cleavages exist, analysis of the socioeconomic context will help explain the incentive to exploit ethnic cleavages to political advantage.

NOTES

1. Larry Diamond, Juan J. Linz, Seymour Martin Lipset, "Introduction: Comparing Experiences with Democracy," in Larry Diamond, Juan

J. Linz, and Seymour Martin Lipset, eds., *Politics in Developing Countries* (Boulder: Lynne Rienner, 1990), 9–34. See also Guillermo O'Donnell and Philippe C. Schmitter, *Transitions from Authoritarian Rule: Tentative Conclusions about Uncertain Democracies* (Baltimore: Johns Hopkins University Press, 1986), and Georg Sorensen, *Democracy and Democratization* (Boulder: Westview Press, 1993).

2. According to John Bowen, Indonesia is a country with substantial ethnic diversity but no ethnic conflict. Even conflicts in East Timor and the northern tip of Sumatra are about control over resources, not ethnic identity. "The Myth of Global Ethnic Conflict," *Journal of Democracy* 7:4 (1996): 11.

3. Terry Lynn Karl, "Dilemmas of Democratization in Latin America" *Comparative Politics* 23:1 (October 1990): 5. See also O'Donnell and Schmitter, *Transitions from Authoritarian Rule.*

4. For a discussion of the problems associated with selection bias and with the particular risk of overestimating effects, see David Collier and James Mahoney, "Research Note: Insights and Pitfalls: Selection Bias in Qualitative Research," *World Politics* 49:1 (1996): 56–91, especially 71–72.

5. Surveying conflicts generally described as "ethnic conflicts," John Bowen argues, in "The Myth of Global Ethnic Identity," that they are more accurately conflicts over economic resources and political control.

6. My description of Nigerian politics draws on that of Larry Diamond in "Nigeria: Pluralism, Statism, and the Struggle for Democracy," in Larry Diamond, Juan J. Linz, and Seymour Martin Lipset, eds., *Politics in Developing Countries* (Boulder: Lynne Rienner, 1990), 351–409, and Peter Lewis, "Nigeria: An End to the Permanent Transition?" *Journal of Democracy* 10:1 (1999): 141–56. For greater detail, see James Coleman, *Nigeria: Background to Nationalism* (Berkeley: University of California Press, 1958); Larry Diamond, *Class, Ethnicity and Democracy in Nigeria: The Failure of the First Republic* (London: Macmillan, and Syracuse: Syracuse University Press, 1988); Richard Joseph, "Africa, 1990–1997: From Abertura to Closure," *Journal of Democracy* 9:2 (1998): 3–17; and Larry Diamond, Anthony Kirk-Green, and Oyeleye Oyediran, eds., *Transition Without End: Nigerian Politics and Civil Society Under Babangida* (Boulder: Lynne Rienner, 1997).

7. Diamond, "Nigeria," 381.

8. Ibid., 392.

9. Ibid., 370.

10. My discussion of the political plan is based on Horowitz's chapter and Gordon P. Means, "Soft Authoritarianism in Malaysia and Singapore," *Journal of Democracy* 7:4 (1996): 103–17. Discussion of the eco-

nomic plan is based on my "A Multi-sector Comparative Analysis of Sources of Growth in the Malaysian Economy" (Williams College, 1988).

11. See Bowen, "The Myth of Ethnic Global Conflict."

12. For discussions of constitutional design, see Andrew Reynolds, "Constitutional Engineering in Southern Africa," *Journal of Democracy* 6:2 (1995): 86–99, and Vincent T. Maphai, "A Season for Power-Sharing," *Journal of Democracy* 7:1 (1996): 67–81.

11

POWER-SHARING VERSUS BORDER-CROSSING IN ETHNICALLY DIVIDED SOCIETIES

PHILIPPE VAN PARIJS

It is a pleasure to comment on such an instructive and gloomy paper.[1] Its instructiveness was particularly pleasurable, because it helped me see in a completely new light whatever I knew about the subject, not, as it happens, by virtue of any expertise I might possess in political theory but, rather, by virtue of having lived for most of my life in what can plausibly be characterized (see below) as a severely divided society: Belgium. Less predictably, the paper's gloominess too was a source of pleasure as I prepared this comment, not at all because I enjoy learning that things go wrong, let alone understanding that they are bound to go wrong, but—quite the contrary—because the little I knew and understood about the subject implied, I thought, that I had some good news for the author. For his paper's central message I understood as follows: while we can get a pretty definite image of the coherent constitutional package needed by a severely divided multiethnic society, there are deep-seated reasons that such societies will adopt instead incoherent hybrids, which will do them no good. The good news will take the form of an argument to the effect that this grim message needs to be drastically qualified. Unsurprisingly (coming from a philosopher), it will rest on two small exercises in conceptual clarification, the crucial relevance of which will be illustrated by my reading of Belgium's constitutional development and debate.

I. WHAT IS A SEVERELY DIVIDED SOCIETY?

Red Spots and Red Spheres

First of all, what is it, in Donald Horowitz's view, that makes a poly-ethnic society qualify as severely divided? By definition, its being prone to (acute, violent) conflict between ethnic groups. Let us take for granted that the notion of an "ethnic group" is clear enough and concentrate on the concept of "conflict-proneness." Conflict-proneness is clearly a dispositional property of the society concerned. But for our purposes, the term "society" is crucially ambiguous. Do we mean "society" in a comprehensive sense that encompasses a country's current constitutional arrangements? Or do we mean it in a lean sense, which counterfactually strips a country of these arrangements? In either case, a society's characterization includes the specifics of its territory and its economy, its ethnic features, including their geographical and social distribution, the overall level and distribution of income and wealth, and so on. But unlike the first interpretation, the second one excludes "constitutional design," understood roughly and pretty narrowly as those rules that directly organize the distribution of political power. The comprehensive interpretation makes the notion of a severely divided society fairly simple, while the counterfactual definition makes it unavoidably tricky. Nonetheless, choosing the comprehensive interpretation would be most unwise, for present purposes. It would soon prove a recipe for depression, as it would turn into an oxymoron not constitutional design as such but any successful constitutional design for a severely divided society: the very success of the design disqualifies the society as a severely divided one.[2] Therefore, unless one takes some perverse pleasure in pursuing the logically impossible, there is no sensible way out of some variant of the counterfactual definition.

But what does it mean to abstract counterfactually from a

country's constitutional design? Does a poly-ethnic society count as severely divided if and only if it would be torn by acute ethnic conflict if it had no constitutional design at all, or perhaps if and only if there exists at least one (sufficiently absurd) constitutional design under which the society would be prone to acute ethnic conflict? Under such characterizations, any poly-ethnic society—indeed, presumably, any society under a sufficiently broad definition of an ethnic group—would count as severely divided. On the other hand, if a society were severely divided only if it was prone to acute conflict whatever its political institutions, we would be back to making successful constitutional design an oxymoron. The appropriate definition must obviously lie somewhere in between. Here is one way of making it precise.

Consider a particular society at a particular time, as characterized by the current values of its nonconstitutional parameters (in a sense that matches the definition of constitutional design adopted above), and think of the set of all logically possible constitutional arrangements for this society as a multidimensional hyperspace, each point in which represents such an arrangement. To make this more concrete, think of this space as a sphere, with each constitutional arrangement represented by a small spot within this sphere, and specified by the values taken by three continuous variables—for example, what percentage of the total vote is required for representation in the parliament, how much veto power there is for ethnic minorities, and how strong the government is with respect to the parliament. Next, color in red any spot that represents an arrangement under which acute conflict is likely, while leaving in white any point that represents an arrangement under which acute conflict is most unlikely, and color the rest in shades of pink.

Under the comprehensive interpretation of what "society" means in that expression, a severely divided society would be one that happens to be in a red area of the sphere. Under the absurdly broad version of the counterfactual interpretation, it would be one whose sphere has at least one red spot: under a sufficiently broad conception of imaginable arrangements, any society, however safely lodged in the middle of a large white area, is severely divided in this sense. Under the self-defeatingly narrow version of the counterfactual interpretation, on the other hand, a severely divided society would be one whose sphere is completely red: no conceivable institutional arrangement could alleviate its conflict-proneness and only the delicate, often painful surgery of secession may enable the red to recede, as the one sphere is turned into two or more. Finally, under the intermediate counterfactual interpretation I propose to adopt, a severely divided society is defined as one whose sphere has a large red area: it is conflict-prone under a large proportion of the constitutional arrangements. The redder the sphere, the more severely divided the society: like fragility or vulnerability, severe division is a dispositional property that admits of degrees. For some countries, the red spots may be so few that the sphere looks white. The desperate cases are those in which red is all over and deep down. Constitutional engineering for deeply divided societies is concerned with the intermediate case, in which there is a serious risk of being in the red area, but also a serious chance of sticking to the white one.

On the background of this conceptual clarification, I can now try to express my first bit of good news. In the dispositional interpretation for which I have argued above, there are far more severely divided societies than is revealed by overt conflict. The United States is hardly less deeply divided than South Africa, or Holland than Ulster. It just so happens that some countries have chosen or stumbled upon institutions that have kept them safely in the white area. Compare the Netherlands and Northern Ireland, for example. Both were carved out of a larger territory (the Spanish Lower Countries, British Ireland) in which Catholics were an overwhelming majority, to form a territory in which the Protestants came to form roughly two-thirds, and the Catholics roughly one-third, of the remaining total. By the beginning of the twentieth century, both had a history of pretty ruthless domination by the Protestant majority and of anti-Catholic discrimination. But in 1917, the Netherlands adopted a pacification settlement that introduced proportional representation, protected both Protestant and Catholic school systems, and ended discrimination against Catholics in access to public sector positions.[3] In Ulster, instead, no such pacification deal was struck. Discrimination and domination continued, at least partly as a direct effect of the political institutions. Proportional representation (in the form of Single Transferable Vote) was introduced by Lloyd

George in 1920 and kept in place in the Republic of Ireland, where the Protestant minority soon dissolved, politically speaking, into a number of Catholic-majority parties. But it was repealed in Ulster in 1929 by the Protestant prime minister James Craig, precisely in order to hinder transconfessional parties.[4]

The good news, for Donald Horowitz and his profession, which is illustrated by this contrast, is of course not, as such, that there are more severely divided societies than they think but that constitutional design (whether deliberate or not) can be so successful in some societies that one loses sight of the fact that they are just as severely divided as others in which conflict rages. Once severe division is interpreted, as it must, as a reddish sphere (of potentialities) rather than a reddish spot (in which one happens to find oneself), constitutional engineering holds great promise.

Shifting Stains

The goodness of this news should not be overstated, however, and the illustration I just gave is not meant to suggest that there are quick fixes. The job is promising but it is not easy. The constitutional engineer's first task obviously consists in locating with some precision the red and white areas, whose sizes and shapes will vary a great deal from one society to another. When naively advocating the import of a ready-made package of rules that has proven its value through years, the clumsy Western do-gooders stigmatized by Horowitz in his contribution are simply oblivious to this fact: a point safely located in an immaculate area of the sphere associated with one country—for example, a presidential system with an assembly elected by first-past-the-post—may be deep inside a dark red portion of the sphere associated with another, in which the ethnic setup is crucially different. The fact that the red patterns vary from one sphere to another does not mean that countries cannot learn from one another. Quite the contrary: there is a lot to be learned from other countries' successes and failures, providing one does not make conflict-proneness an attribute of isolated constitutional devices, nor even of whole constitutional frameworks, but of a combination of a system of devices and the background nonconstitutional conditions. Even though no two countries are anything like identical along these dimensions, insight into the mechanisms that under-lie conflict-proneness and conflict-inhibition in one country can help guide choices in another. This is exactly what is at work when Horowitz ventures to say, for example, to South Africa: "Don't go there, it's red. Go there, you'll be safe."

The job does not stop at identifying the contours of the red and white areas, however, for the wisest recommendation is not always that one should move to the nearest white spot. Often reaching the red area will require moving along two or more di-mensions at once. If one moves along one of these dimensions and gets stuck, one may end up in a darker red area than the one one was trying to steer away from. When making recommenda-tions, one should therefore anticipate the possibility that one may be able to go only part of the way. One must also try to guess what the winds and slopes will be, driving the reform further or pushing it back to where it started.

All this seems hard enough. But there are more sophisticated tasks still,[5] for the contours of the red area are not fixed. Demo-graphic or economic changes, for example, may upset the ability of current institutions to keep conflict-proneness under check, and constitutional engineering should anticipate such shifts of the red area and design institutions accordingly.[6] As a very simple illustration, take a country, such as Belgium, in which the consti-tution can be changed only with a two-thirds majority. If the ma-jority ethnic group represents 60 percent of the population (which is currently the case in Belgium), this rule protects the minority group against a constitutional change unilaterally im-posed by the majority. But if demographic trends lead to the ma-jority ethnic group's forming more than two-thirds of the popula-tion, then the current arrangements, without undergoing any change themselves, may suddenly find themselves in the turbu-lent red area.[7]

Or take the following, slightly more complex illustration, also taken from the history of Belgium. Throughout the nineteenth century, Belgium was marked by a sharp contrast between its mainly rural North (Flanders) and its far more industrialized South (Wallonia), with the result that, as from 1884, Flanders sends 100 percent of Catholics to Parliament, and Wallonia a majority of liberals. In 1893, the country moves from highly restricted male suffrage (only taxpayers vote) to universal male suffrage with plural voting (one additional vote for married taxpayers, one or two additional votes for the educated), using a plurality type of electoral system with small multimember constituencies and a double ballot. As a result, the newly created socialist party obtains representation in Parliament, where Liberals and Socialists together win 40 of Wallonia's 62 seats, while the Catholic party wins all 90 seats in Flanders and Brussels at the 1994 national election.[8] Obviously, the Catholics can retain power with a comfortable, overwhelmingly Flemish parliamentary majority. The government, which had no Wallone member at all in the 1880s, will have no more than one in the 1890s.[9] As the population of Flanders kept growing faster than that of Wallonia, while Wallonia remained far more industrial, there was no prospect of a change in the underlying situation.

It may therefore be tempting to claim that, by the end of the nineteenth century, severely divided Belgium was well into the red area, and to understand in this light the bold, unprecedented leap Belgium ventured in 1899, when it became the first country to adopt proportional representation (PR). Thus, D. Johnson[10] asserts that "the list-proportional system was introduced in Belgium in 1899 to remedy some of the irreconcilable differences between the Walloons and the Flemish," while D. M. Farrell[11] conjectures that what drove the move was Belgium's desire "to adopt an electoral system which could equalize the representation of the different communities involved." Such interpretations derive from the false presumption that if an area is red now, it must always have been so.[12] In fact, the 1899 reform was not motivated by the desire to alleviate an ethnic conflict, nor did it result in extinguishing an ethnic tension, which simply did not exist. But whatever it was driven by and achieved at the time, it certainly helped Belgium stay clear of the red area as the latter expanded through the following decades. Let me spell this out.

The history of proportional representation in Belgium starts with the creation of the Association réformiste pour l'adoption de la représentation proportionnelle (1881). One of its founding members is Victor D'Hondt, author of the first books advocating the list variant of PR, as opposed to the Single Transferable Vote variant advocated by Thomas Hare and John Stuart Mill.[13] An international conference was organized in Antwerp in 1885 to discuss the relative merits of STV and list PR. It closed with a motion advocating the D'Hondt system and asserting "that proportional representation is the only means of assuring power to the real majority of the country, an effective voice to minorities, and exact representation to all significant groups of the electorate."[14] Note that the "minorities" referred to are ideological, not ethnic minorities. The results of Belgium's 1894 election did come as a shock that noticeably strengthened the case for PR, but this had nothing to do with ethnic divisions. The fact that, with about 50 percent of the vote, the Catholic party could get nearly 75 percent of the seats simply did not seem fair. Moreover, some of the most forward-looking Catholics could see that, if the 1893 reform was only a first step to a "one man, one vote" electoral system, there was a serious risk that the socialist party, still in its infancy but growing fast, would end up squeezing out the liberal party altogether and obtain an absolute majority, as a result of industrialization and rural exodus spreading to Flanders. Hence, the Catholic prime minister Beernaert, a member of D'Hondt's association, proposed list PR in 1894 but was defeated and resigned. There followed some unsettled years, culminating in strikes, physical violence inside Parliament, further resignations, and finally the adoption of list PR by a narrow majority on the 29th of December 1899.[15] Because the average magnitude of the PR districts was small, larger parties retained a strong advantage, and the Catholics' absolute majority survived until the introduction of "one man, one vote" universal suffrage in 1919, but the reform did secure that all three parties were significantly represented in all three regions.

Throughout this period all sorts of arguments were used.[16] Some were contingent upon the specific variants under consideration (for example, the "immoral" alliances for the second ballot) and others related to the essential difference between plurality and PR (for example, the number of viable parties). Some were unashamedly partisan while others were overtly impartial. And among the latter, some were consequentialist (the long-term public interest resulting from inclusion or stability) while others were not (fairness, genuine democracy). But nowhere is there a trace of any reference to "the irreconcilable differences between the Walloons and the Flemish." Why not? Because at the time Belgium was still run by a francophone elite that was ruling throughout the country. There may have been only Flemings in the national government, but the language they spoke at government meetings was exclusively French (as it remained well beyond the middle of the next century), and the fact that Wallonia was in effect run by an overwhelmingly Flemish government was not perceived, as such, as a serious problem.[17] The fundamental cleavage, so threatening that the national motto had to be "L'union fait la force," was still the countrywide ideological divide between Catholics and liberals, not the ethnic divide between Flemings and Walloons.

Yet, it became true, half a century later, that had the old plurality system been kept and thereby the ideological minorities deprived of any representation in whole regions, "the regional polarity would have been made more acute, hence nation-wide agreement would have been made harder to achieve and the unity of the State, indeed of the country itself, would have been endangered."[18] Owing to the steady progress of the "Flemishization" of the Flemish territory and its elites throughout the twentieth century, it had become correct to say, by the middle of the century, that "majority voting, if it were introduced, would divide the state so deeply that its continued existence would be in doubt."[19] Though not driven at the time by any concern with ethnic conflict, the move made in 1899 (and carried further later on through an increase of effective district magnitude) had kept the country for decades out of an area that was still white when Belgium left it but had gradually become dark red. The red stain, however, kept expanding further—culminating in the expulsion of the French section of the Catholic University of Louvain from the Flemish town of Leuven in 1968 and the subsequent splitting of all three national parties along ethnic lines—and by the 1960s it was clear that further constitutional reform was urgently needed to steer clear of the red. Belgium was then gradually turned into a federal state (1994), with significant regional autonomy, with veto powers for both linguistic communities in the form of supermajority requirements on touchy issues, and with guaranteed equal representation in the federal government. Concern with the red stain, this time, was clearly on everybody's mind.

II. WHAT IS A COHERENT PACKAGE?

Consociationalism and Its Rival

This extended example was introduced to illustrate the difficulties that arise—both when looking backward in order to explain and when looking forward in order to advise—when the red stain shifts, that is, when the extent to which a society is severely divided changes through time. The last episode of the example, however, leads naturally to the second conceptual issue I want to raise: What counts as a coherent constitutional package, and hence what the relationship is between the competing views of what this package should be. For jointly with proportional representation, the three features introduced in Belgium from the 1970s to alleviate the ethnic conflict are precisely the features listed by Don Horowitz as the defining features of consociationalism. Hence the arrangement currently in place in Belgium would seem to offer a paradigmatic example of what he presents as the main rival of the "incentives approach," which he himself advocates. But is it really? Some doubt is bound to arise, as one considers Horowitz's two main objections to consociationalism. One is that it is unable to mitigate conflict because it generates no electoral support for ethnic compromise—an objection that is certainly not lacking relevance in the Belgian context and to which I shall return shortly. The other objection is that consociationalism "provides no room for a feature vital to democracy: opposition"—an objection that can only strike me as bizarre, not because I do not believe in the importance of opposition but because I fail to see why consociationalism, as characterized and hence as illustrated by Belgium, should rule it out. Belgian politics displays daily both the salience of the four characteristic features of consociationalism and the presence of an active, vocal opposition: the government is made up of an equal number of Flemings and francophones, but backed only by a subset of the parties in Parliament—currently the socialists and Christian-democrats—leaving a diverse opposition made up of liberals, ecologists, and nationalists from both linguistic communities to vigorously challenge the government from all sides. To sort this out, some further conceptual clarification is in order.

To keep conflict-proneness under check in poly-ethnic societies—that is, to keep clear of the red area—there are basically three methods. The first one—devolution—consists in reducing what is at stake at the level of the country as a whole. Since Karl Renner's[20] pioneering advocacy of institutional devices for accommodating diverse nationalities, it has come in two varieties: territorial federalism and personal federalism. How much the former can help depends on the separability of territories, that is, on the extent to which ethnic groups are concentrated in territorially contiguous areas or on the contrary dispersed throughout the country. How much the latter variety can help depends on the separability of competencies, that is, on the extent to which ethnically contentious policy areas can meaningfully be assigned to a decision-making body distinct from the one in charge of competencies with an irreducibly central spatial dimension.

If devolution in either variant could go all the way, nothing of significance would be left to decide at the central level, and the problem would not be solved but dissolved with the disappearance of the deeply divided society into two or more homogeneous societies. Under most conditions, this is not possible, and some arrangement must therefore be devised for poly-ethnic governance of whatever is left at the center. There are two basic methods for trying to foster accommodation and compromise at this level. One is commonly called "consociationalism." It consists in making political *power-sharing* between ethnic groups possible, or rewarding, or even compulsory. It has been advocated most systematically by Arendt Lijphart,[21] but is traced back by him to the 1979 British Nobel laureate in economics Arthur Lewis.[22] The other is sometimes referred to as the "incentives approach." It consists in making political *border-crossing* between ethnic groups possible, or rewarding, or even compulsory. It is being advocated most systematically by Donald Horowitz,[23] but was anticipated in Seymour Martin Lipset's[24] emphasis on the importance of crosscutting cleavages for the political dynamics of the United States.

Note that even though these two methods will unavoidably lead to different specific institutional proposals in given historical conditions, they are not defined by specific institutions. This was stressed from the outset by Lijphardt: "The grand coalition cabinet is the most typical and obvious, but not the only possible, consociational solution for a fragmented system. The essential characteristic of consociational democracy is not so much any particular institutional arrangement as the deliberate joint effort by the elites to stabilize the system."[25] Analogously, Horowitz notes: "The incentives approach does not require specific structures. It is, for example, at home with different electoral systems, depending on the context . . . provided that the system is strongly conducive to interethnic moderation in the appeal for votes. . . ." This interpretation of both consociationalism and its alternative as methods rather than as specific institutional blueprints should help us sort out the puzzle with which we started about the relationship between consociationalism and opposition.

One way in which power-sharing can be organized is by treating ethnic groups as subpolities and using ethnically based parties as the building blocks of central politics. This corresponds to a narrower characterization of consociationalism, which Horowitz sometimes adopts. If power-sharing can only be institutionalized using such ethnic blocks, in the form of a guaranteed presence in the legislative and the executive, mutual veto powers, and so on, then there is a serious tension between consociationalism and a lively opposition. But power-sharing between ethnic groups can also operate with either poly-ethnic parties—as it does in Switzerland—or poly-ethnic families of mono-ethnic parties—as it does in Belgium.[26] These variants of consociationalism can still impose ethnic constraints on the composition of the executive or the assembly, or require separate majorities on certain issues. It is perfectly compatible with a lively opposition, including on interethnic issues, though not with one consisting of the whole of one ethnic group. Hence, the objection that rests on the claim that opposition is essential to democracy is quite relevant to the ethnic-block variant of consociationalism but not to consociationalism as such.

Border-Crossing for a Power-Sharing Society

Conceptual clarification, on the other hand, can do nothing to counter the other objection Horowitz raises against consociationalism. As confirmed by the political history of Belgium—especially since, in the aftermath of the Louvain affair, all national political parties split up along ethnic lines—consociationalism does nothing to generate electoral pressure toward ethnic compromise. Admittedly, compromise needs to be reached at a post-electoral stage, whether because of the need to form a government or because of the mutual veto powers conferred by super-majority requirements. But this is consistent with electoral pressure that drives mono-ethnic parties to try to outbid one another in terms of ethnic toughness and intransigence.[27] This generates a structural discrepancy between the platforms parties are driven to propose to their mono-ethnic electorates and the compromises power-sharing rules force government parties to settle for. The political forum does not construct a common interest. Instead, the whole of political life is essentially perceived as a strenuous bargaining between the distinct interests of the ethnic groups, with the government parties invariably selling out to the other side.

As an observer of the strain thus systemically generated by Belgium's current variant of consociationalism, I can only be favorably predisposed to the alternative, border-crossing approach, which emphasizes the importance of incentives for "pooling votes across ethnic lines," for "luring votes across group boundaries" (as Horowitz puts it). Indeed, I am convinced that conflict-proneness would be far better checked—that Belgium would dwell at a safer distance from the red stain—if arbitration between ethnic groups were done not ex post between the sharply diverging platforms that mono-ethnic parties committed themselves to defend but ex ante within the platforms of poly-ethnic parties put forward to poly-ethnic electorates. The final settlement would then be (perceived as) the outcome of a confrontation between rival views of the general interest, rather than a painful compromise between the particular interests of ethnic groups. And this obviously requires that one should make at the very least possible, preferably also rewarding, and perhaps even compulsory, the fishing for votes across ethnic borders. It is therefore not surprising that a number of Horowitz-like proposals have recently sprung up in the Belgian context.

Thus, the Flemish political scientist Wilfried Dewachter, who had long been advocating on independent grounds the double-ballot direct election of the prime minister, has recently opted for a variant in which both the prime minister and the deputy prime minister are directly elected, with the constraint that one should necessarily belong to one linguistic group and the second to the other.[28] It is of course of the utmost importance that the Flemings should not elect one and the Francophones the other, in the way the Greek and the Turkish Cypriots elected the president and vice-president, respectively, in Cyprus's short-lived "consociational" constitution of 1960–63. The candidates must come in bilingual tickets (in Dewachter's proposal, only at the second ballot) with ethnic groups lumped together in a single constituency.[29] One problem with such a proposal is analogous to the one pointed out by Horowitz in connection with the 1978 Nigerian constitution. It is fine to build border-crossing incentives into the election of the executive, but if the executive needs the confidence of an assembly subjected to the same old incentives, precious little may have been gained. A natural response, for advocates of the above proposal, is to extend the double ballot single-member system to parliamentary elections. Of course, most of the corresponding single-member districts will be mono-ethnic. But as the party system adjusts to the direct election of the executive, one can expect two cross-ethnic party blocs to form and to compete countrywide on the basis of platforms consistent with the one put forward for the crucial election of the prime-ministerial ticket. Unfortunately, for reasons spelled out above in the discussion of PR, this would be a most risky move for Belgium to make, as the emerging pattern of representation is likely to be very different in the North and the South, with the result that the elected executive is likely to enjoy dangerously slender parliamentary support from one of the two linguistic groups.

The alternative is to stick to both parliamentarism and proportional representation, while forcing vote-fetching across the linguistic border at the elections for the House of Representatives (the only chamber in which the government needs a majority in Belgium's bicameral Parliament). One option, inspired by an aspect of the system currently in place in Mauritius and recently proposed by the constitutional lawyer Francis Delpérée, consists in giving each elector two votes at these elections. One would be used, in the usual way, to elect, say, 130 of the 150 representatives in relatively small multimember constituencies. The second one would be used to fill the remaining 20 seats by asking voters of each of the two communities to choose ten representatives among candidates from the other community.[30] Border-crossing will thus be institutionalized, and the House of Representatives will comprise members of both communities whose task will be to represent—in the way they vote and even more importantly in the explanation of their vote to the community to which they belong—the interests of the other community. This is an interesting proposal that is worth pondering. As far as the creation of centripetal forces is concerned, here is the most serious difficulty I believe it raises.

Clearly, the impact of the scheme would be at best negligible, at worst seriously counterproductive, if candidates for the special seats could be "pseudomembers" of the other community—say, Flemings living in Wallonia and defending Flemish-nationalist positions or francophones living in Flanders and belonging to a single-issue party defending their own interests. For there is then a serious risk that campaigns would soon focus on concentrating votes on these Trojan horses instead of "wasting one's vote" on "real" members of the other community. The francophones of Brussels's Flemish periphery—less than 1 percent of Belgium's population—might then end up with 10 out of 150 representatives. To prevent such derailing, one can hardly put much hope in a language test (let alone a blood test!) or in a substantive screening of electoral platforms in order to prevent the special seats from being usurped by nonmembers of the relevant community. But it is possible to have the lists of candidates for the special seats endorsed by their own communities. This could be done quite simply by requiring these lists to be presented by the parties competing for the electors' first vote and by allocating the special seats of one community exclusively to those parties that obtain more than, say, 5 percent of the first vote in the constituencies of that community: no hope then, for single-issue francophone parties in Flanders or single-issue Flemish parties in Wallonia, and competition for the special seats will really be between the parties of one community for the votes of the other community.

The next question is whether the role thus given to political parties may thwart the impact hoped for. The people elected to the special seats may well want to be reelected. But they will beware of diverging too markedly from their party's line because they can be reelected only if endorsed by their party, whereas if their own voters are disappointed and therefore unlikely to re-elect them, their party may still offer them, as a reward for sticking to the line, a potentially victorious position in the election for the standard seats. The personal action of the holders of the special seats is therefore unlikely to have a great impact, especially as one cannot expect a party's big names to accept being relegated to one of them. However, the parties themselves will factor into their strategies what they may lose as a result of disappointing the voters from the other community. The smaller the number of special seats, the more rewarding a tough line will remain, and the more damaging a conciliatory stance. But as their number rises, a party cannot ignore this source of potentially crucial gains and losses, and it will have to care, to an extent unimaginable in the present context, about developing an appropriately inclusive discourse and recruiting political personnel able to address the other community in its own language. As the share of special seats increases, however, the intrinsic tension with the proportionality principle grows, which may jeopardize the scheme's legitimacy in the eyes of the community that is losing out.[31] This trade-off may not be fatal, but it invites a search for alternatives.

A second, quite distinct way of trying to engineer vote-fetching across the linguistic border at parliamentary elections relies on the creation of a countrywide constituency. As such, this measure is both too much and too little. Too much, because it would abolish any guaranteed representation for any part of the country, and each group's fear of being seriously underrepresented would therefore secure the persistence of mono-ethnic parties. Too little, because overbidding by nationalist parties will still make it a losing proposition for countrywide parties to form again, with platforms designed to appeal to both ethnic groups. Some versions of the proposal, however, may avoid both difficulties. Here is one.

Introduce a German-style dual system, with each voter casting two votes for the election of the members of the House of Representatives. Using the first of the two votes, keep allocating 100 of the 150 seats with a list PR system in fairly small multimember constituencies (for example 11, corresponding to the provinces, instead of the current 20), so as to make sure every part of the country is appropriately represented. Using the second vote, allocate the remaining 50 using open list PR, with the possibility of multiple votes on the same list, in a single countrywide constituency. The allocation of the first category of seats is made using the D'Hondt formula, with no apparentement across provinces—which amounts to a variant of PR that is quite favorable to (locally) large parties. The allocation of the second category, on the other hand, is made so as to achieve maximum proportionality in the House as a whole, with no overall threshold, *among those parties that have achieved, say, at least 0.5 percent of the vote in each of the eleven provinces or maybe 3 percent of the vote in each of the three regions.*[32] Seats obtained by these parties in the provincial constituencies are taken into account in the overall proportional allocation. Seats obtained in the provincial constituencies by parties who do not present candidates in the countrywide constituency or fail to reach the quota in at least one of the provinces or regions are retained by them.

The parties' best responses to these new rules are obvious enough: the former countrywide parties will reunite, or at least form common lists with single platforms at the federal level, and with candidates who will try to appeal to voters of both groups. The nationalist parties are also welcome to bid for votes in the countrywide constituency, but obviously they stand a chance only if they manage to gang up around a common platform—which may be easy enough if the key issue is autonomy, but is altogether out of reach if borders and net transfers are the key issues. In the latter case, nationalist parties are not excluded but will have to narrow down their hopes to reaching the provincial constituencies' pretty high effective threshold. The central purpose, however, is not to get rid of any specific parties but to reshape political competition and rhetoric, so that they will consist again in confrontation not between the interests of mono-ethnic blocks but between alternative versions of the common good.

"Incoherent": Hybrid or Centrifugal?

The various proposals thus briefly presented illustrate, for the severely divided society I am most familiar with, what the second, border-crossing approach might look like. But given the extent to which this society already uses, as mentioned earlier, paradigmatically consociational, power-sharing devices, is this not, at the same time, a crystal-clear illustration of an "incoherent" package? Horowitz "want[s] to insist on coherence as a virtue of constitutional design for severely divided societies," and the requirement of "coherence" or "consistency" keeps popping up throughout his contribution. But what is "coherence"? Horowitz repeatedly suggests that a coherent package is the opposite of a "hybrid" package, as illustrated by the Fiji Islands or Ulster, that is, a package that puts together bits of consociationalism, of the incentives approach, of simple majoritarianism, and so on. Under this interpretation, coherence requires us to choose between the power-sharing approach and the border-crossing approach, and therefore the vote-pooling measure suggested above would by definition make Belgium's constitutional design "incoherent" and should therefore be rejected.

But there is another way of understanding "coherence" or "consistency." The reason Horowitz says he "want[s] to insist on coherence as a virtue of constitutional design for severely divided societies" is that "their centrifugal forces are so strong that without equally strong, consistent, centripetal institutions their divisions tend to become acute." A coherent package, on this second interpretation, is not by definition one that is not a "hybrid" but, rather, one whose components interact in such a way as to be "centripetal," as to produce accommodation and compromise. Under this interpretation, there is no reason to suppose that coherence requires us to make an exclusive choice between the three methods of conflict mitigation—devolution, power-sharing or border-crossing—which does not mean that specific devices may not turn out to be incompatible. For example, a variety of consociationalism organized around mono-ethnic parties with mono-ethnic electorates is obviously incompatible with the possibility, let alone the encouragement or obligation of vote-pooling. But these are not only formally compatible with power-sharing devices such as proportional representation, supermajorities, or guaranteed presence of ethnic groups in the executive. They may well combine, as suggested above, to produce a more centripetal outcome. In this sense, a "hybrid" package can be more coherent than a "pure" one. The requirement of coherence, then, simply reflects, rather than a fixation on "purity" (with a given nomenclature of ideal types), a down-to-earth search for a set of rules of the game that, taken as a whole, systematically defuse potential ethnic conflict.

No less than the first one, this second exercise in conceptual clarification can be interpreted as good news for Donald Horowitz. For suppose he is stuck, as most of the time he seems to believe he is, with the first construal of the coherence requirement. What is needed in a severely divided society must then be either consociationalism, which is coherent but won't work, or the incentives approach, which is coherent and will work. But, for deep-seated reasons that Horowitz sketches and illustrates, opportunities for significant constitutional reform are rare, and often produce hybrids rather than coherent packages. No wonder therefore he sounds gloomy. But suppose we decide instead to drop all concern with coherence as ideal-typical purity, and interpret instead the coherence requirement in the second direction delineated above: what we are looking for is a set of rules of the game that jointly generate a conflict-mitigating dynamics. Territorial autonomy is then bound to help under circumstances in which ethnic groups are sufficiently concentrated. And so are some devices that make it possible, rewarding, or compulsory to share power *and* to cross borders. What and how much is required will depend on variable, though specifiable circumstances, but the three methods can certainly be combined, and not all features of any particular method need to be introduced in one go—even though, for reasons mentioned earlier, the order in which features are introduced must be carefully thought through.

This does not detract from the importance of Horowitz's observation that for any particular country, opportunities for significant reform are few and far between and that when they occur, people often make a mess of it. But as the recent political histories of Italy, Japan, or eastern Europe show, situations that seemed completely frozen can suddenly come unstuck. And when this happens, well-intentioned insiders must be ready, duly equipped with principled and detailed proposals whose likely consequences in the relevant particular context have been properly thought through, at least in part thanks to the sort of perceptive and imaginative comparative research in which Donald Horowitz has been engaged. This message is nothing new. It is, for example, at the core of the memoirs of Jean Monnet, the man who changed the shape of Europe more deeply than Hitler, de Gaulle, and Thatcher together, through shrewd, sometimes counterintuitive yet amazingly successful constitutional engineering for a severely divided continent.[33] But whether new or not, I hope it will help Don Horowitz cheer up, shake off the despondency reflected in his paper. Gloominess is misplaced. "Never doubt that a small group of thoughtful committed citizens can change the world: indeed, it's the only thing that ever has." So at least Margaret Mead is quoted as saying on a bumper sticker that caught my eye on Berkeley's Telegraph Avenue while I was concocting my comment on Horowitz's paper.

NOTES

1. An earlier version of this paper was presented as a comment on Donald Horowitz, "Constitutional Design: An Oxymoron?" at the annual meeting of the American Society for Political and Legal Philosophy (San Francisco, January 5–6, 1998). Unless otherwise specified, attributions to Horowitz are references to this paper. I am grateful to Don Horowitz for the stimulation provided by his paper, his reactions to my verbal comments, and the part of his work I took this opportunity to read, and to Paul Janssens for checking (and correcting) my interpretation of the political history of Belgium.

2. A conceptual choice of this sort must underlie Horowitz's dismissal (above) of consociational arrangements as irrelevant: "they are more likely the product of resolved struggles or of relatively moderate cleavages than they are measures to resolve struggles and to moderate cleavages."

3. See Arend Lijphart, *The Politics of Accommodation, Pluralism and Democracy in the Netherlands* (Berkeley: University of California Press, 1968).

4. See David M. Farrell, *Comparing Electoral Systems* (Hemel Hempstead: Prentice Hall/Harvester Wheatsheaf, 1997), 112–15.

5. Even if one were only concerned, as I shall suppose throughout is the case, with conflict-proneness. But there is no reason that the

consequentialist evaluation of political institutions should confine itself to their impact on acute ethnic conflict or even, more broadly, on democratic stability—even though there are no doubt circumstances in which there are good reasons to give this dimension top priority. But among locations that are outside the red area, there is no good reason to decree that they are all equivalent or that the optimal one is the one most remote from the red border. A just or good or decent society is not simply one in which ethnic groups do not kill one another. It may also be one, for example, in which the interests of younger or future generations are not sacrificed to older or present ones, and the design of political institutions might be of crucial importance in this respect (see Philippe Van Parijs, "The Disfranchisement of the Elderly, and Other Attempts to Secure Intergenerational Justice," *Philosophy and Public Affairs* 27:4 (1998): 292–333). Or one may be dissatisfied with a system that secures ethnic peace but at the same time disempowers some ethnic minorities, thus preventing them from defending their material interests as much as the sustainable achievement of distributive justice would require. The balance between two poly-ethnic conglomerates stabilized by the U.S. plurality system, for example, may be quite effective to keep the country out of the red. But, as argued by Lani Guinier, *The Tyranny of the Majority: Fundamental Fairness in Representative Democracy* (New York: Free Press, 1994), for example, this may come at a heavy cost for the weaker, underrepresented minorities. If a more comprehensive (and defensible) view is taken of the overall objective, even reforms that take the risk of moving into a pinkish area would be fully justified if this were the price to pay for leaving a very dark area in terms of social justice.

6. The contours of the red area are not only not fixed, they may also be responsive to the nature of the constitutional arrangement itself. Hence, constitutional engineering should not only anticipate exogenous movements of the stain but also try to bring about its endogenous shrinking. Presumably, the maxim "if you want peace, pursue justice" is relevant here, or the recommendation that, in multilingual societies, one should not go for some fuzzy bilingualism (as was tried in Belgium and Canada) but for a firm application of the territorial principle, as was in place from the start in the Swiss confederation (see, e.g., André Donneur, "Un nationalisme suisse romand est-il possible?" in *Vous avez dit Suisse romande?* (Lausanne: Institut d'études politiques, 1984): 25–52; Alexandre Papaux, "Droit des langues en Suisse: Etat des lieux," *Revue suisse de science politique* 3:2 (1997): 131–34.

7. Note that Switzerland, with a Germanic majority of more than three-fourths, has a different rule, which requires approval both by an overall majority and by majorities in a majority of cantons (see Peter

Moser, "Why Is Swiss Politics So Stable?" *Swiss Journal of Economics and Statistics* 132:1 (1996): 31–61, at 43).

8. The population is then overwhelmingly French-speaking in the South (Wallonia), with a German-speaking minority in the South-East; it is overwhelmingly Dutch-speaking in the North (Flanders), with French spoken by part of the urban middle classes; it is mainly and increasingly French in Brussels, the capital of the kingdom completely surrounded by Dutch-speaking territory.

9. See Lode Wils, *Van Clovis tot Happart. De lange weg van de naties in de Lage Landen* (Leuven-Apeldoorn: Garant, 1992), 190 (French translation: *Histoire des Nations belges* (Ottignies: Quorum, 1996)); and Xavier Mabille, "De l'indépendance à l'Etat fédéral," in A. Dieckhoff, ed., *La Belgique. La Force de la désunion* (Bruxelles: Complexe, 1996): 19–46, at 41.

10. D. Johnson, *Public Choice: An Introduction to the New Political Economy* (Mayfield, Calif.: Bristlecone Books, 1991).

11. Farrell, *Comparing Electoral Systems*, 61.

12. Analogous interpretations seem far more relevant for the introduction of list PR a few years later in Finland (1906) and of the Single Transferable Vote in the Republic of Ireland (gradually as from 1918). In Finland, "all parties except the Swedes [a comparatively privileged ethnic minority strongly represented in the former Estate of the nobility] were in favour of a unicameral system, and when the Swedes realized that this would probably prevail, they held out for a system of PR for the unicameral parliament, as the only guarantee of the continued representation of minorities in parliament" (Andrew McLaren Carstairs, *A Short History of Electoral Systems in Western Europe* (London: George, Allen & Unwin, 1980), 113). In the first Irish election under home rule (1918), First Past the Post was used everywhere except for one constituency where the Single Transferable Vote variant of PR was proposed and adopted in order to encourage political participation by the Protestant minority. Sinn Féin won a dramatic victory except in that constituency, where Protestants obtained impressive results. The Unionists hailed STV as "the magna carta of political and municipal minorities." The principle of PR was then incorporated in the first Irish constitution (1922) and its STV variant chosen, more out of ignorance of other systems than as a positive choice (see again Farrell, *Comparing Electoral Systems*, 112–15).

13. See Victor D'Hondt, *Question électorale. La représentation proportionnelle des partis par un électeur* (Bruxelles: Bruylant, 1878); and Victor D'Hondt, *Système pratique et raisonné de représentaion proportionnelle* (Bruxelles: C. Muquardt, 1882); Thomas Hare, *Treatise on the Election of Representatives, Parliamentary and Municipal*, 2d ed. (London: Longman,

Green, Longman & Roberts, 1861); and John Stuart Mill, *Considerations on Representative Government* (1861), in *On Liberty and Other Essays*, ed. J. Gray (Oxford: Oxford University Press, 1991), 203–467.

14. Carstairs, *A Short History of Electoral Systems in Western Europe*, 3.

15. Ibid., 49–56.

16. See Léon Moreau and Charles Goossens, "L'évolution des idées concernant la représentation proportionnelle en Belgique," *Revue de droit international et de droit comparé* 35 (1958): 378–93.

17. There were some faint, hardly audible noises on the Wallone side, for example, the writer Albert Mockel suggesting in 1897, as a remedy to the antagonism between Walloons and Flemings, "a complete administrative separation between Flanders and Wallonia, with a Parliament for each of them": Flanders would have a conservative Catholic government and Wallonia a liberal-socialist one, and the constant clashes of interests between the agricultural North-West and the industrial South-East would be avoided. But it is only as from 1912, when Catholics unexpectedly retained an absolute majority, that a real autonomist movement got off the ground in Wallonia (Jules Destrée, *Wallons et Flamands. La Querelle linguistique en Belgique* (Paris: Plon, 1923), 181–82; Wils, *Van Clovis tot Happart*, 193–95).

18. See Moreau and Goosens, "L'évolution des idJes concernant la reprJsentation proportionnelle en Belgique," 387.

19. Carstairs, *A Short History of Electoral Systems in Western Europe*, 57.

20. Karl Renner, *Das Selbstbestimmungsrecht der Nationen, in besonderer Anwendung auf Oesterreich* (Leipzig & Wien: Franz Deuticke, 1918), 67–85.

21. See Arend Lijphart, "Consociational Democracy," *World Politics* 21 (1969): 207–25; *Democracy in Plural Societies* (New Haven: Yale University Press, 1977); "Multiethnic Democracy," in *The Encyclopedia of Democracy*, ed. S. M. Lipset (Washington, D.C.: Congressional Quarterly Press, 1995): 853–65 ; and "The Puzzle of Indian Democracy: A Consociational Interpretation," *American Political Science Review* 90:2 (1996): 258–68.

22. W. Arthur Lewis, *Politics in West Africa* (London: Allen & Unwin, 1965).

23. See Donald L Horowitz, *Ethnic Groups in Conflict* (Berkeley: University of California Press, 1985); *A Democratic South Africa? Constitutional Engineering in a Divided Society* (Berkeley: University of California Press, 1991); "Democracy in Divided Societies," *Journal of Democracy* 4:4 (1993): 18–38.

24. Seymour Martin Lipset, *Political Man: The Social Bases of Politics* (Baltimore: Johns Hopkins University Press, 1981).

25. Lijphardt, "Consociational Democracy," 213.

26. The relationship between consociationalism and opposition is not the only issue that the Belgian example should help clarify. See, e.g., Brian Barry ("Political Accommodation and Consociational Democracy," in Barry, *Democracy and Power* (Oxford University Press, 1991), 100–35, at 135): "But would it be a contribution to social harmony if each ethnic group were represented by a single monolithic organization? If it were so in Belgium, then Belgium would be, as far as I know, unique in the annals of human history. Except where it is the prelude to peaceful scission of the state, a situation in which conflicting ethnic groups are mobilized behind monolithic organizations is a situation of potential civil war or of civil war averted by effective oppression by one group of the other." Barry's forceful indictment of a mono-ethnic-party-based consociationalism, as advocated for example by Kenneth McRae for Canada and Ulster, is not an indictment of consociationalism (qua power-sharing) as such. ("The Consociational Model and Its Dangers," in Barry, *Democracy and Power* (Oxford University Press, 1991), 136–55, at 139, 145.)

27. At a national election of the late 1980s, the electoral slogan of the leader of the Parti socialiste (Wallonia's main party) was "Why do you think they do not like me?"

28. Wilfried Dewachter, "De verdere democratisering van de Belgische politiek," *Res Publica* 10:2 (1968): 253–78; Wilfried Dewachter, "Une nouvelle technique d'élection directe du gouvernement," *Res Publica* 34:1 (1992): 75–85; "Changer la démocratie pour sauver la solidarité?" (Université catholique de Louvain: Chaire Hoover d'éthique économique et sociale, 1996).

29. A similar proposal had been sketched by the (then) director of the Flemish liberal party's study center, Stefan Ector (1993). The idea of a mixed copresidential ticket is also suggested for divided societies by Matthew S. Shugart and John M. Carey, *Presidents and Assemblies* (New York: Cambridge University Press, 1992), 101–2, 219.

30. See Francis Delpérée, *La Démarche citoyenne* (Bruxelles: Labor, 1998); Francis Delpérée and F. X. Dubois, "Le double vote ou le vote multiple," in Groupe "Avenir" de l'Université catholique de Louvain, *Des Idées et des hommes. Pour construire l'avenir de la Wallonie et de Bruxelles* (Louvain-la-Neuve: Academia-Bruylant, 1999), 69–84.

31. If the number of standard seats in each community is proportional to its size, the scheme generates overrepresentation either of the smaller community itself (if the special seats are distributed in proportion to the sizes of the populations they are meant to represent) or of its interests (if they are distributed in proportion to the sizes of the populations from which their incumbents are drawn) or both (under any intermediate formula). This is bound to look unfair to some members of the

larger community, especially if the proposal is coming from the smaller one. The only way of circumventing this dilemma consists in abandoning proportionality for the standard seats at the expense of the smaller community. For example, with 60 percent of Flemings and 40 percent of francophones, a 10/10 division of the 20 special seats can be reconciled with overall proportionality (in terms of both which community the representatives belong to and whom they represent), i.e., a 90/60 division of the 150 seats, if the standard seats overrepresent (in both senses) the bigger community (80/50 instead of 78/52). As soon as the number of seats is no longer marginal, serious departure from proportionality along one of the three dimensions mentioned may start jeopardizing the legitimacy of the scheme.

32. The idea of nationwide constituencies for either the House or the Senate is also defended in Steven Vansteenkiste, "Staatsstruktuur moet via federale rol parlement versterkt worden," *De Standaard* 2:9 (1993): 8; and Gérard Roland, Toon Vandevelde, and Philippe Van Parijs, "Repenser la solidarité entre les régions et entre les nations," *La Revue nouvelle* 105 (mai–juin 1997): 149–57. In the absence of regional or provincial quotas, however, the incentive for parties to provide platforms that are appealing to both ethnic groups is far too weak, as the individual candidates' desire to gather preference votes across the border will be constantly thwarted by their party's concern not to lose out to more-nationalist competitors. Regional quotas need to be set higher than provincial ones to avoid the risk of their being satisfied by the vote of linguistic minorities in border areas (a sharply francophone party could conceivably collect 1 or 2 percent of the votes in the Flemish region by mobilizing the francophone minority living in the part of Flanders around Brussels).

33. Jean Monnet, *Mémoires* (Paris: Fayard, 1976).

12

PROVISIONAL PESSIMISM: A REPLY TO VAN PARIJS

DONALD L. HOROWITZ

Philippe Van Parijs has provided a well-considered critique that takes the arguments of my essay seriously, agreeing with some of them and challenging others, always having regard to evidence. Authors can hardly wish for more than a careful, respectful reading. Grateful as I am for having received one, I shall try here to correct some misinterpretations of my work and that of others, as well as to sharpen up some remaining differences. I shall argue that Van Parijs underrates the need for strong institutions to counter conflict in severely divided societies.[1] Two of his examples, Ireland and Belgium, are inapposite to the argument he attempts to make about the utility of half-measures—a point I shall demonstrate without going much beyond the evidence Van Parijs himself adduces. Similarly, some misunderstanding by Van Parijs of Arend Lijphart's theory of consociational democracy and of my own approach to incentive-based methods to reduce ethnic conflict results in an overestimate of the degree to which mix-and-match strategies will achieve the desired objective.

Preliminarily, I explicitly concede that severely divided societies can make progress even if they adopt half-measures or, perhaps more likely, in spite of their adoption of half-measures or even no measures at all. It should not be thought that everything turns on the institutional structure of a divided society. Quite the contrary: even well-designed institutions are likely to make only a small impact on severe ethnic conflicts, and those conflicts may evolve in one direction or another regardless of the shape of the institutional structures. Institutions do not explain most of the conflict variance. Their impact remains important because marginal change is valuable and because formal institutions are amenable to deliberate intervention. The point I would make is that those who wish to intervene deliberately in severe conflicts have to use the tools at hand. Although reformers habitually try to change interethnic attitudes, and occasionally they have some success, the institutional structure is certainly more malleable than is the configuration of interethnic attitudes; and, among institutions, the most powerful structures that are only modestly powerful to begin with are, in my view, the electoral system and the territorial arrangements, devolved or otherwise.

My starting-point, therefore, is a relatively modest set of aims and a sense that many severely divided societies will more or less muddle along for shorter or longer periods, with cyclical ups and downs in conflict and violence, while others descend into more serious and protracted episodes of civil war, genocide, and uncivil peace. In none of these phases is there a strong sense of common citizenship transcending ethnic lines, and it is the uneasiness that flows from the often well-founded suspicion that some groups would like to dominate others that makes such countries uncomfortable places in which to live. In such places, opinions cannot be argued, for they go straight to the problematic question of community. Intimacies cannot be shared, for aspirations diverge. Traditions cannot be celebrated jointly, for they are often contested. Public life is segmented, but contact cannot be avoided. This is a picture of a stunted community.

I have sketched the forces that seem to me to produce strongly centrifugal tendencies in such societies, and I have contended that a strong and consistent prescription of innovations is required if institutions are to be able to counter these tendencies in a significant way. It is quite wrong to think that I favor a coherent package as an exercise in "ideal-typical purity."[2] Purity is the last thing one can expect in institutional configurations. What I mean by coherence is a tendency for parts of the package to work together rather than to cancel each other out or simply prove too

weak in the aggregate to promise any serious centripetal movement. So far, it seems to me, there is little evidence that the requisite packages are likely to be adopted, but I want to reiterate in
no uncertain terms that this is an entirely provisional judgment;
my research is far from complete. On some other matters, however, I think there is already plenty of evidence, some of which
does not support Van Parijs's judgments.

It is very difficult to make a convincing case, as Van Parijs attempts to do,[3] that the difference in Protestant-Catholic relations
in Northern Ireland compared to the Irish Republic is a function
of the benign impact of proportional representation, specifically
the single transferable vote (STV), in the Republic. Not only are
Protestants a small minority in the Republic, but they are in no
position to challenge the legitimacy of the state or to threaten to
control it. In the North, the fears of Protestants are exacerbated
by their minority status in all of Ireland and by their sense that
many Catholics do not accept the boundaries of the current state
or the legitimacy of the regime. To compare the North and the
Republic on these dimensions is to compare incomparables. And
if STV were the decisive difference between the two, then how do
we explain the facts that Northern Ireland had an STV election
in 1973, at a time when the British government was pushing
power-sharing, and that STV did exactly nothing to foster interethnic accommodation? The resulting power-sharing cabinet
shared power only briefly and was out of office in short order, despite STV.[4]

Like Arendt Lijphart, Van Parijs seems to think that proportional representation (whether of the STV or list-system variety)
is likely to have beneficial effects on ethnic conflict, and he cites,
in addition to Ireland, the example of Belgium, which adopted
PR in 1899. Unfortunately, the Belgian example does not support
the thesis—and not merely because Belgium remains a precarious society. PR did not save Belgium; the configuration of its
cleavages and parties saved PR from exacerbating ethnic conflict.
Had the Belgium of a century ago been divided between Flemings and Walloons in the way that it now is, and had those groups
been formed into two ethnically based political parties, PR would
have meant the permanent exclusion of the minority, a truly ex-
plosive situation.

As Van Parijs notes, however, ethnic divisions had not really emerged strongly in Belgium then. Rather, two other cleavages were predominant in the society and in the party system: between Catholics and Liberals (proclerical and anticlerical, in other words) and between those two bourgeois parties and the Socialists. By the time of PR, Belgium's two cleavages had produced a three-party system, and the existence of more than one cleavage made it very difficult for this double conflict, with its tripolar face, to become a more dangerous, exclusionary, single-cleavage, bipolar conflict. In due course, the ethnic cleavage was added to the two earlier-emerging cleavages, but by then the party system was so entrenched that ethnicity did not entirely supplant the earlier cleavages, and ethnic parties coexisted with parties founded along the other two cleavage lines. Even then, when the conflict arrived, it took a lot more than basic consociational methods to handle it.

Now imagine for a moment a counterfactual not considered by Van Parijs. Suppose PR had been adopted when Flemings and Walloons were coming into increasing conflict, and suppose further that the clerical-anticlerical and class conflicts were so muted or insignificant that parties were not organized around them. Flemish and Walloon parties would then have emerged, and PR would have provided such "fair" representation that the Flemish majority could expect to be in power in perpetuity and the Walloon minority could expect to be out of power for just as long. In such circumstances, nothing about PR would save Belgium from the problem of bifurcation, and those are common circumstances around the world. Perhaps the peculiar identity and composition of Brussels might have mitigated the conflict somewhat, although this is uncertain; but if it had, that would not be a point in favor of PR. Rather, this circumstance, like the earlier configuration of cleavages and parties, would be an argument in favor of the complexity of alignments and the multiplicity of parties that prevents bifurcation and so prevents the perfection of inclusion and exclusion that PR can help achieve when ethnic identities are more salient than others.

Note, too, that the Belgian story, so well told by Van Parijs, even if it points a different moral from the one he draws, also suggests a strong causal role for sequencing. The order in which events occur is a greatly underrated causal variable in social life. In terms of the prospects for interethnic accommodation, it is discouraging that deliberate constitutional engineering typically comes so late in the development of conflicts.

Van Parijs suggests that Belgium's political system is consociational, and in the sense that it contains devices for consensual decision-making, it is consociational. But it does not habitually operate on the basis of an inclusive or "grand" coalition of the sort recommended by Lijphart for divided societies. At any given moment, some parties are in power and some are in opposition. Now it is true that Lijphart has said various things at various times about the need for a grand coalition, but the logic of the consociational thinking requires, as I said in the essay on which Van Parijs has commented, what Lijphardt calls an "elite cartel" embracing leaders of all the groups to keep the peace by conspiring against the extravagant demands of their more ethnocentric followers.[5] When each ethnic group is represented by more than one party, and some of these parties are not included in the governing coalition, the result is intraethnic opposition of a decidedly conflict-producing sort.

In my view, the only way out of this problem is to counter the electoral rewards for politicians opposing interethnic compromises. What is to prevent the erosion of the electoral support enjoyed by the compromisers when their compromises are attacked by party leaders from their own group? The only durable offsetting reward in democratic conditions has to be offsetting electoral support, but where will it come from? In a polarized environment, that necessary offset can be produced only by electoral rules that reward compromise, rules of the sort I have described elsewhere, so that the compromisers' loss of votes to parties of the same groups that attack the compromises can be compensated by votes across the ethnic divide. Consociational theory, wedded to list PR, provides no such rewards. Every ethnic list competes against every other. Van Parijs seems to think that consociational theory makes power-sharing electorally rewarding, but there is no reason in theory and there is no reason in experience to think that this is so.

That leaves the question of whether it is possible to combine "devices that make it possible, rewarding, or compulsory to share power *and* to cross borders."[6] Before I respond to this, I want to make two preliminary remarks.

First, contrary to Van Parijs's impression,[7] I do not for a moment advocate rules, electoral or otherwise, that would make what Van Parijs calls "border crossing" compulsory. On the contrary, my aim is to use the market in votes to let politicians make their own decisions about where their interests lie. One of my main criticisms of consociational theory is precisely that it makes interethnic cooperation compulsory. Politicians have a way of rejecting what is compulsory but not rewarding to them.

Second, following Lijphart, Van Parijs identifies consociationalism with power-sharing and considers "border crossing" to be something else, desirable, perhaps, but different. In point of fact, if incentives to cooperate across ethnic lines work as intended, the result is interethnic power-sharing, and it is misleading for proponents of consociational theory to appropriate the term.

Is it, then, possible to mix consociational devices with incentive-based devices? Naturally, if cooperative norms of a consociational sort emerge from incentive-based structures, then there will be some overlap in political practice. But the question here is a matter of institutional design. Tempting though it may be to have one's political cake and also devour it, there is a fundamental incompatibility that cannot be elided. At the heart of consociational theory lie ethnically based parties that rely on monoethnic support and compromise after elections. At the heart of incentive-based electoral ideas are ethnically based parties that, in search of marginal votes across ethnic lines, compromise before elections and may even form interethnic coalitions that put up candidates jointly for election. The two models are in tension, to say the least, and any electoral system that aims to do some of one and some of the other will have precisely the problem of incoherence that I have been emphasizing. The attractiveness of a mix-and-match system, even to nonparticipant analysts, is, then, yet another source of likely hybrid institutions that I failed to enumerate in my original essay. There are unavoidable choices to be made, but experience suggests (again, provisionally) that they will not be made.

NOTES

1. By *severely divided societies*, I mean those in which ethnic-group identities have a high degree of salience, exceeding that accorded to alternative identities (including supraethnic, territorial, ideological, and class-based alternatives) and in which levels of antipathy between ethnic groups are high. Such a definition allows us to reason about whether a society so constituted at Time One is affected one way or another by an institutional innovation adopted at any time after Time One, as measured by the effects of the innovation at Time Two, and so avoids the problem of endogeneity cited by Van Parijs in the first section of his comments. Compare the not-too-dissimilar definition of a deeply divided society employed by Eric A. Nordlinger, *Conflict Regulation in Divided Societies* (Cambridge: Harvard University Center for International Affairs, monograph no. 29, 1972), 9. On the more general methodological problem, see Gary King, Robert O. Keohane, and Sidney Verba, *Designing Social Inquiry* (Princeton: Princeton University Press, 1994), 185–95, 221–23.

2. Philippe Van Parijs, "Power-Sharing Versus Border-Crossing in Ethnically Divided Societies," this volume, p. 314.

3. Ibid., pp. 299–300.

4. See Richard Rose, *Northern Ireland: Time of Choice* (Washington, D.C.: American Enterprise Institute, 1976), 29–31, 76–93.

5. Arendt Lijphardt, "Consociational Democracy," *World Politics* 21:2 (January 1969): 207–25, at 213. On the "grand coalition," see Arend Lijphart, *Democracy in Plural Societies* (New Haven: Yale University Press, 1977), 25–36.

6. Van Parijs, "Power-Sharing Versus Border-Crossing," p. 314 (emphasis in the original).

7. Ibid.

INDEX